M000266465

COLLECTING CIGARETTE LIGHTERS

A Price Guide

By Neil S. Wood

*L-W Book Sales
& Publishing*

10166903

The current values in this book should be used only as a guide. They are not intended to set prices, which vary from one section of the country to another. Auction prices as well as dealer prices vary greatly and are affected by condition as well as demand. Neither the author nor the publisher assumes responsibility for any losses that might be incurred as a result of consulting this guide.

12-99-24 (6) LAD 10-99
10-06 Sod 10-06 34(11)
9-08 LAD 5-07 35(11)

Additional copies of this book may be ordered from:
L-W Book Sales
P.O. Box 69
Gas City, IN 46933

$24.95
Add $2.00 for shipping.

1st Printing
ISBN#0-89538-056-0

Printed by: Image Graphics, Paducah, KY

ACKNOWLEDGMENTS

Thanks to the following people for helping make this book possible & contributing lighters:

Wes & Elaine Hart
Wayne Stoops
Dorothy Miller
Foster's Antiques
Jim & Erin Richards
Mary & Harry Dilley
David Dilley
Lael Boren
Mark Cole
Gene & Stephanie Bartel
Judith Sanders
On the Lighter Side

Clubs you may be interested in joining:

On the Lighter Side, Inc. - International Lighter Collectors

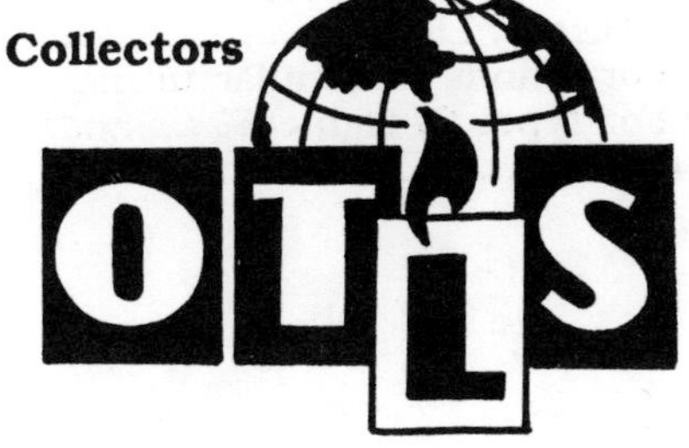

Contact: On The LIGHTER Side
International Lighter Collectors
136 Circle Dr.
Quitman, TX 75783-1824
Ph. (903) 763-2795
Fax: (903) 763-4953

Please send Self Addressed Envelope.

PLPG - Pocket Lighter Preservation Guild

Contact: PLPG
11220 West Florissant, Suite 400
Florissant, MO 63033
Ph. (314) 838-7543

Yearly Dues: $30

TABLE OF CONTENTS

INTRODUCTION

I have seen a need for a price guide on lighters for many years. After waiting on an experienced collector to write one, I decided to research it myself. After many months and more money than I would like to say, this book is the result. Over 95% of the lighters are owned by L-W Books. Many dealers and collectors helped guide me, but I am sure mistakes were made. I am sure this is not totally a complete book but it does fill a void. I have tried to make it as helpful as possible. Therefore, I have included two indexes in this book. If you have a Zippo with a fish on the front of it, you can either find it by looking in the brand index or you can look it up by going to the types of lighters index and looking for it under fish. You may also cross-reference them by first looking under the fish and finding what pages the fish lighters are on then go to the brand index and find what pages correspond with the pages for fish. I hope you enjoy this book and improve your collection.

PRICING INFORMATION

I have priced all lighters as in good working order. A lighter mint in box will be worth more (vintage ones much more). Non working lighters will be worth less. Remember the prices stated in this guide are retail prices that a collector should be willing to pay for lighters to add to his or her personal collection.

Happy Hunting!

Pictures in this book that have been numbered read from left to right, top to bottom.

Example:

1.	2.	3.
4.	5.	6.
7.	8.	9.
	10.	

LIGHTERS THAT USE BUTANE FUEL

Adcan
Admiral
Allround
Arteb
Astronaut 888
Audi
Augusta
Baronex
Benlow
Bentley
Ben Wade
Bijou
Binalite
Bison
Boston
Braun
Brio
Bronica
Brotherlite
Budget
Bugatti
Butler
Calculighter
Capri
Carna D'Ache
Cartier
Cat's Eye
Charmant
Christian Dior
Classic
Clipper
Colibri
Comoy
Consul
Cord
Cordless Iron
Corona
Cosmic
Crown
Derringer
Diamant
Diplomat
Doncor
Duncan
Dunhill
Dupont
Edinex
Erhard
Espirit Gas
Evans
Extar
F.B.M.
Felter
Feudor
Fisher
Flaminaire
Fleury
Garant
Gas Boy
Gasomatic
G.B.D.
Gemini
Givenchy
Goddess
Gold Ingot
Gold View
Golf
Goya
Guy
Hadson
Harvard
Hings
Hirota
Ibelo
Imco
Iwahori
Jeans-Flip
Jet Lite
Jewel Gas
JJJ
K77 G
Kabari
Karat Gas
Kawee
Kaywoodie
K.B.L.
Kingflame
Kingsway
Kleer Vue
Koei
Kotana
Kreisler
KW
Lasatron
Leo
Lilliput
Litex
Luna
Maba
Marksman
Martin
Maruman
Matchbox
Matchless 3000
Max
Maxim
Medico
Mikado
Milord
Mini Gas
Modern
Myfriend
Mylflam
Myon
Narumi
National
Nichika
Novo
Orlik
Oro
Ostine
Panther
Parker
Partner
Peacock
Pearl
Penguin
Penna
Pet
Peterson
Philips Haircare
Picolo
Pierre Gardin
Pierre Mondor
Piezolite
Pillar
Pipeboy
Pipeflam
Playboy
Plufill
Polly Gaz
Polo
Poncho
Prebenholm
Prince
Prontolite
Pulsar
Pyxis
Regal
Rogers
Roland
Ronson
Ross
Rossa
Rowenta
Royal Musical
Rubin-Gas
Safari
Saffa
Sarome
Savinelli
Scripto G
Seikolite
Sharp
Sigma
Silvermatch
Sim
Solomon Dimple
Starlon
St. Louis
Studio
Sun
Swan
Swiss Gas
T Mini
Tanita
Thunderbird
Titan
Tokyo Pipe
Trigger
Tsuge
Twiggy
Vinci
Whisper Flame
Win
Windmaster
Windmill
Zaima
Zilon
Zimmerblaze
Zippo
Zoomer

INTERESTED IN BUYING

"TRENCH" LIGHTERS AND OTHER VINTAGE OR UNIQUE LIGHTERS

ALSO PRE-1960 ZIPPO POCKET LIGHTERS
WITH ADVERTISING
AND ZIPPO TABLE LIGHTERS

ELAINE'S TIQUES

WES & ELAINE HART
963 Westhaven St.
Columbus, OH 43228

Ph. (614) 870-7141

For A Periodic Auction Catalog of Lighters
(Fully Illustrated)

write to:
JACK SEIDERMAN
1631 N.W. 114 AVE.
PEMBROKE PINES, FL 33026

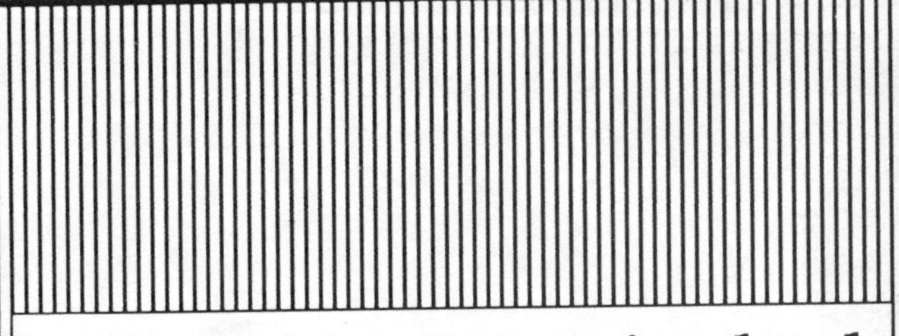

Look For An Upcoming book on Lighters and Smoking Paraphernalia from:

L-W Book Sales
P.O. Box 69
Gas City, IN 46933

"FOSTER'S LAST STAND"
Antiques and Collectibles

GEORGE L. FOSTER
(317) 675-3391
(317) 675-4724

118 N. Main Street
Tipton, Indiana 46072

Cigar Lighter.

55452 Cigar Lighter, complete with colored globe, either amber, white, blue or ruby. There are two lighters to be used with alcohol. The vase is hand decorated.

1892

IMPERATOR CIGAR LIGHTER

One pressure does the work; absolute satisfaction guaranteed.

N718–Burns benzine; a single loading will last a week in general use, or fifty minutes' continuous burning; simple in construction; easy to keep in good working order; made of special composition metal; heavily nickel plated; size 2x1½x½ inches. Each in a box with full instructions.

1913

Showing how Wonderliter is used.

No. 566209, Each. Gem Pocket Wonderliter. Polished Nickel. With Ring for Waldemar Chain. Striker has everlasting steel point.

1915

Automatic Flaming Cigar Lighters

S523

S974

No. S523. Cosmo Simplex Cigar Lighter, convenient vest pocket size, rounded ends, nickel plated, gears easily removed and refilled either with wick or with new flints, the tension readily adjusted by a screw at bottom; in efficiency and appearance equal to any lighter made. A corking fine item for scheme, premium, advertising and mail order propositions. One dozen in box. Gross... Dozen...

No. S524. Extra Flints for above. Dozen ....

No. S972. Watch Shape Flaming Cigar Lighter, exact shape of a 12 size hunting watch, heavy nickel plated, highly burnished, with crown and antique bow. Pressing crown springs up the lid, ignition follows. Screw at bottom for releasing interior gear for refilling, etc. Flat model, convenient for vest pocket wear; a strictly up-to-date lighter. Dozen...........

No. S963. Extra Flints, these will fit lighters Nos. 972 and 974. Dozen ....

No. S974. Flaming Cigar Lighter, 2¼x1¼ in., flat round edge model, depressed panel on one side, highly nickel plated and polished, filler in back unscrews, permits the gear to slide out for refilling, etc. Strictly high grade in quality and finish; small enough to conveniently wear in vest pocket, with ring for hanging on key chain. Dozen............ **3.50**

No. S1657. Cigar Lighter and Cigar Cutter Set, one of the most popular combinations to be had. The cigar lighter is well made and finely finished, gives instantaneous flaming light. Cigar cutter of tempered steel, regular shear loops, nickel plated, with protecting pin to prevent closing over center. The entire set is finished equal to the highest priced goods made. An especially fine premium article.
Per dozen sets.. **1.50**

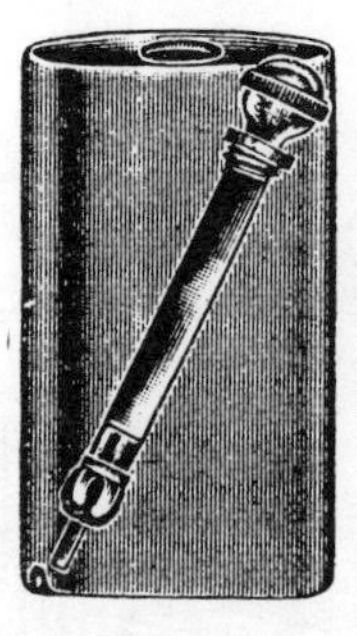

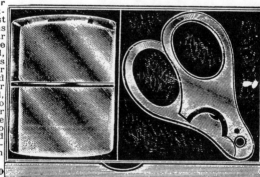

No. S957. Wonderliter, size 2x1⅛ in., small, neat, compact thin model, weight 1 ounce, fine nickel plated and polished. No springs, wheels or weights, top screws in, at end of which is steel striker. No extra flints required as a large piece of sparking metal is fastened in base of lighter the entire width. Scratch steel strike across sparking metal same as you would a match and it lights instantly. Guaranteed. With ordinary care will last a long time, fluid need be replenished only very infrequently. The best, most practical sure pocket lighter ever made. Will be the world's biggest seller.
Per dozen ....

1914
N. Shive Co. – Chicago

CATALOG CUTS

SAFETY FUSE OR CIGAR LIGHTERS

Just the lighter for the **soldier,** sailor, automobilist and outdoor **man.** Will light in the strongest **wind, in** fact, the stronger the wind **the** stronger the light. No benzine **or al**cohol required, simply turn wheel **with** thumb to produce spark and **wick ig**nites. To put out light pull **down wick** and ball automatically **closes wick** opening and extinguishes light.

No. 400—Fuse or Cigar **Lighters,** nickel plated brass **frame and** sparker container, **hardened cut** steel wheel, complete with **6 inches** of wick and ball and chain extinguisher, w't per doz. ½ lb.,

1922

No. 864105, Wonderliter, $2.50
Table Lighter and Ash Tray.
Lights by merely drawing the striker across Sparking Metal, is everlasting.
Antique Brass Finish.

1918

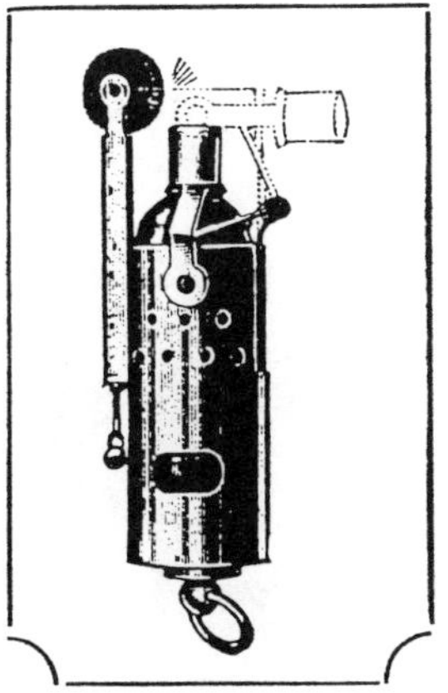

No. 4574 — Windlighter. Nickel finish throughout. To light, pull up outer guard, turn wheel; wind cannot blow out light when in use. Complete with ring on end for attaching to wach chain.

1937

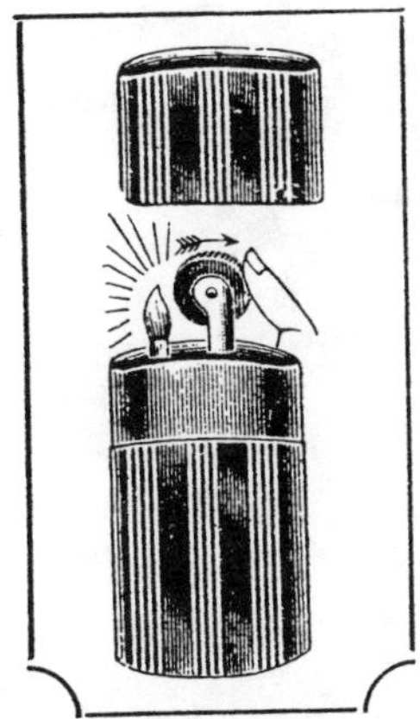

No. 4549 — Strikalite Midget Pocket Lighter. A very convenient flat lighter. Entirely engine turned, in nickel finish. Twelve to carton.

1937

CIGAR LIGHTER

This new electric convenience is neatly molded in a mahogany tinted porcelain, which will perfectly match your radio set or furniture. Has push-button contact and removable element. Convenient silk cord, which may be permanently connected to a nearby fixture. Does away with unsightly matches and offers a novelty for your home. Shipping weight, 1½ lbs.
57K3388—For 110-volt city current only...............

1926

No. 442914, ...
Table Lighter.
Sterling Silver.
Gray Finish.
Height, 3½ inches.
Hammered Design.

1934

Electric Cigar or Cigarette Lighter

Convenient for smoker —protection for home. A neat, attractive item for the library table, dining-room or buffet. Attaches to lighting socket. Slight pressure on button in the handle to light—release pressure and light is off. Includes abt. 4 ft. of cord and 2-piece attachment plug.

Shpg. wt., 10 ozs.

1926

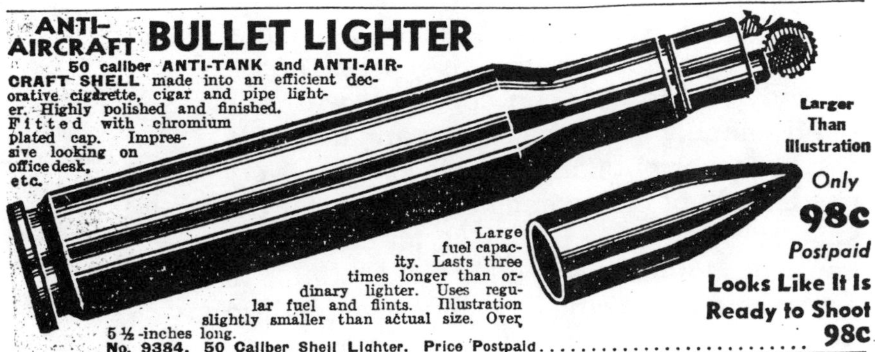

1943

ELECTRIC LIGHTER AND TRAY

No. E150. A smart looking set that anyone would be proud to own. Attractively designed. Consists of black tray with well for ashes and cigarettes and electric lighter to match with metal figure on top. Uses electricity only when lighting—shuts off when set on tray or placed right side up. Excellent as a bridge prize or Christmas gift. Weight, per set, 1 lb.

Selling price, 89c Sample, **59c; Dozen, $6.50**

1939 Catalog

MEN'S 3-PIECE LAMP SET

No. M326. All pieces match perfectly. Consists of one attractive desk lamp, height overall, 10 inches with black enameled base, fabrikoid covered post, paper, parchment shade, complete with cord, plug and socket; one cedar lined cigarette box with fabrikoid covered body, metal top and sides; one metal ash tray with two rests. A gift which will please any man; a fine prize. Weight, each, 1 lb. 8 ozs.

Suggested selling price, $1.75

Sample, **98c**; Dozen, **$11.40**

1939 Catalog

The "Kramer" perfect pocket lighter. It is easy to fill, easy to clean and ever reliable. You will fill the reservoir with gasoline and it is ready to use. You can operate it with one hand – simply press the button and instantly you have a bright flame, ample for your every need. It is not only a splended lighter for the smoker but is also useful as an emergency lamp for motorists and others. It is simple in construction, nothing to get out of order, and we guarantee it to the fullest extent.

1919 Illustration

NOVELTY CIGAR LIGHTER FOR SMOKER TABLE

No. M166-RS. A white metal that always stays bright. Makes an excellent gift or bridge prize. This comes in Lighthouse style. Height, about 4½ inches. Weight, each, 6 ozs.

Selling price, 50c

Sample, **29c; Dozen, $2.45**

TABLE LIGHTER

No. M62. The rich coloring and beautiful finish of the base make these lighters very attractive. Fitted with a dependable lighter. The tri-colored base which comes in assorted colors is stunning and appealing. Looks like Catalin. Height, overall, 2½ inches. Weight, each, 5 ozs.

Selling price, 50c

Sample, **23c; Dozen, $2.20**

FLINTS AND WICKS FOR LIGHTERS

No. M111-I. Each envelope contains one wick and two flints. Will fit all styles of pocket lighters.

Selling price, 5c

Sample, **3c; Dozen, 25c;** Gross, **$2.75**

Per 1,000 Pkgs., **$13.50**

AIRPLANE MODEL LIGHTER

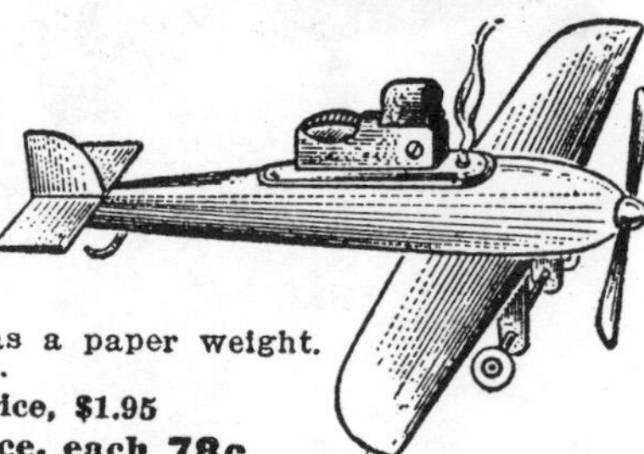

No. M 1 7 6. Made entirely of metal and nickel plated. Has a wing spread of 4½ inches. The lighter part is in the cockpit of the plane. This lighter makes a very unique table decoration and can also be used as a paper weight. Weight, each, 8 oz.

Selling price, $1.95

Wholesale price, each **78c**

1939 Catalog

CATALOG CUTS

Combination Pencil and Cigar Lighter

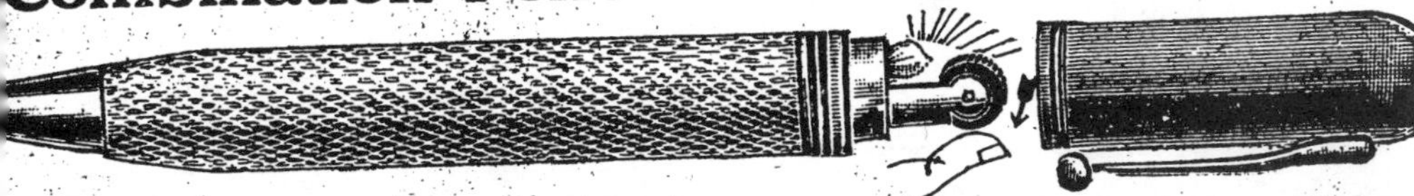

Combination Cigar Lighter and Mechanical Pencil. The cap conceals a lighter, in the space usually set aside for the eraser. To light, turn the wheel with the Made entirely of metal, with highly polished finish. A very popular and useful

25. Combination Cigar Lighter and Pencil. Price Postpaid............25c

1943

AJ2570.................
Evans automatic table lighter. Jade green Evanite base. Non-tarnishing chromium finish lighter. Large fuel capacity. Height 2½ in., diameter 2 in. A sturdy and practical model.

1939

Electric Cigaret Lighter

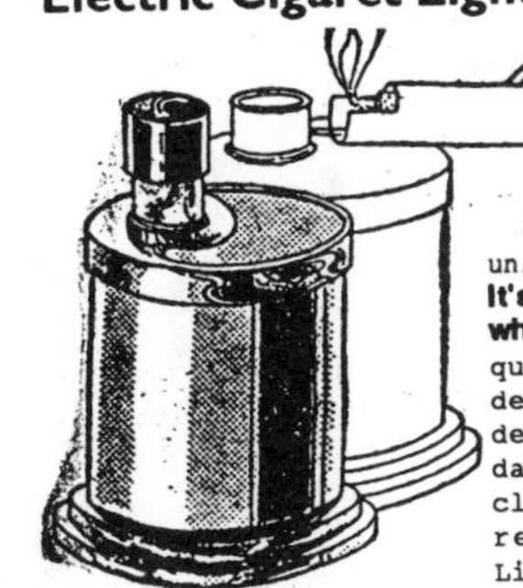

No Wires
Uses Ordinary
Batteries

Wireless electric lighter unit, touch contact and **PRESTO! It's lit! No flints. No sparking wheel.** It lights easily and quickly. A fine lighter for desk, or table. Beautifully designed. Operates on standard flashlight cell, included with lighter. Uses regular lighter fluid. Lights cigarets, cigars or pipes. Large flame. Chrome finish.
No. 9366

1943

Ladies' Combination Cigarette Case, Compact and Lighter

No. 9N-639

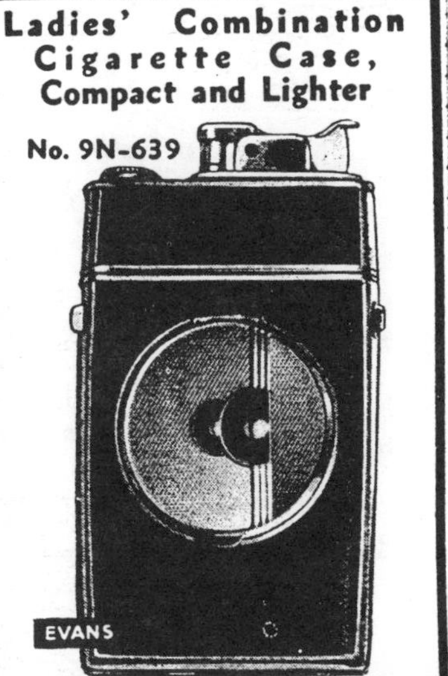

Colors: Black, Green, Burgundy. Knife-edge model. Chrome finish. French enamel front. Fitted with large mirror, loose powder container and full size rouge. Famous Evans Trigo-lighter on top. Each.....

1935

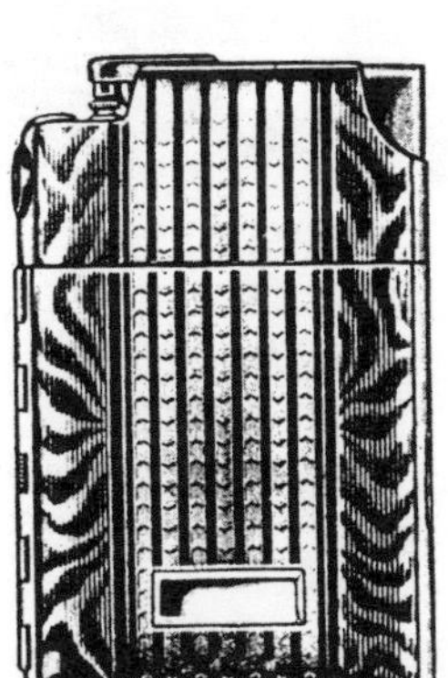

GG1625 - - - - - - - -
Perm-A-Plate—Cigarette Case and Slide-A-Lite combination. Hand engine turned on black French enamel. Beautiful natural gold effect.

1940

EVANS COMBINATION LIGHTER AND CIGARETTE CASE

No. 206—Non tarnishing chromium finish with hammered front. Has monogram shield. Lighter is the Evans TRIGO-LIGHTER—the lighter that never fails.

OUR PRICE

EVANS TRIGO-LIGHTER

No. 502 — Lights every time, simply press the handy button—only one hand required. Handsome design. Heavy chrome plate will retain its lustrous finish. The perfect lighter that every smoker will appreciate.

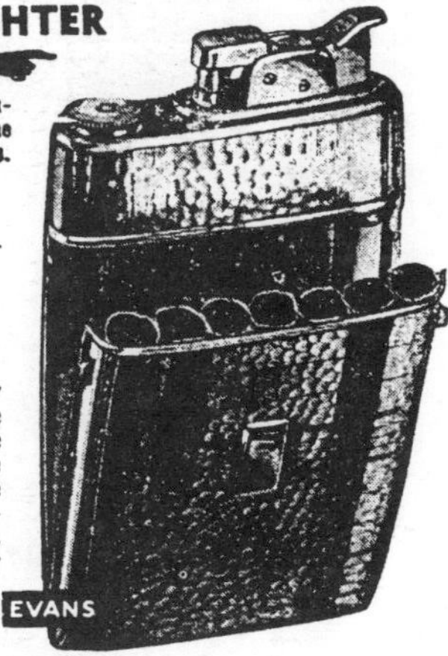

1935

Lighted Cigarette Dispenser

Delivers A Lighted Cigarette!

This handy dispenser fits on dashboard of your car. Just press the button on the side and **presto!** a lighted cigarette ready for you to smoke and enjoy comes out. You don't have to take your eyes off the road; you can keep one hand on the wheel all the time. Most drivers find it awkward to light a cigarette while driving. This new invention makes it a pleasurer. Device operates off the battery so there is **no fuel, no wick, no constant changing or attention required.** Takes but a few minutes to install. Nearly everyone who sees it will admire it. Will operate from dry cells if you desire to install it in your home. Or you can connect it to your house current if a transformer be used. Using ordinary No. 6 dry cells they will last for a long time.
No. 9348

1943

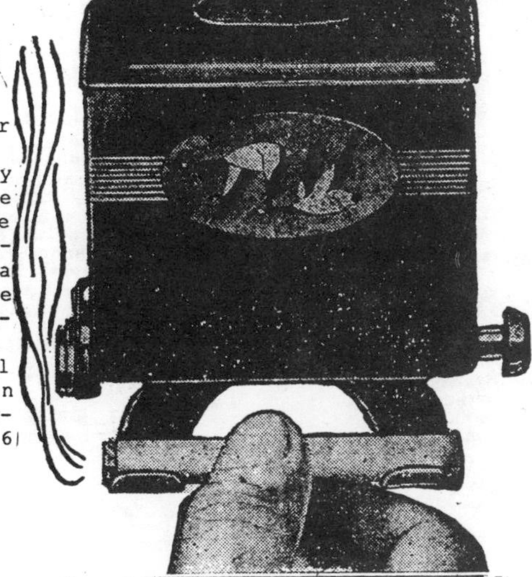

"A Light at Your Fingertip"

GLOLITER Combination GEAR SHIFT BALL AND CIGARETTE LIGHTER

A combination gear shift ball in attractive Catalin colors, plus a flameless lighter. It's airtight gear shift socket prevents fluid from evaporation which assures consistency of performance.

Comes with universal type bushing to fit all cars. **98c**
M4236—Compl.

Contains no flint—needs no electricity—no sparks—no wires. Not affected by wind or rain.

SMART—HANDY—DEPENDABLE

1939

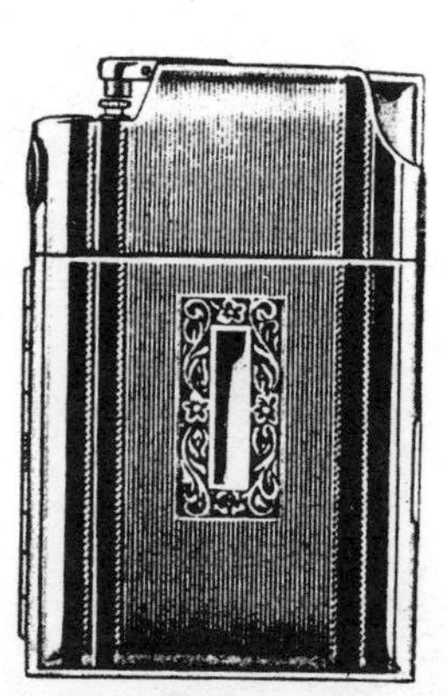

GG1626 - - - - - - - - -
Perm-A-Plate—Cigarette Case and Slide-A-Lite combination. French enamel in black. Hand engine turned and engraved. Beautiful natural gold effect.

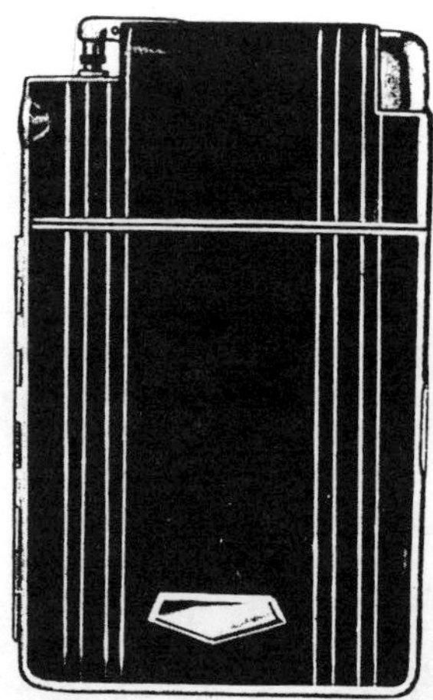

GG1627 - - - - - - - -
Perm-A-Plate—Cigarette Case and Slide-A-Lite combination. French enamel in tortoise shell. Beautiful natural gold effect.

1940

America's largest-selling smoking tobacco

Feb. 1, 1954

No. 4878—Catlin Table Liter. Genuine Evans Liter imbeded in a multi-colored catlin case. Height 2 inches. Felt on bottom to prevent scratching.

1930

HAMILTON Desk Lighter

Marine Style–Turn the Wheel–Lights Up

Here's just the right nautical touch for desk, smoking stand or den—a ship's wheel lighter that never misses. Just turn the wheel and it lights up with a steady lighthouse flame. **Designed with all the smooth trimness of true marine engineering and finished in brilliant chromium or brass that will not tarnish or stain.** Holds oceans of fluid so that it will go week after week without being refilled, lighting up faithfully at the flick of a finger. Lighter stands 5 inches in height,

No. 3QR7561B. Brass finish.

No. 3QR7562C. Chrome finish.

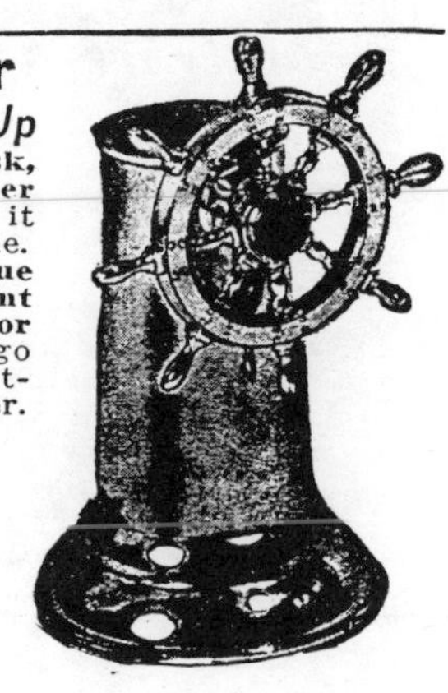

1940

LEKTROLITE "NO FLAME" LIGHTERS

RKS IN ANY WIND

ern flameless, faultless lighter—just puff, and it lights—even heavy wind. No wheels—nothing to manipulate—won't wear Has the looks, too—makes sales for dealers everywhere.

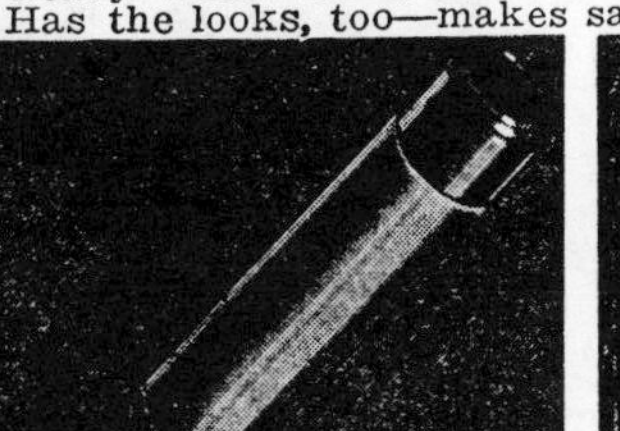

POINT MODEL. Lights unngly every time — neat, no s—no fuss, no odor, no stains. d by everyone for dainty appearance, compactness and simty of operation. Slim, cylinstyle in satin black finish. h bottle of fluid in box.

3QR-G12.

ESTA GLOPOINT. Same, ased colors, contrasting tips. n fluid in box.
3QR-G15.

PLASTIQUE MODEL. Light weight, thin, smaller than a book of matches—a real beauty — **lustrous chrome trim** with body in assorted colored patterns. Positive, dependable action. Merely puff and it lights, even in a gale. In box with fluid.
No. 3QR-P12.

Nov. 21, 1941

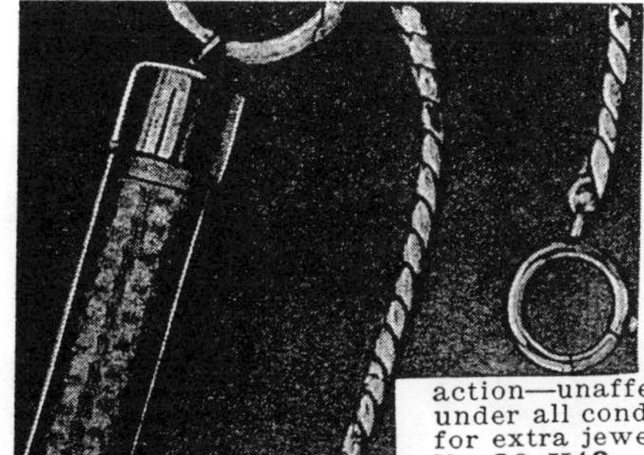

LEKTROLITE KEYCHAIN MODEL

Giving or getting, it's always right with LEKTROLITE. Especially, if it's this smart, modern style — a distinctive model with cord type Chain and fine quality key holder richly gold plated. Equipped with efficient LEKTROLITE mechanism—positive in action—unaffected by wind—dependable under all conditions. In gift box designed for extra jewelry.
No. 3Q-K12.

LEKTROLITE NEW PIPE LIGHTER

When lighting up your pipe with this LEKTROLITE you get the fragrance of tobacco smoke immediately, not the unpleasant taste of matches as is the case when lighting up the old way. It's built on the same LEKTROLITE principle — IS FLAMELESS—lights anywhere in any wind. Lustrous black plastic finish. Boxed with bottle of fluid complete.
No. 3Q-R11.

A Sure Light for Your Pipe

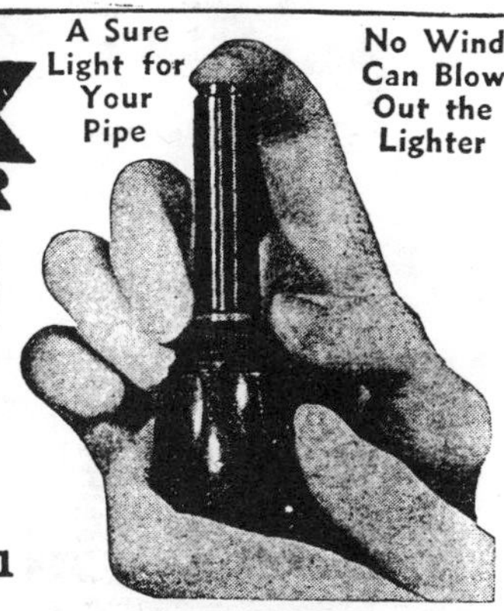

No Wind Can Blow Out the Lighter

Nov. 21, 1941

THE NEW

LEKTROLITE

LEKTROLITE PENCIL MODEL

CJ4802 Black Enamel

CJ4803 Chromium finish....

Smart new style with a Lektrolite lighter on one end, automatic pencil on the other. Just lift the cap off and a flameless lighter is available. Pencil of finest quality, propels, repels and expels. Solid chromium finish or black and chromium. Length 5½ in. Splendid useful gift.

Smokers everywhere are hailing this modern lighter with puffs of delight. Neither wind, nor rain, nor sleet prevents its instant, flameless light. You just lift the cap, place your cigarette or cigar at the lighter's tip and at the first inhalation a soft red glow lights it. No flints, no flame, no wheels, no buttons, no mechanism, no gadgets, no tricks. Enjoyment at the first puff—gone is the acrid, sulphur, match taste. Lektrolite comes in many modern, attractive, compact models with automatic refill. A guarantee that speaks for itself.

CJ4804 Sterling Silver....

CJ4805 14 Kt. Solid Gold.....

Finest quality engine turned, in sterling silver or 14 kt. solid gold. Shield for engraving. Simply lift the cap and there's a soft glow ready to light cigarette or cigar. Complete with supply of fluid. Fine gift box. Splendid gift or presentation. Illustration actual size.

CJ4806 Chromium ....
CJ4807 Colored Enamel—Black or Green ....
Effective transparent enamel and chrome, or all chromium. Smart cylindrical style, handy for pocket or ladies' purse. Simply lift the cap and there's a soft glow to light cigarette or cigar. Available in black, or green. Specify color desired. Complete with supply of fluid in filler container. Fine gift box. Illustration actual size.

NO FLINTS • NO FLAME • NO WHEELS • NO BUTTONS
NO BATTERIES • NO MECHANISM • AUTOMATIC REFILL

1934

The Lincoln Automatic

The New Standard Lighter of the World

Regular Size.

No. **4169** Ostrich ....
No. **4170** Alligator ....
No. **4171** Pin seal..........

Junior Size.

No. **4172** Pin seal.........
No. **4173** Tan alligator.....
No. **4174** Green morocco...

The features embodied in the Lincoln Automatic Lighter will make it the most welcomed and practicable gift of its kind, regardless of price.

1. An automatic lighter where cover remains open without holding—a very much desired feature.

2. Fewer and stronger parts—simplicity in itself.

3. Parts extra heavy, made of high-grade steel, hardened and ground for perfect alignment and ease of operation.

4. Sparking wheel milled from Victor crucible steel. Cuts flint smoothly and will last a lifetime.

5. Special feature ball-bearing rack which operates flint-cutting wheel. Reduces friction, eliminates wear and produces extreme ease of operation.

6. All lighters leather covered.

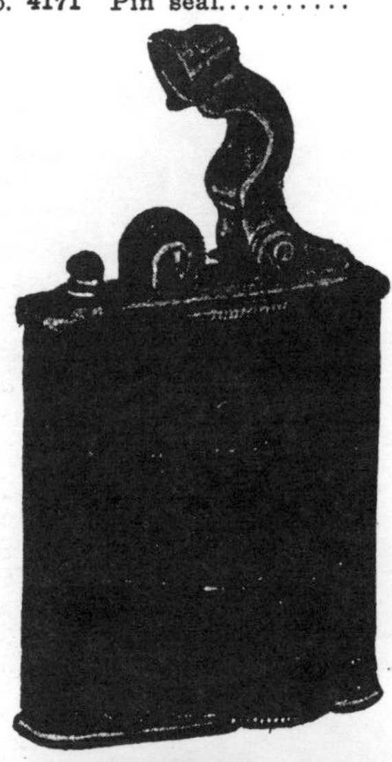

Regular Size.
Open.

Junior Size.
Open.

RONSON DE-LIGHT - AUTOMATIC

A most welcome gift. Perfectly constructed with watchlike precision. Here is a lighter small and thin enough to fit in the vest pocket or handbag. Perfect performance, beauty of design and finish with a large fuel capacity, giving maximum service with minimum attention. Sells at half the price with twice the performance of any other high-grade lighter made.

No. **4175** Black leather covered...............................
No. **4176** Red leather covered.................................
No. **4177** Green leather covered...............................

SILVER PRINCE

Automatic self-lighter. Simple - practical. Either (left or right) operates. One motion of thumb automati ignites wick. One motion of thumb, pressing snuffer position, extinguishes light. Has beautiful lines with c top.

No. **4178** Sterling case ....

1929 CATALOG PAGE

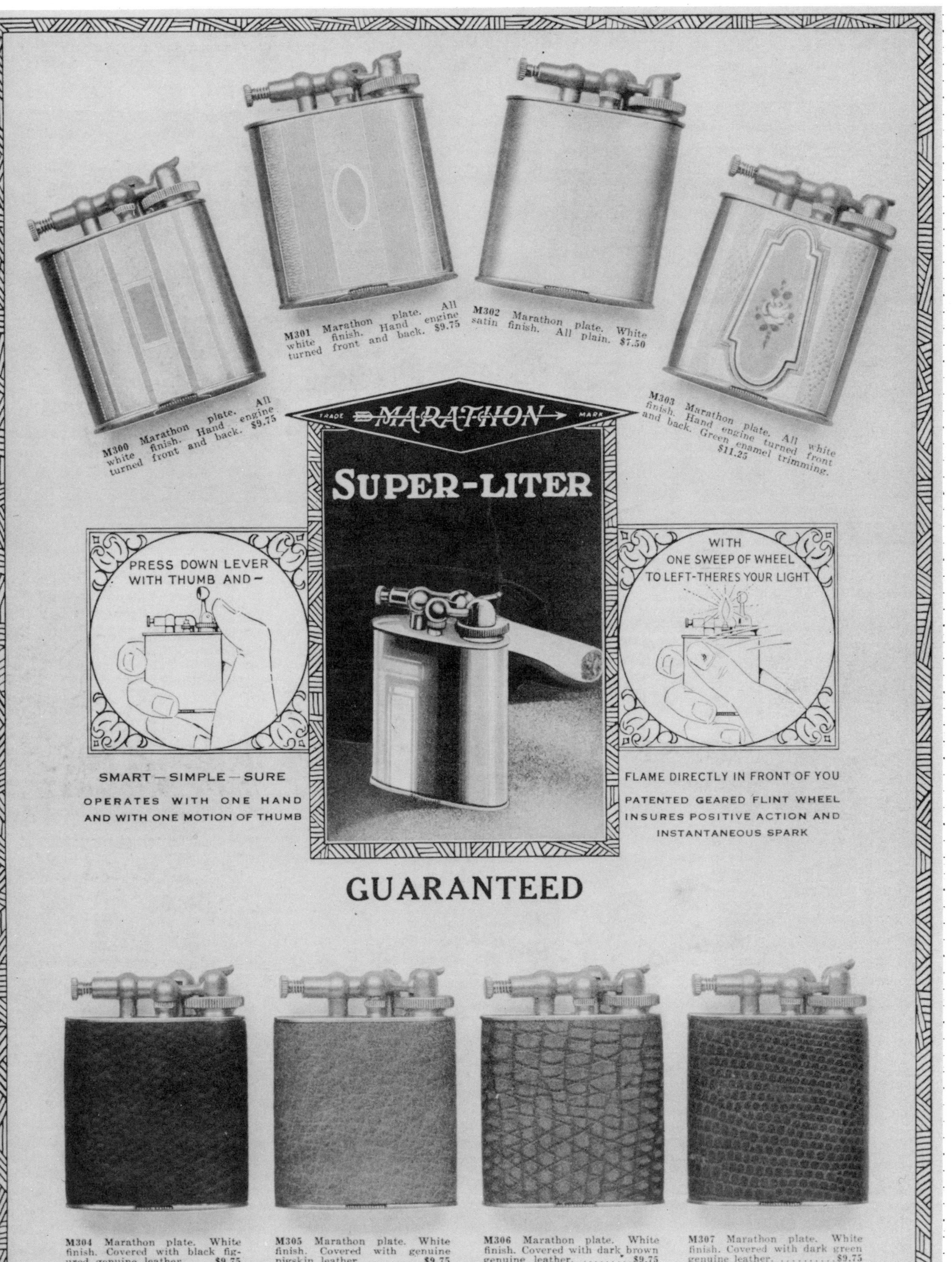

M300 Marathon plate. All white finish. Hand engine turned front and back. $9.75
M301 Marathon plate. All white finish. Hand engine turned front and back. $9.75
M302 Marathon plate. White satin finish. All plain. $7.50
M303 Marathon plate. All white finish. Hand engine turned front and back. Green enamel trimming. $11.25
TRADE MARATHON MARK
SUPER-LITER
PRESS DOWN LEVER WITH THUMB AND—
WITH ONE SWEEP OF WHEEL TO LEFT-THERES YOUR LIGHT
SMART — SIMPLE — SURE
OPERATES WITH ONE HAND AND WITH ONE MOTION OF THUMB
FLAME DIRECTLY IN FRONT OF YOU
PATENTED GEARED FLINT WHEEL INSURES POSITIVE ACTION AND INSTANTANEOUS SPARK
GUARANTEED
M304 Marathon plate. White finish. Covered with black figured genuine leather. .. $9.75
M305 Marathon plate. White finish. Covered with genuine pigskin leather. $9.75
M306 Marathon plate. White finish. Covered with dark brown genuine leather. $9.75
M307 Marathon plate. White finish. Covered with dark green genuine leather. $9.75

1930 CATALOG PAGE

Lincoln Automatic Lighter

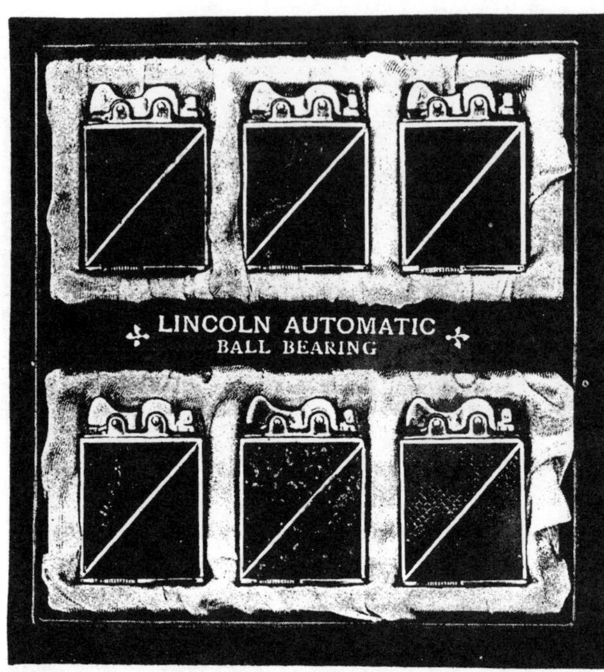

DE LUXE BAR ASSORTMENT

No. N1087 . . . .

Six genuine assorted leather covered Lincoln Automatic DeLuxe Bar Lighters, nickel plated—diagonal bar—sides very thin and compact. Individual boxes part of special display pad.

No. N1088 With Initial . . . .
No. N1089 Without Initial . . . .

FEATURING INTERCHANGEABLE INITIALS

FIFTY INITIALS FREE WITH EACH ASSORTMENT OF SIX

Special display pad, silk lined, contains six Lincoln Automatic Lighters, covered with genuine leather, nickel silver, bezels and initials. Initial It while your customer waits—takes less than a minute.

No. N1090 Grotto . . . .
No. N1091 Ostrich . . . .
No. N1092 Marlboro . . . .
No. N1093 Red and Green . . . .
No. N1094 Snake . . . .
No. N1095 Black . . . .

No. N1096 Lizard . . . .
No. N1097 Ostrich . . . .
No. N1098 Black . . . .
No. N1099 Green . . . .

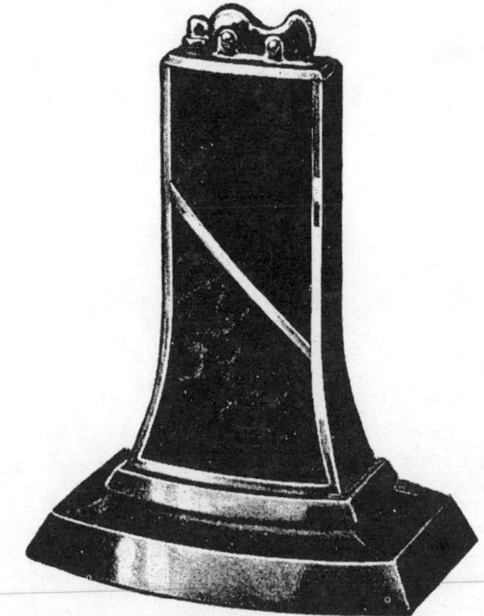

No. N1100 Marlboro . . . .
No. N1101 Red and Green . . . .
No. N1102 Snake . . . .

FEATURES OF LINCOLN AUTOMATIC

1—Automatic lighting and cover remains open without holding. A very much desired feature, found only in the Lincoln Automatic.

2—Fewer and stronger parts—simplicity in itself.

3—Parts extra heavy, made of high grade steel, hardened and ground for perfect alignment and ease of operation.

4—Sparking wheel milled from Victor Crucible steel. Cuts flint smoothly and will last a lifetime.

5—Special feature Ball Bearing rack which operates flint cutting wheel. Reduces friction, eliminates wear and produces extreme ease of operation.

THE LINCOLN AUTOMATIC
TABLE LIGHTER

Especially designed for beauty, ease of lighting and handling. Height, 5½ inches; width, 1½ inches by ½ inch thick at top. Base, 4 inches long by 3 inches wide. Insures extremely large fuel capacity.

Furnished in three different leather combinations. Metal parts heavily nickel plated. Weight, ¾ pound.

1930 CATALOG PAGE

Douglass Precious Metal Lighters

CREATED BY WADSWORTH—FAMED FOR WATCH CASES

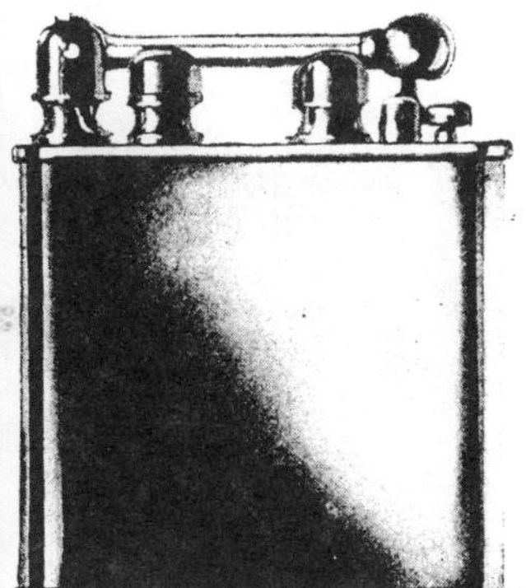

No. N1163 Gold filled
14k gold filled.
No. N1163½ Sterling
Plain design, for monograms or emblems.
No. N1163
No. N1163½

No. N1164 Sterling silver
Engine turned and signet design. A model much in favor.

No. N1165 Gold filled
14k gold filled.
No. N1165½ Sterling
Engine turned and plain with signet.
No. N1165
No. N1165½

No. N1166 Gold filled, 14k
Engine turned design.

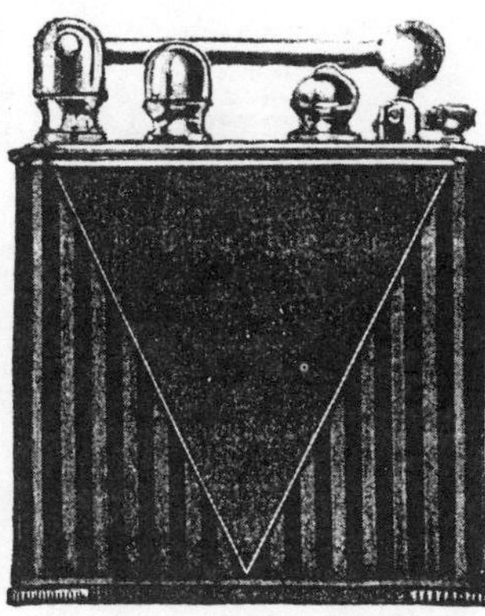

No. N1167 14k gold filled
This model, with a fresh, sparkling turn in design.

WADSWORTH, the master designer of America's finest watch cases, has put his genius in a group of cases for DOUGLASS LIGHTERS. 14k gold filled and sterling silver in all its treatments with engine turning and enamels. These select Douglasses mark a new day in the highest class lighters. Some show the modern-trend lines and angles. Others find their inspiration in classic designs.

All are Douglass Silhouettes—thin, graceful, worthy of the company they keep.

No. N1168 14k gold filled
No. N1168½ Sterling silver.
A beautiful design in the checker decoration.
No. N1168
No. N1168½

No. N1169 14k gold filled
No. N1169½ Sterling silver.
Delicate inlaid lines of enamel.
No. N1169
No. 61169½

No. N1170 14k gold filled
No. N1170½ Sterling silver.
Delicate inlaid lines of enamel.
No. N1170
No. N1170½

No. N1171 14k gold filled
No. N1171½ Sterling silver.
Delicate inlaid lines of enamel.
No. N1171
No. N1171½

No. N1172 14k gold filled
No. N1172½ Sterling silver.
Engine turned design with small squares enameled.
No. N1172
No. N1172½

1930 CATALOG PAGE

Douglass Automatic Lighters

PRESS THE TRIGGER—THERE'S YOUR LIGHT

No. N1135 . . . .

The lowest price of all Douglasses, yet with all Douglass' mechanical advantages. Made of sturdy polished nickel.

No. N1136 Black . . . .
No. N1137 Brown . . . .
No. N1138 Snake . . . .

Sturdy polished nickel case covered with above leathers.

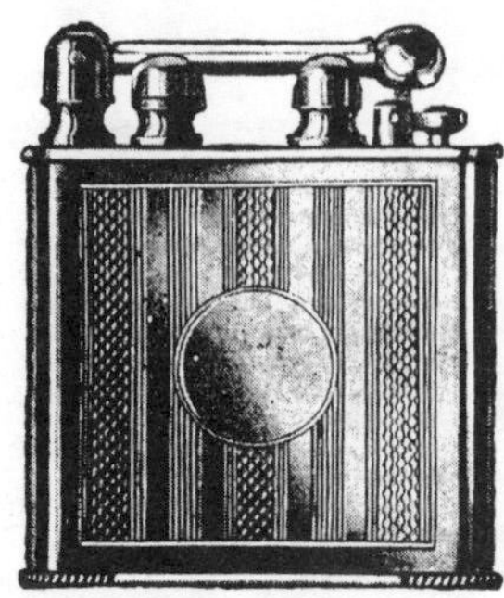

No. N1139 . . . .

A polished nickel plated model in the thin silhouette style, like a modern watch with chased lines, as shown.

No. N1140 Alligator . . . .
No. N1141 Black . . . . . .
No. N1142 Brown . . . . . .

Silhouette style, extra thin mode covered with above leathers.

No. N1143 . . .

Silhouette style (extra thin model), silver plated with chased design.

Refinements

have brought Douglass Lighters to a new perfection

The Douglass automatic principle marked a new day in lighters. The first Douglass models are giving faithful service yet. But there have been many small improvements. A tighter cap prevents evaporation, better springs assure livelier sparks—every threatened weakness has been overcome. Douglasses today have reached the highest plane of lighter performance.

No. N1144 Ostrich
No. N1145 Pig Skin
No. N1146 Snake
No. N1147 Pin Seal
No. N1148 Alligator
No. N1149 Br. Lizard

Silhouette style, silver plated, leather covered.

No. N1150 Red & Black
No. N1151 Blue & Black
No. N1152 Green & Black

Silhouette style, silver plated, with above enameled combinations.

No. N1153

Silhouette style, gold plated.

No. N1154 Red & Black . .
No. N1155 Blue & Black
No. N1156 Green & Black

Silhouette style, gold plated with above enameled combinations.

No. N1157 Ostrich . . . .
No. N1158 Pig Skin
No. N1159 Snake
No. N1160 Pin Seal . . .
No. N1161 Alligator . . .
No. N1162 Br. Lizard . .

Silhouette style, gold plated with above leather coverings.

1930 CATALOG PAGE

No. 400—Goldplated lighter with bronze figure,

THESE NEW STYLE AUTOMATIC SWISS-MADE DESK AND TABLE LIGHTERS HAVE PROVEN TO BE THE BEST SELLERS OF THE YEAR.

No. 403—Goldplated lighter with bronze figure on Brazilian Onyx pedestal,

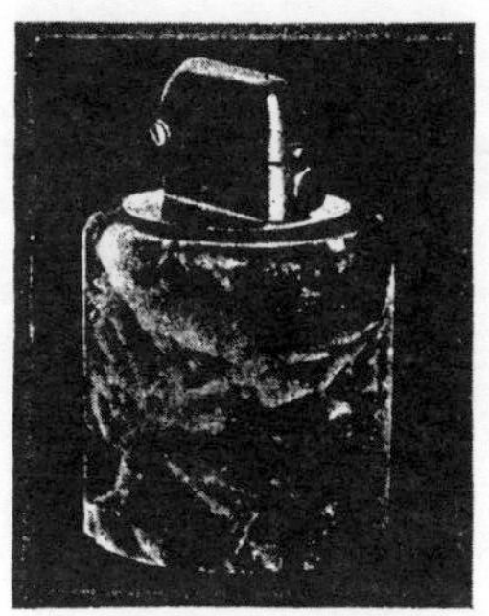

No. 520—Goldplated lighter with Brazilian Onyz base,

No. 500 —Nickelplated lighter with Italian Marble base

Many Other Beautiful Styles and Designs to select from.

THORENS, Inc.

450 Fourth Avenue
New York, N. Y.

No. 300—Goldplated lighter with Synthetic Ivory base,

LEVIN BROS., TERRE HAUTE, IND.

Again "Match King" Sets the Pace!

Never Lags in Sales—Produces the Volume Dealers Want and

If Unchanged Would Still Be the Greatest Dependable Lighter on the MARKET

—Yet It Is NOW Tremendously

IMPROVED!

—so that the NEW models have made them once more

America's Greatest Sellers

A nationally advertised and extensively used product—NEW, yes, but a constantly growing favorite. Hits the "bullseye" every time for sales. The idea once suppressed now an actual reality! Does away entirely with the obsolete systems of automatic lighting and makes available a sure light—no mere flicker but a real flame that gives you time to "light up" cigar, cigarette or pipe. Lights and burns like an ordinary match.

Win Sales With "Match King"

Match King Model 75

Improved handsome Match King with the removable flint feature — acknowledged fast seller. This small size makes it sufficiently compact to be conveniently tucked away in vest pocket or milady's purse. Made in convenient oval shape and finished in chromium—available in assorted subjects of 12 different kinds on display card.

J4253—Match King Model 75.

Match King Two-Piece Combination Set

Consists of Cigarette Case and LIGHTER

Sensational value is this matched two-piece combination set. Consists of cigarette case holding full pack and a major model Match King lighter. Case is finished in chromium with baked-on enamel colorings. Set is cellophane wrapped and boxed.

J4254—Match King Combination Set. Set

Match King Model 60

Compact, light weight "Match King" made of bakelite and produced in a pleasing array of eye-catching colors. Its oval shape gives it elegance and makes for more convenience when tucked away in vest pocket or in ladies' purse. These come packed 12 assorted in special display box.

J4256—Match King Model 60.

Match King Model 15

Extremely attractive pocket model made in a series of assorted popular designs, finished in varied colors. 1 doz. assorted in sales-stimulating display box.

J4255—Match King Model 15.

You cant make MONEY unless you try

Offer FLASHY Practical Premiums

CIGAR LIGHTERS ARE MORE POPULAR NOW THAN EVER BEFORE

Feature These Special LIGHTERS

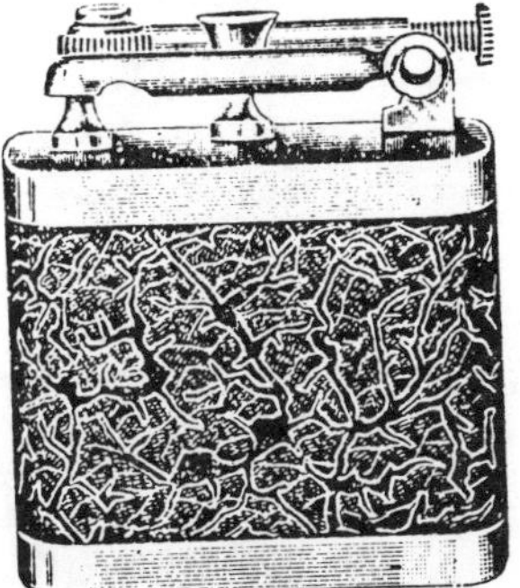

Miniature Size Vest Pocket Lighter

J93—Vest Pocket Lighter. Offered at a price that makes it especially attractive for premium purposes. Nickel plated trim, covered with imitation leather in assorted colors. Doz. in box.

Combination Watch and Pocket Cigar Lighter

J92—Watch Lighter. Assorted chromium and gold plated, fancy shaped lighters, fitted with 6-jewel cylinder movements, black numerals and hands. In this unusual combination the operator of punch boards has a real attraction to get the money. Any man who sees this fine outfit will want one and no doubt will take a "chance" to win it.

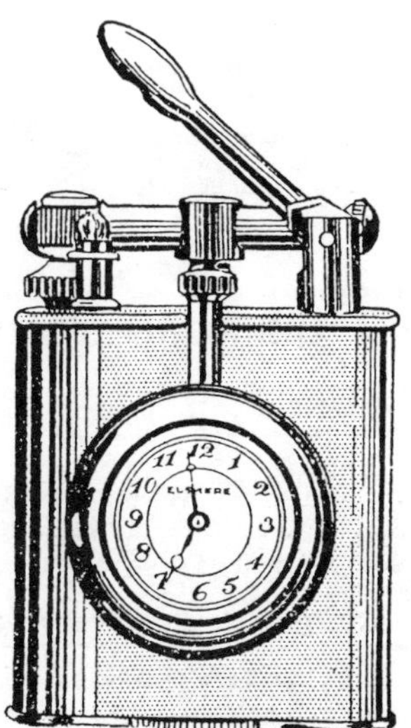

NEW Combination Pencils and LIGHTERS

Innovations That Appeal, Catch the Eye and Make Sales for You

These Pencil Lighters are distinctly new and are an answer to the quest for a practical device of this kind that dealers might handle profitably at a popular price.

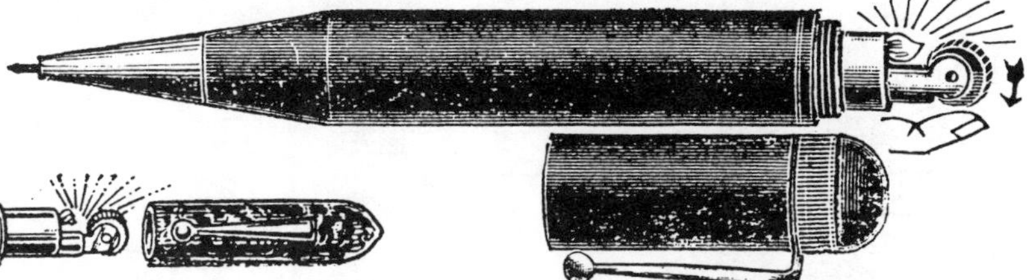

J3120—Combination Pencil Lighter. An exceptionally good looking pencil made of metal and finished in nickel and black. Repels, expels and propels the lead, just like any other more expensive pencil will do. The lighter section incorporates reservoir for fluid with wheel and wick. Flares up instantly to provide a light for all kinds of smokes. Has attached pocket clip. Length 5¼ in.

J3121—Combination Pencil Lighter. Lovely oversize composition barrel in onyx and charming color contrasts. Performs efficiently to propel, repel and expel the lead just like any ordinary much more expensive pencil. Embodies in addition to pencil feature complete section with reservoir, wheel and wick for lighting all kinds of smokes. When cap is screwed on lighter is concealed from view, accordingly it appears like mechanical pencil only. A genuine bargain at our low price. Length 4¼ in.

1939 CATALOG PAGE

OWL LIGHTER

No. M73. Novelty lighter, yet practical. Convenient to carry in pocket or purse. Owl head cover. Thumb wheel action. May be had in either nickel or enamel finish. Weight, per dozen, 3 ozs.

Dozen, 35c; Gross, $3.95

No. M245. Air-ship shaped cigarette lighters made of highly polished nickel finish with assorted colored silk tassels. An ideal premium number. Length approximately 2¼ inches. Weight, each, ½ oz.

Sample, 6c;
Dozen, 50c; Gross, $5.75

OCTAGON SHAPED LIGHTERS

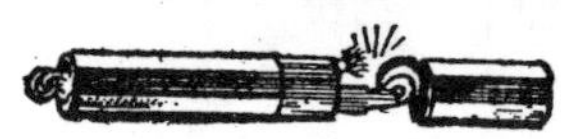

No. M243-H. Octagon shaped pocket lighter. Nickel plated. Suitable for ladies' handbag or for men. Weight, each, 1 oz.

Selling price, 15c

Wholesale Sample, 6c;
Dozen, 35c; Gross, $3.65

No. M239-I. Octagon shape pocket lighter. Same as above but is shorter, lighter weight case.

Sample, 3c; Dozen, 30c; Gross, $2.98

OCTAGON LIGHTERS WITH TASSEL

No. M244. Pocket or handbag lighter with colored silk tassel. Nickel finish. Octagon shape. Weight, 1 oz.

Selling price, 15c

Wholesale Sample, 5c;

Dozen, 35c; Gross, $3.75

BULLET SHAPE LIGHTER

No. M51. A novelty lighter yet practical. The shell end covers the lighter part. Nickel finish outside. A fast seller. Weight, each, ½ oz.

Selling price, 10c to 25c

Sample, 5c; Dozen, 40c; Gross, $4.45

IMPORTED LIPSTICK LIGHTER

No. M253-H. Imported lipstick lighters, less expensive quality, same shape as above.

Selling price, 15c

Sample, 6c; Dozen, 48c; Gross, $4.45

★ MIDGET LIPSTICK LIGHTER ★

No. M249-S. Convenient to carry in pocket or purse. Made of metal finished with chip-proof, hard-baked enamel which comes in assorted colors. Trimmed with silver colored metal. Fitted with high grade tool steel sparking wheel. Twelve assorted colored lighters on a card. Weight, per card, 10 ozs.

Selling price, 25c

Sample, 9c; Dozen, 98c; Gross, $11.50

No. M212-O. A light with every strike. Simple to operate, nothing to get out of order. Made of highly polished nickel finish.

Selling price, 15c

Sample, 7c;
Dozen, 69c; Gross, $7.98

★ COMBINATION LIGHTER PENCIL ★

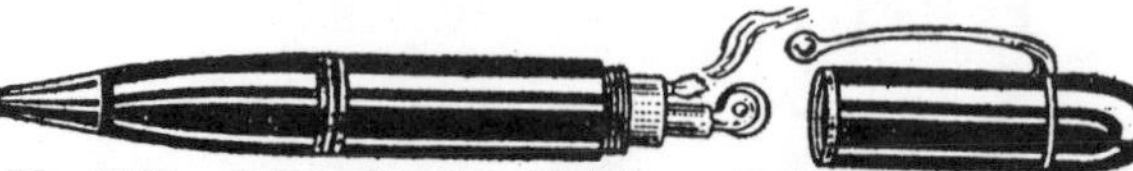

No. M43. Solid black, highly polished, exceptionally fine finish, good quality throughout. Mechanical pencil repels and expels, lighter always works. Each in a box. Weight, each, 1 oz.

Selling price, 25c to 35c

Sample, 12c; Dozen, $1.15; Gross, $12.90

Display cards for above, 5c each.

PENCIL AND LIGHTER

No. M53-U. Same as above but has enameled metal barrel in assorted colors. 1 dozen in display carton. Weight, dozen, 7 ozs.

Selling price, 15c

Sample, 8c; Dozen, 85c; Gross, $9.90

POCKET LIGHTER

No. M38-BO. Very attractive. Comes in beautiful assorted marble-like finish; nickel trimmings. A smooth working, durable lighter. Weight, each, 1 oz.

Selling price, 35c

Sample, 16c; Dozen, $1.58

Gross, $17.75

AUTOMATIC POCKET LIGHTER

No. M60. Fitted with efficient, dependable mechanism. Case is made of black or brown fancy bakelite case. Works smoothly and will give complete satisfaction. Weight, each, 1 oz.

Selling price, 50c

Sample, 14c; Dozen, $1.35
Gross, $15.60

FLINTS AND WICKS FOR LIGHTERS

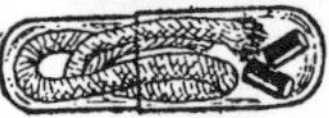

No. M111-I. Each envelope contains one wick and two flints. Will fit all styles of pocket lighters.

Selling price, 5c

Sample, 3c; Dozen, 25c; Gross, $2.75
Per 1,000 Pkgs., $13.50

JUNIOR MODEL MATCH KING

No. M172. Made of bakelite with fancy overlay design. Special thumb piece. Weight, each, 1 oz.

Selling price, 25c

Sample, 14c; Dozen, $1.45

EXTRA FLINTS FOR ABOVE LIGHTER

No. M174-S. To fit our No. M172 Match King Lighter.

Selling price, 15c

Sample, 9c; Dozen, 96c; Gross, $10.90

"MATCH KING" THE EVERLASTING MATCH

No. M169. A match of a million lights. No wick, no wheels, no springs. Does away with old style matches. Can be lit and relit simply by striking it again and again. Bakelite case in assorted colors, nickel knob. Uses any lighter fluid. Weight, 1 oz.

Selling price, 50c

Sample, 29c; Dozen, $2.95

No. M173-S. Extra flints to fit our No. M169 Lighter.

Sample, 9c; Dozen, 96c; Gross, $10.90

LIKES OUR VARIETY AND QUALITY

I consider you the one outstanding concern in your line of business. I have sold for a number of concerns in the past, but none of them could compare with you in the high quality of merchandise and the large variety to choose from.

—J. W. Bowden, Louisiana.

1939 CATALOG PAGE

BALL MODEL CIGAR LIGHTER FOR SMOKER TABLE

No. M35. Fine as a premium or prize. Ball shaped. Nickel finish. Dependable. Ideal as a desk or table lighter. Weight, 4 ozs.

Selling price, 50c
Sample, 18c; Dozen, $1.95; Gross, $21.60

AUTOMATIC TABLE LIGHTER

No. M25. A dependable lighter that will give good service. Has an attractive body which comes in assorted colors; polished metal top and bottom. Fitted with a simple lighting mechanism—press lever and the wick lights. Ideal for office, home, den, desk or table. Height, 3½ inches. Each in a box. Weight, 3 ozs.

Selling price, 50c
Sample, 18c; Dozen, $1.95; Gross, $21.60

AUTOMATIC PISTOL LIGHTER

No. M37. Handy and convenient. When trigger is pulled, the lighter is ready for use; when released the light is extinguished. Small, compact and can be carried in vest pocket. Nickel-like finish top and trigger, black composition butt. Weight, each, 2¼ ozs.

Selling price, 95c
Sample, 45c; Dozen, $4.75

AUTOMATIC LIGHTER

No. M30. Looks like a watch. The stem presses in and operates the flint wheel. Nickel plated. Sturdily constructed. A real practical lighter. Weight, each, 2 ozs.

Selling price, 69c
Sample, 39c; Dozen, $3.95

CAMERA LIGHTER

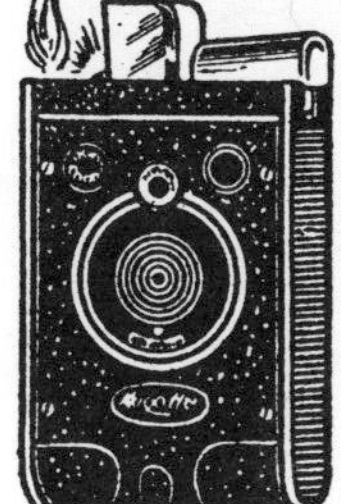

No. M69. Consists of black composition case made to represent a small camera. Has nickel plated automatic lighting mechanism fitted inside. Merely press top and presto! it lights. You will be proud to own one of these fast-selling novelty lighters. Length, 2¼ inches. Weight, each, 2 ozs.

Selling price, 50c
Sample, 17c; Dozen, $1.75

TWO-WHEEL LIGHTER.

No. M72. Has a highly polished nickel plated case. Fitted with an efficient and dependable mechanism. A turn of the two smooth-running wheels gives an instant spark. Each in a box. Height, 2½ inches. Weight, each, 1 oz.

Suggested selling price, 50c to 75c
Sample, 25c; Dozen, $2.45

FLINTS AND WICKS FOR LIGHTERS

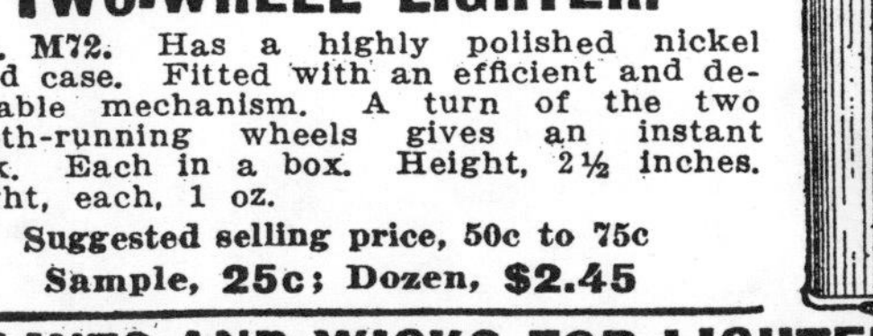

No. M111-I. Each envelope contains one wick and two flints. Will fit all styles of pocket lighters.

Selling price, 5c
Sample, 3c;
Dozen, 25c; Gross, $2.75
Per 1,000 Pkgs., $13.50

WINDPROOF ZIPPO LIGHTER

No. M250. Thousands of Zippos have given constant, faultless service since its production.

Here are the features:

Windproof—lights instantly; protector feature makes it stay lighted.

One hand control—convenient and safe for motorists, sportsmen and travelers.

Large capacity—a filling lasts two weeks with usual use.

Smart appearance—stainless chromium finish. Weight, each, 3 ozs.

Selling price, $2.00
Sample, $1.29; Dozen, $14.40

CHROME WIND-PROOF LIGHTER

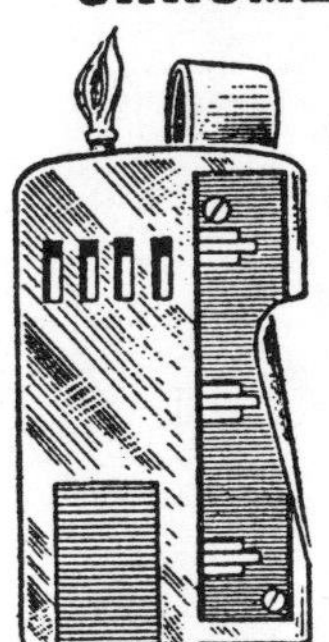

No. M177. A better quality lighter with a chrome plated case. Has a perforated chimney which protects the flame from the wind. Automatic flint control. Large tank for fuel supply. Can be used to light pipes, cigars, cigarettes and start a fire. Will burn any of the common lighter fluids. Easy one hand action. Closes automatically. Weight, each, 1½ oz.

Selling price, $1.00
Wholesale Sample, 42c;
Dozen, $4.75

AUTOMATIC STORM LIGHTER

No. M91. Handsomely designed nickel plated lighter. Dependable full automatic action. Simply press side, top will open and light. Bottom tank can be taken out and used as pipe lighter. Can be lit in draft or gale. Comes in assorted nickel designs. Each in box. Weight, 2 ozs.

Suggested selling price, 50c
Sample, 29c; Dozen, $2.95

WIND-PROOF LIGHTER

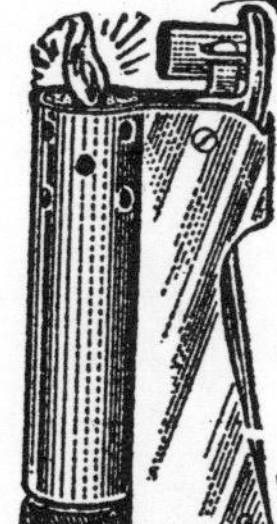

No. M32. A shielded flame at the "press of a thumb." Has a perforated "chimney" which protects the flame from wind; automatic flint control; large tank for fuel supply; and nickel plated case. Can be used to light pipes, cigarettes or start fires. It is convenient to carry in pocket or purse. Will burn any of the common lighter fluids. Just the thing for golfing, hunting, fishing, automobiling or where a shielded, wind-proof flame is desired. Weight, 1½ ozs.

Selling price, 35c
Sample, 12c; Dozen, $1.15; Gross, $13.45

WIND POCKET LIGHTER

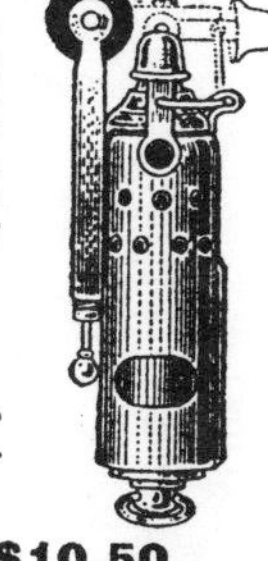

No. M33. Will light cigarette, cigar or pipe in a heavy wind. Fitted with a sliding cylinder which protects the flame from wind and danger of being blown out. Fine for hunters, golfers, sportsmen, fishermen, etc. Small enough so it can be carried in pocket very conveniently. May be had in nickel or brass finish. Weight, each, 1 oz.

Selling price, 25c
Sample, 10c; Dozen, 89c; Gross, $9.95

No. M64. Same as above but has streamlined case.

Selling price, 25c
Sample, 9c; Dozen, 90c; Gross, $10.50

LIGHTER FLUID

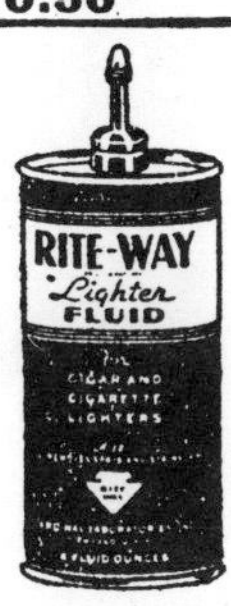

No. M59. Lights instantly. No smoke or odor. A dependable, high quality fuel for all cigarette lighters. Cans provided with sealed-tip filler spout. This bright, attractive can sells on sight. Weight, each, 6 ozs.

Suggested selling price, 10c to 15c
Sample, 7c; Dozen, 75c; Gross, $8.64

We can supply you with any electro as illustrated in this catalog at 35c each. Electros cannot be returned for credit.

1941 CATALOG PAGE

DUNHILL *"Silent Flame"* LIGHTERS

FOR PIPES . Cigars and Cigare

Silent Flame—a new principle that produces efficient, lasting lighting service. **A smooth, perfect flame obtained in an instant** by merely pulling out the cylindrical holder and touching it to the side of the case. **Burns like a match**—without a flicker.

DUNHILL Triangular TABLE LIGHTER

A novelty in artistic simplicity of design that makes it as unusual ornament for table or desk. In addition to its unusual appearance it contains the most efficient, dependable lighter ever developed—the famous Dunhill "Silent Flame." When the stem is removed from the center and held against the side of the lighter it silently bursts into a smooth, perfect flame, ideal for cigar, pipe or cigarette. Its gleaming chrome finish adds distinction to home or office.

No. 3QD150.

★

DUNHILL TURN-O-TOP Lighter-Dispenser

Combination Dunhill Silent Flame Lighter and cigarette dispenser. Turn the top and a cigarette pops up. Then get a light just as easily from the "Silent Flame." In genuine leather with saddle stitched trim in rich chestnut brown (dark). Size 3¾ in. high, 4 in. wide.

No. 3QD310.

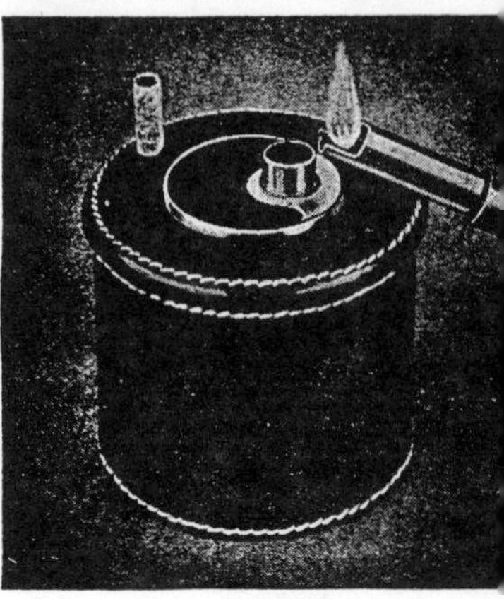

Table Lighters

N7586 - Antimony Lighters. Asstd. styles consisting of Dogs, Lions, Elephants and Tigers, average height 1 1/2 in., individually boxed. Each animal equipped with hinged head and complete lighter therein.

Dunhill Lighter

"Silent Flame" Appears When Body of Fan Dancer Is Touched

Everyone likes to use this attractive and mirth-provoking "Silent-Flame" table lighter. Lighting operation is simple—just remove lighter stick, which inserts in base and holds wick and fluid, touch tip to the body of the "Fan Dancer", and Presto! . . . There's a flame! Contact completes an electric circuit. The base is attractive brown bakelite. Size 5" high — 3" square.

No. 155H250 — Fan Dancer. Shpg. wt. 2 lbs.

BEATTIE JET LIGHTER

Here is a pipe and cigarette lighter that was designed to fill a long-felt need. Tilt it for pipes — and in a few seconds a jet of flame gushes out to pipe bowl. Easy to light. No pressure is necessary. Use it upright for cigarettes and cigars. SELLS ITSELF. Once its practicability is demonstrated, pipe smokers buy on sight. Durably constructed and attractively finished in black enamel.

No. 56V395—Beatty Jet Lighter. Shpg. wt. ½ lb.

1945 CATALOG PAGE

Every smoker knows that the distinguished name of Dunhill means outstanding performance and supreme quality. Fine craftsmanship and choice materials give unequalled value guaranteed by the famous Dunhill name.

STERLING SILVER WINDPROOF

In wind or storm you can light your cigarette outdoors with this De Luxe fuel-less lighter. A simple flip of the wheel ignites the chemically pretreated wick in the best or the worst weather. Ideal for servicemen and sportsmen. It gives dependable service every time. **$5.00**

Add 20% U. S. tax **1.00**

$6.00

alfred dunhill SERVICE LIGHTER

SERVICE is the key feature of this smartly styled lighter. One touch of the thumb and it is open and lit, ready for action! A gale-proof case protects the flame. The generous fuel capacity assures faithful service and complete dependability.

NEW MODEL
NEW LOW PRICE

ENAMEL FINISH $1.00

dunhill
50 LIGHTER FLINTS

DUNHILL LIGHTER FLINTS

For maximum efficiency and for economy, too, get a supply of these top grade flints.

50 for $1.00

AONIAN FLINTS

Keep a supply of these sure - shot flints for all standard lighters.

5 flints
10c

AONIAN FLINTS AND WICKS

4 flints and a wick
10c

AONIAN FLINTS

for lightning service, fit your lighter with free-sparking Aonian flints.

30 for 50c

THOREN'S BELBLUE

For economy's sake get this wooden cylinder containing the superior quality Thorens Flint.

40 for 50c

GEORGE YALE ★ 1083 SIXTH AVENUE (near 41st Street) ★ NEW YORK 18, N. Y.

1945 CATALOG PAGE

Thorens
"The Lighter That Works"
PRODUCT OF SWITZERLAND
THORENS WINDPROOF
has a built-in wind guard for flame protection in every kind of weather. Chrome Finish.
$4.00
SATISFACTION GUARANTEED OR MONEY BACK
THORENS AUTOMATIC
lights at instant pressure and locks for safety when not in use. Chrome Finish.
$5.00
NEW IMPROVED
FOXHOLE BLACKOUT LIGHTER
This amazing lighter needs no fuel but burns at any time in any weather. A simple turn of the wheel ignites the chemically pre-treated wick. Its absolute dependability is a boon to those who demand consistent service. With 2 extra Wicks and 18 extra Flints.
$1.50
FOXHOLE BLACKOUT LIGHTER
EAGLE FLINTS and WICK
for all "rope" model lighters. Includes 2 flints.
15c
MIGHTY MIDGET
Convenience and dependability are paired in this 2½" cigarette lighter, made of vari-colored enamelled metal.
69c
BALL OF FLAME
Made with a special wick to create a torch-like arch of flame, this lighter is indispensable to pipe and cigar smokers. The ball end contains extra flint
89c
NO REQUEST NEEDED FOR G I XMAS GIFT: SEPTEMBER 15-OCTOBER 15!

1946-47 CATALOG PAGE

DISTINCTIVELY STYLED FIRST QUALITY LIGHTERS

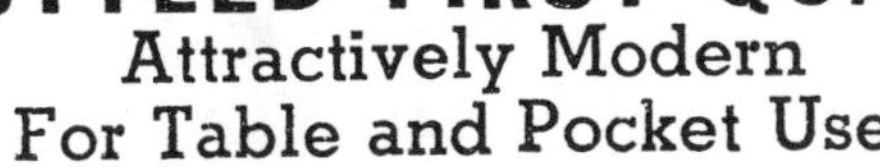

Attractively Modern For Table and Pocket Use

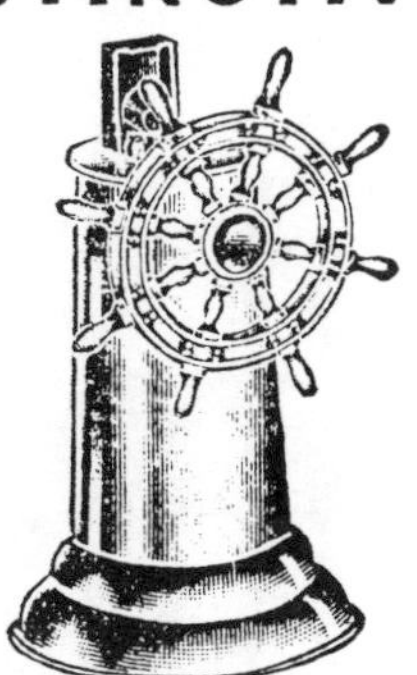

No. 1199—Deluxe Marine Lighter. Beauty and usefulness combine to make this a delightfully new and different cigarette lighter. The little ship's wheel is exact in design down to the tiniest little rivet. Turn the realistic ship's wheel and a steady dependable flame is produced by which a cigar or cigarette can be lighted. Crafted of finest quality steel with an exquisite, sparkling chrome plated finish. Ideal for dens, offices or anyplace where beauty is a dire necessity. Strong sturdy spring assures powerful flashing spark from extra long flint. Large capacity fuel compartment. One filling will last a month under ordinary use. Height, 5 inches.

GIANT TABLE LIGHTER No. 1181

Each

Giant Table Lighter. It's a super jumbo extra large table lighter that is made exactly like a small pocket size automatic lighter. A brilliant idea that finds a humorous welcome on desk, table or bar. Massive in size, it is heavily constructed and modernly designed with chrome plate finish and covered with simulated Lizard, Alligator and Morocco in black and tan. Has instant lighting automatic mechanism and features a precision milled ignition wheel. Extra large fuel compartment—one filling lasts 30 days under ordinary use. One extra piece of flint is furnished with each lighter. Individually boxed. Height, 4 inches.

No. 1197—Horses Head Table Lighter. Way in the lead and still going in popularity. A novel new distinguished looking table lighter that is just the thing for home, office or club. Exceptionally well made of sparkling gold-like die-cast metal, molded into an appealing replica of a horses head. Dependable lighter mechanism in top can be easily removed for refilling. Base is conveniently padded with soft cushiony felt to insure against marring glossy furniture surfaces. Height 4¾ inches.
Each ....

No. 1195—Oxford Table Lighter. The very newest in a modern all around table lighter. Round chrome plated top is securely countersunk into a sparkling crystal clear transparent lucite base cut into a majestic pyramid shape. Has ample fuel capacity and adjustable flint tension. Features simple reliable mechanism that lights with a flick of the finger. Thoroughly dependable, this perfected lighter is a favorite for home or office. Height, 3 inches; width, 2⅞ inches.

No. 1196—Oxford Table Lighter. Same style as above but in assorted breathtaking transparent colors

No. 3057 — Lektrolite Flameless Lapel Cigarette Lighter. A lighter with the endearing appeal of a treasure. There's no other lighter like it. Simply insert end of cigarette, inhale, and presto—it's lighted. No wheels, no wicks, no flints, no sparks—nothing but a dependable light every time—even in a gale. Has a smart Lumigold case enriched with a glistening simulated gold cap and a fine genuine braided leather thong lapel button. A lighter of great distinction. Attractively packaged with 1 oz. container of fluid.

No. 3056 — Lektrolite Flameless Key-Chain Cigarette Lighter. It's the one lighter that's ornamental as well as useful. Crafted like fine jewelry it has a Lumigold case with sparkling simulated gold cap and short stirrup-model key-chain attached. Beauty with a purpose for people who like the practical. Insert end of cigarette, inhale, and you have an instant light. No moving mechanical parts—nothing but a dependable light every time—even in a storm. Appealing packaged with 1 oz. container of fluid.

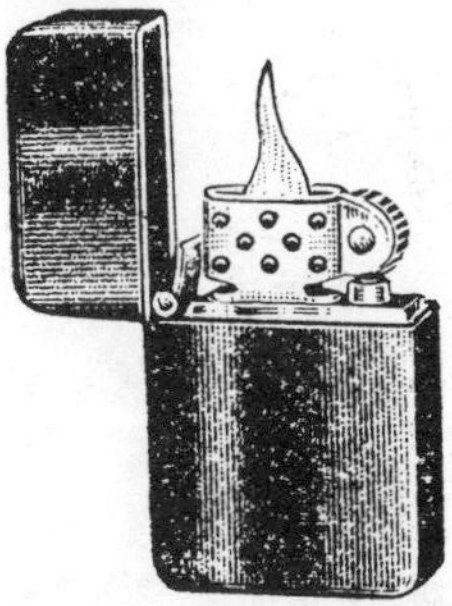

No. 1171 — Zephyr Windproof Lighter. Windproof and dependable. it lights instantly under all conditions, even in gale, storm or blizzard. Modernly designed to provide the utmost in durability, it comes in assorted two-tone metallic and enamel finish or attractive hammerloid finishes. With a spring actuated top that is easy to open, it features a heavy metal die-cast case that contains a reliable compact lighter unit having an extra heavy nickel plated flame guard of sturdy one-piece construction. Flint tension is easily adjusted by means of a concealed set screw.

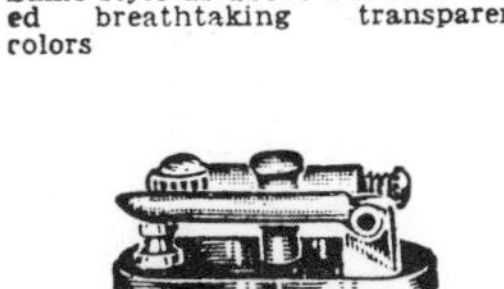

No. 1198—Cigarette Lighter. Compact, easy to carry around, dependable and safe. Marvelously constructed to withstand an unmentionable amount of punishment. Features easy-to-load strong spring tension flint chamber. Just a flick of the thumb and a powerful spark is produced to ignite the long lasting wick. Has long snuffing arm to safeguard against smoldering wicks. Large fuel capacity. One filling will last a week or more under ordinary usage. Height, 1¾ inches; width, 1½ inches.

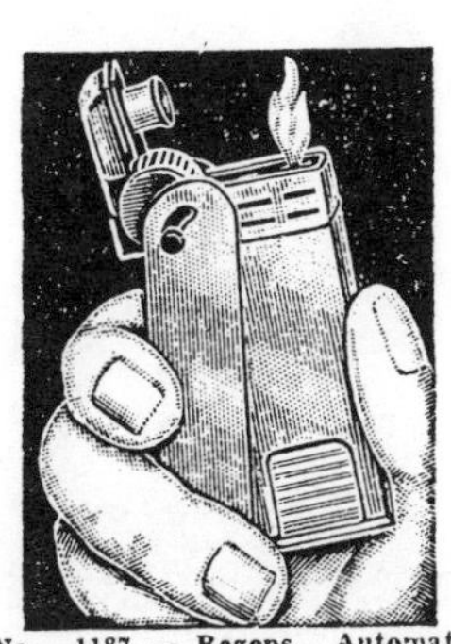

No. 1187 — Regens Automatic Storm Lighter. A new and different lighter that lights automatically by gently pressing the sides, producing a steady flame, amply protected against wind and storm. As an extra convenience, easy removal of outer casing forms a torch for lighting pipes. Expertly constructed of polished nickel plated steel. Length, 2¼ inches. Packed each in box, one dozen in colorful, illustrated display carton.

No. 1157 — Lektrolite Flameless Cigarette Lighter. A new sensational lighter that has no gadgets to get out of order, no wheels to spin, no spark, no flare—absolutely flameless. Just insert tip of cigarette, push button-end in, draw on cigarette and it's lit. Lights any time, anywhere, under all conditions. Sturdily made of lustrous plastic in gleaming black and bright red color combinations. Also included with each lighter is a 1 oz. can of genuine Lektrolite lighter fluid. Each in display box.

No. 3060—Wind Proof Lighter. A massively designed pocket lighter in a modern featherweight style that is ideal for all smokers who desire a lighter of real distinction. Made of the finest die-cast metal and polished to a sparkling mirror-like finish, it has a hammered-effect design with convenient space for monogram. Features thumb-type wheel that gives off a powerful spark to light the long lasting wick. Entirely windproof, it will light in the strongest wind or gale. Has spacious fuel compartment.

233-243 No. Water Street GENERAL MERCHANDISE COMPANY Milwaukee 1, Wisconsin

Hard-to-get Windproof Lighters

Immediate Delivery

No. 1620 — Kem Bottle Lighter. A real novelty in a sensational pocket lighter that is tremendously popular with men and women. Made of heavy metal in the exact shape of a miniature bottle. Features a highly polished nickel plated finish with a jet-black enamelled band that is decorated with four aces. Has a dependable lighter unit having an easy-to-fill fuel compartment. Another plus feature is the adjustable flint tension for sure-fire lighting ability. Height, closed, 2½ inches. Put up one dozen on a colored display card.

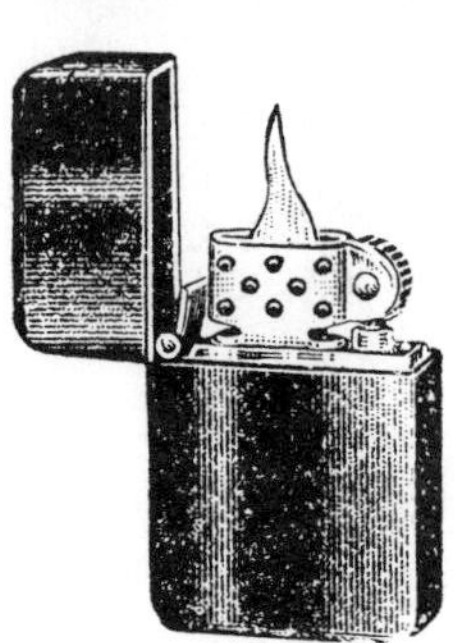

No. 1151 — Superior Windproof Lighter. A sensational lighter that is tops in durability, quality and popularity. Lights in a jiffy in gale or storm—absolutely windproof. Features heavy metal case attractively finished in crackle enamel. Also has perforated wind guard, adjustable flint tension and strong spring-snap top. Each in box.

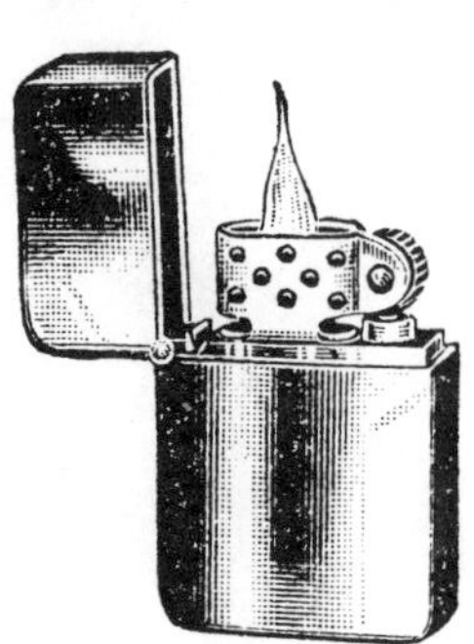

No. 1152 — Zephyr Windproof Lighter. Sparkles like a jewel in its lustrous highly polished mirror-like chromium finish. Sensational windproof style known for its unfailing dependability. Sturdily constructed of heavy metal with strong spring actuated top. Features large fuel capacity, adjustable flint tension and perforated wind guard. Each in box.

No. 1619—Wind Boss Pocket Lighter. The smoker's choice, this sensational lighter is leak proof and wind proof—scientific wind guard assures an instant light under all conditions. Though small in size, it has a new style fluid-conserving inner seal that provides hundreds of lights between refills. Excellent for men or women, it has a beautiful enamel finish in assorted green, white, blue and red colors. Length, closed, 2⅝ inches. One dozen on display card.

No. 1184 — Bowers Storm Master Lighter. The very newest in a good all-around pocket lighter for pipes as well as cigarettes. Made in latest windproof style having an extra wide thick wick for longer life, greater fuel economy and unfailing reliability. Crafted of solid brass that sparkles like gold with its highly polished mirror finish. Easy to fill, too—has no screws to remove. Another sales feature is the easily adjustable flint tension that provides an instant light with a flick of the thumb. Height, closed, 2 inches. One dozen on flashy display card.

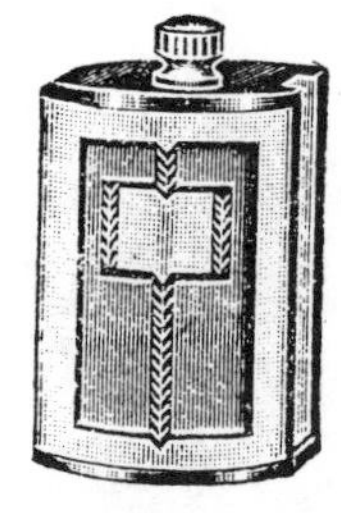

No. 1611—Match King Pocket Lighter. No mechanical wheels, gears or springs to get out of order—no moving parts at all. Newest thin style that fits vest pocket or purse. Single filling lasts a week or more. Made entirely of sturdy metal with assorted decorative designs. Supplied in assorted colors and finishes.

No. 1618 — Flare Pocket Lighter. A luxurious long slender lighter that features a highly polished nickel plated finish. Has simple sturdy dependable lighter mechanism that assures years of satisfactory service. Ample fuel capacity—a single filling lasts 2 weeks or more. Excellent for pocket or purse. Each in box.

No. 1155—Oxford Lighters. Made for lasting durability, this excellent lighter has a large fuel capacity and a dependable compact mechanism that is built for service. Case is enameled in assorted colors, including blue, red and lustrous black. Length, 2½ inches. One dozen on display card.

No. 1156—Oxford Chrome Lighters. Same lighter as above but with highly polished chrome finish.

No. 1624—Oxford Junior Lighter. Same as enameled lighter listed above but in smaller junior size. Length, 2⅛ inches. One dozen on display card.

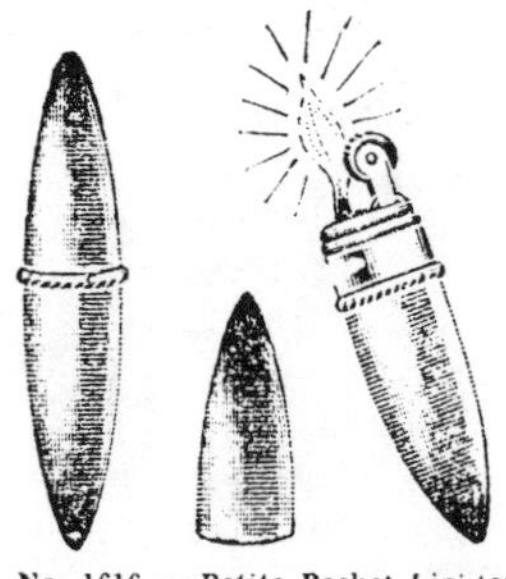

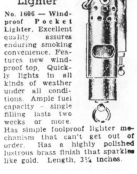

No. 1616 — Petite Pocket Lighter. A modernly styled purse or pocket size lighter. Beautifully made of heavy metal with attractive enamel finish in assorted gay colors. Has reliable lighter mechanism with adjustable flint tension. Easily refilled. Delightfully dainty, this lighter is preferred by many women. Length, 3 inches.

No. 1600 — Handy-Lite Cigarette Lighter. No wheels, no gears, no mechanism! Excellently made of high quality stainless steel, it fits vest pocket or purse. To operate, simply pull out striker, and with a single short firm stroke a steady flame is produced. A very dependable lighter for cigars, cigarettes, or pipes that is in public demand. Put up 12 lighters on attractive, colorful display card.

No. 1610 — Allbright Gold Plated Cigarette Lighter. A remarkable cigarette lighter — unequaled in beauty and tops in utility. Excellently styled and expertly constructed, its modern, graceful lines are enhanced by rich lustrous gold plating. Assorted engraved chased designs, each a masterpiece in patterned loveliness, add an air of dignity to each lighter. Thoroughly dependable perfected lighter mechanism makes it a favorite with all users. Height, 2½ inches. Packed one dozen lighters in colorful box.

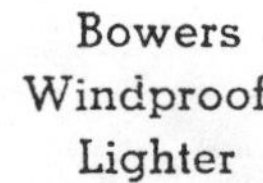

Bowers Windproof Lighter

No. 1606 — Windproof Pocket Lighter. Excellent quality assures enduring smoking convenience. Features new windproof top. Quickly lights in all kinds of weather under all conditions. Ample fuel capacity — single filling lasts two weeks or more. Has simple foolproof lighter mechanism that can't get out of order. Has a highly polished lustrous brass finish that sparkles like gold. Length, 3¼ inches.

1953 CATALOG PAGE

WINDPROOF
Chromium, Engine turned
No. 301.....

NOTE: Enamels and leathers are packed
Six assorted black and tortoise to carton.

WINDPROOF
Black Enamel, Engine turned
No. 302......

WINDPROOF
Tortoise Enamel, Engine turned
No. 302.....

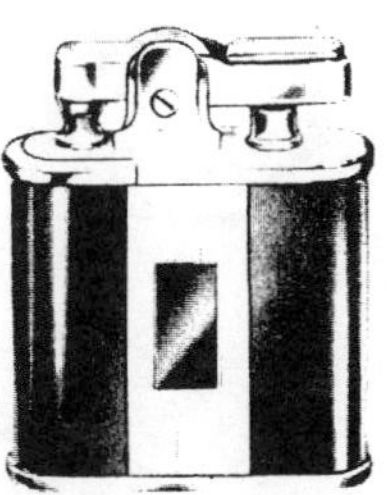

WINDPROOF
Black Enamel, Engine turned
No. 302.....

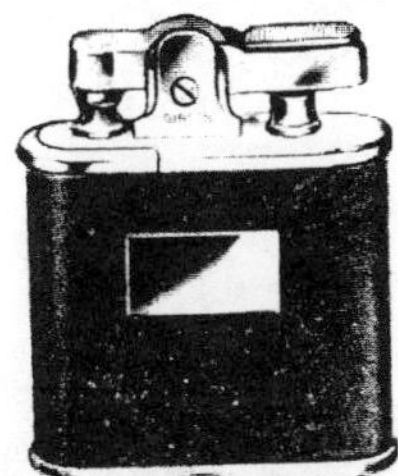

WINDPROOF
Genuine leather, Ostrich grain
No. 303.....

WINDPROOF
Genuine leather, Alligator grain
No. 303.....

"A" DEAL

One Dozen assorted GIBSONS. — Assorted properly by the popular demand for each model.

Consists of:

Six No. 101 STANDARDS.
Two No. 201 THINLITES.
Four No. 301 WINDPROOFS.

"B" DEAL

One Dozen assorted Engine turned black and tortoise GIBSON Enamels. Assorted properly by the popular demand for each model.

Consists of:

Six No. 102 STANDARDS.
Two No. 202 THINLITES.
Four No. 302 WINDPROOFS.

FULLY AUTOMATIC FULLY GUARANTEED

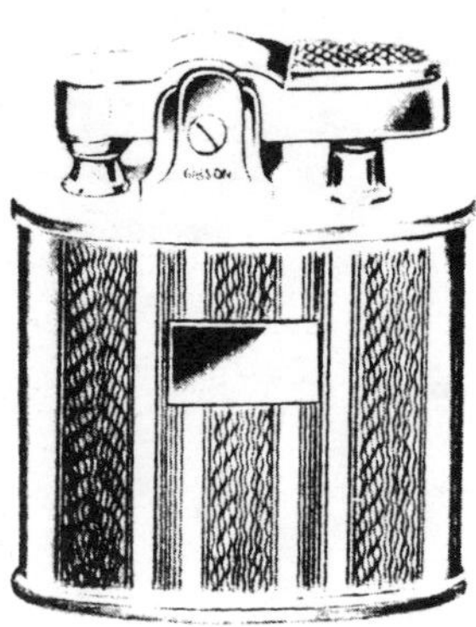

STANDARD
Chromium, Engine turned
No. 101.....

STANDARD
Black Enamel, Engine turned
No. 102.....

STANDARD
Tortoise Enamel, Engine turned
No. 102.....

STANDARD
Black Enamel, Engine turned
No. 102.....

STANDARD
Genuine leather, Alligator grain
No. 103.....

STANDARD
Genuine leather, Lizard grain
No. 103.....

STANDARD
Genuine leather, Lizard grain
No. 103.....

THE GIBSON LIGHTERS pictured on these two pages show a comprehensive line of basic demand models in chromium, enamels and genuine leathers, attractively gift packaged, forcefully displayed.

GIBSONS create an immediate desire for possession. **GIBSONS** are backed by an unconditional guarantee.

ONE MILLION GIBSONS SOLD IN 1952

THINLITE
Tortoise Enamel, Engine turned
No. 202.....

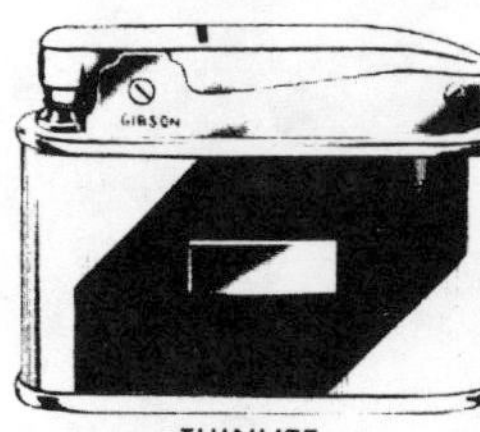

THINLITE
Black Enamel, Engine turned
No. 202.....

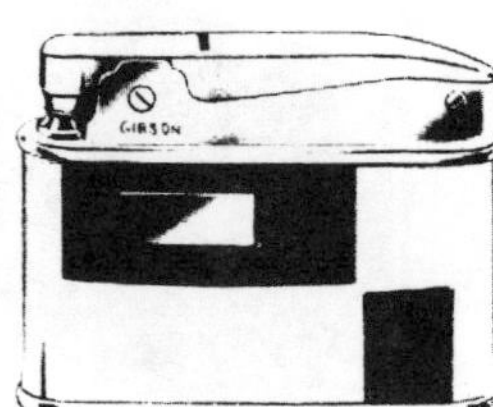

THINLITE
Tortoise Enamel, Engine turned
No. 202.....

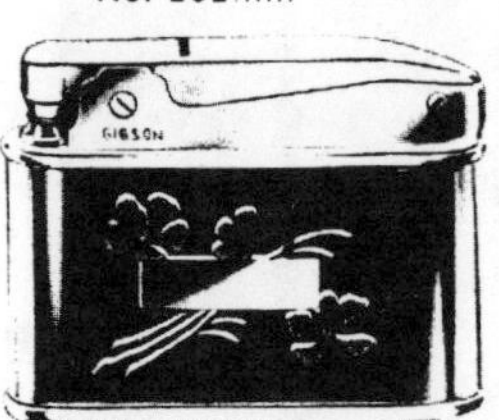

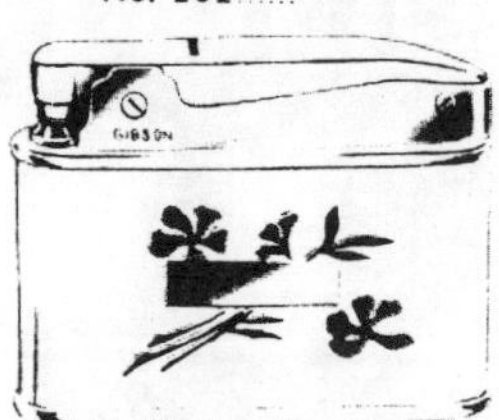

THINLITE
Enamel Floral design, Engine turned
No. 202F.....

THINLITE
Chromium, Engine turned
No. 201.....

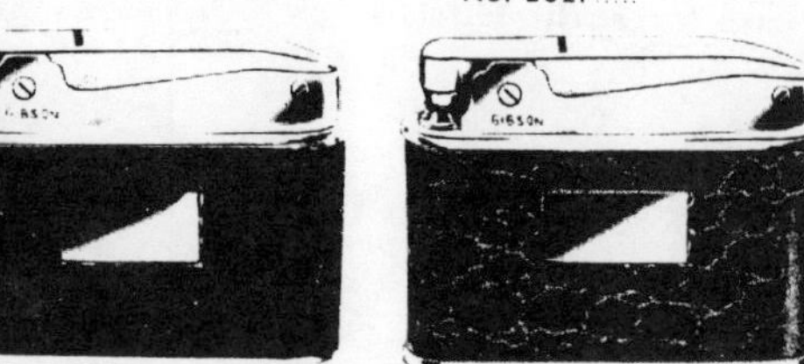

THINLITE
Genuine leather, Lizard grain
No. 203.....

THINLITE
Genuine leather, Alligator grain
No. 203.....

THINLITE
Genuine leather, Lizard grain
No. 203.....

ΓE: Enamels and leathers are packed
Six assorted black and tortoise to carton.

#C600 PHOTO-LITER

The
Ritepoint PHOTO-LITER

Photos Are Accurate and Personal...

Keep Your Building or Product Always in View

#C340 PHOTO-LITER

SPECIFICATIONS

Photo panels are available for the #C340 and #C390 long reservoir pocket models and the #C600 table-desk model only. A good sharp glossy photograph or snapshot of subject to be reproduced must be furnished by customer. If retouching is necessary, a net extra charge will be made, based on amount of work involved. We will prepare prints in a standard size ⅞" high by 1⅛" wide for horizontal display, and the same sizes reversed for vertical display. Photos available in black and white only.

Photos can be laminated for either single or back-to-back display. List prices include one color printing on back side of single photo for all models, and one color printing on one side of wick chamber for #340 model on orders for back-to-back photos. For back-to-back photos for #390 and #600 models a ¼" high white space at top or bottom of photo can be provided for printing signatures, cuts or limited copy. Imprinting this space on both sides with the same copy in one color is included in list prices.
See price list for net extra charges for photo-panels.

New! Deluxe!

#690 POCKET-DESK LITER COMBINATION

A PERFECT PAIR WITH DOUBLE DUTY ADVERTISING VALUE

- A #390 pocket and #600 table-desk liter packed together in beautiful gift box.
- Available with advertising copy, chrome initials or plain.
- Your choice of Crystal, Topaz, Emerald or Ruby colors.
- Individual corrugated mailers
- The #690 combination can be supplied with miniatures and photo-panels at same extra charge for each Liter as listed for individual Liters.

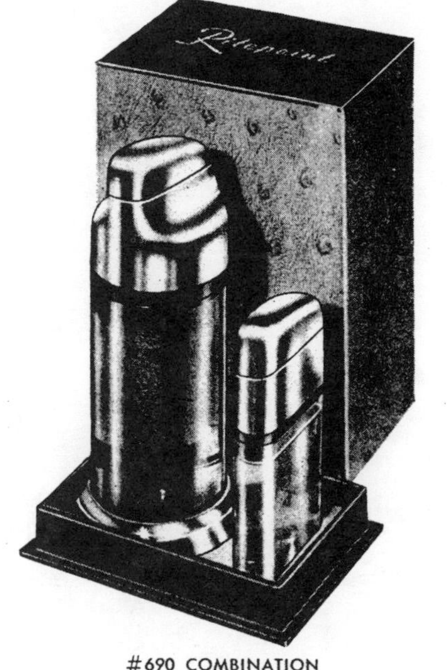

#690 COMBINATION IN GIFT BOX

Ritepoint Liters are shipped—Full of Fuel—Ready to Use Your Advertising Begins Immediately!

Packaged in Gift Box *at* . . . NO EXTRA CHARGE!

ATTRACTIVE GIFT PACKAGE

RITEPOINT TABLE-DESK LITERS

are packed in Gift Boxes with crepe padding. Complete illustrated Instruction Booklet and Guarantee packed in each Gift Box with LITER. Each Gift Box is packed in chip board sleeve.

RITEPOINT POCKET LITERS

are packed with cotton padding in handsome silver and black metal gift box with hinged top, at no extra charge. Instruction booklet, packed with each liter.

INDIVIDUAL MAILING PACKAGING . . . *Liters Ready for Mailing*

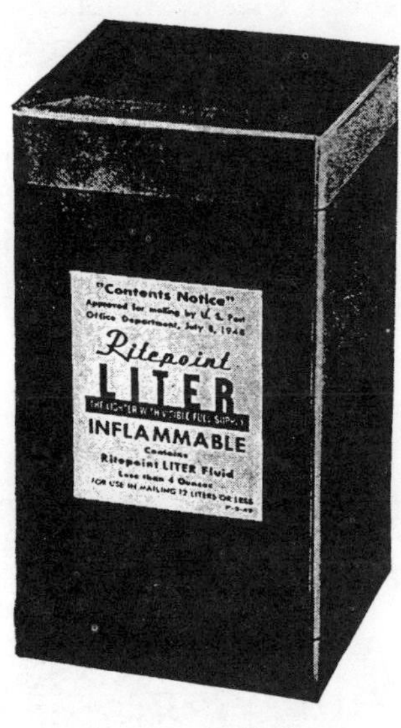

Special Mailer with Table-Desk Liter inserted—

By compliance with U. S. Post Office Department Regulations "Ritepoint LITERS" may be mailed individually, with reservoirs full of fuel.

To comply with these regulations use Ritepoint Individual Mailing Packaging.

Liters to be mailed must not have fuel transferred from reservoir to wick chamber. Gift Box must be placed in double corrugated mailer. All seams of mailer must be sealed with gummed tape; contents notice glued to one side of mailers must not be covered by labels or tape. Place addressed label on one side of mailer opposite contents notice.

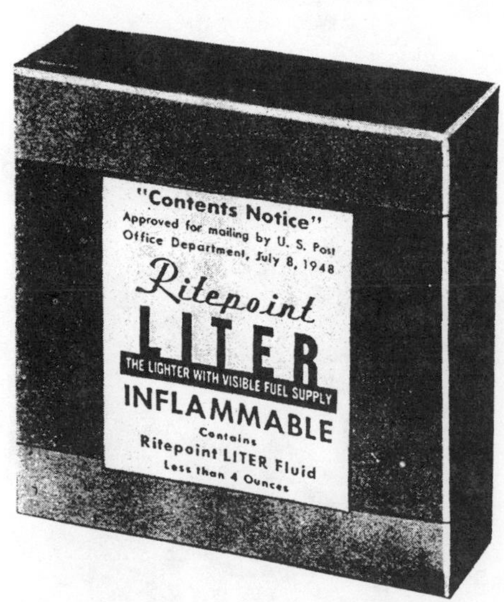

Special Mailer with Pocket Liter inserted —

LITERS in Mailers may be mailed by Parcel Post as Fourth Class Matter

NATIONALLY ADVERTISED *Ritepoint* **GUARANTEED**

GOLFER

Sports Liters

THE PERFECT GIFT FOR ALL GOOD SPORTS

FULL COLOR REPRODUCTIONS OF AMERICA'S MOST POPULAR GAMES AND SPORTS ON WHITE PANEL IN #390 POCKET LITER AND #600 TABLE-DESK LITER

SPORTS LITERS FURNISHED IN CRYSTAL ONLY

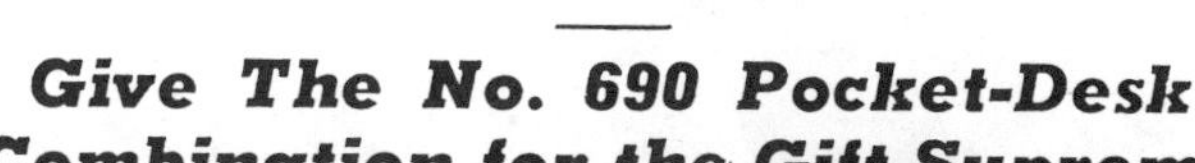

Give The No. 690 Pocket-Desk Combination for the Gift Supreme

BOWLER

HUNTER

NO EXTRA CHARGE FOR BEAUTIFUL COLOR SPORT SCENES

SAIL FISH

ASSORTED SPORT SCENES ARE AVAILABLE AT NO EXTRA CHARGE

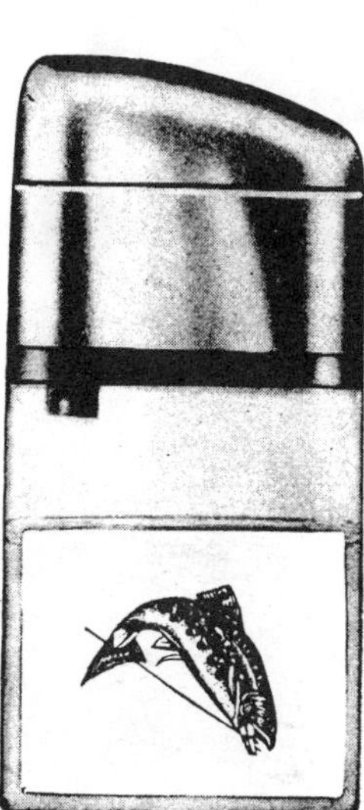
TROUT

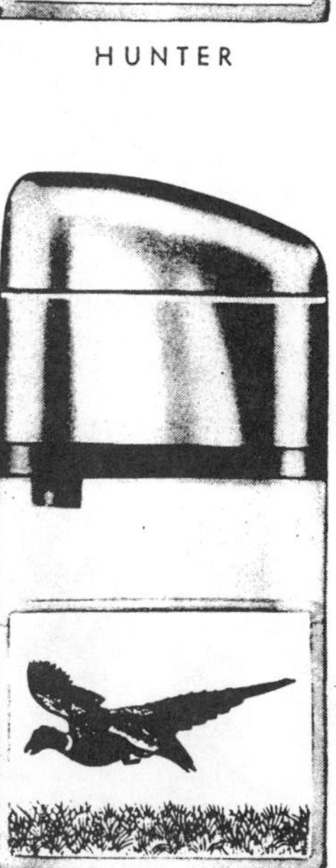
PHEASANT

Advertising copy, if wanted, is printed on reverse side of panel in any color or colors of ink. Price includes sport scenes in full color only. For two color imprint add standard 2 color printing charge.

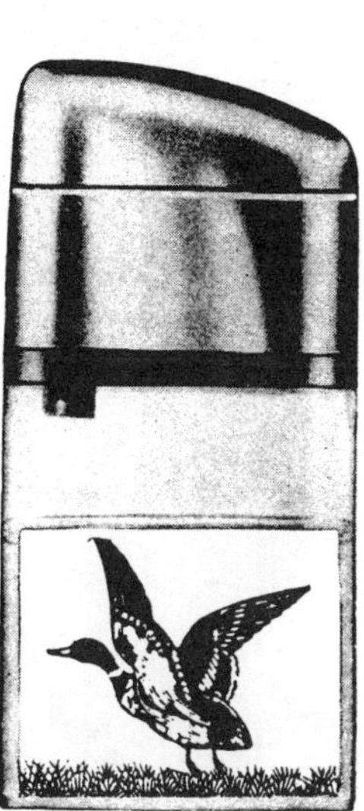
DUCK

1929 CATALOG PAGE

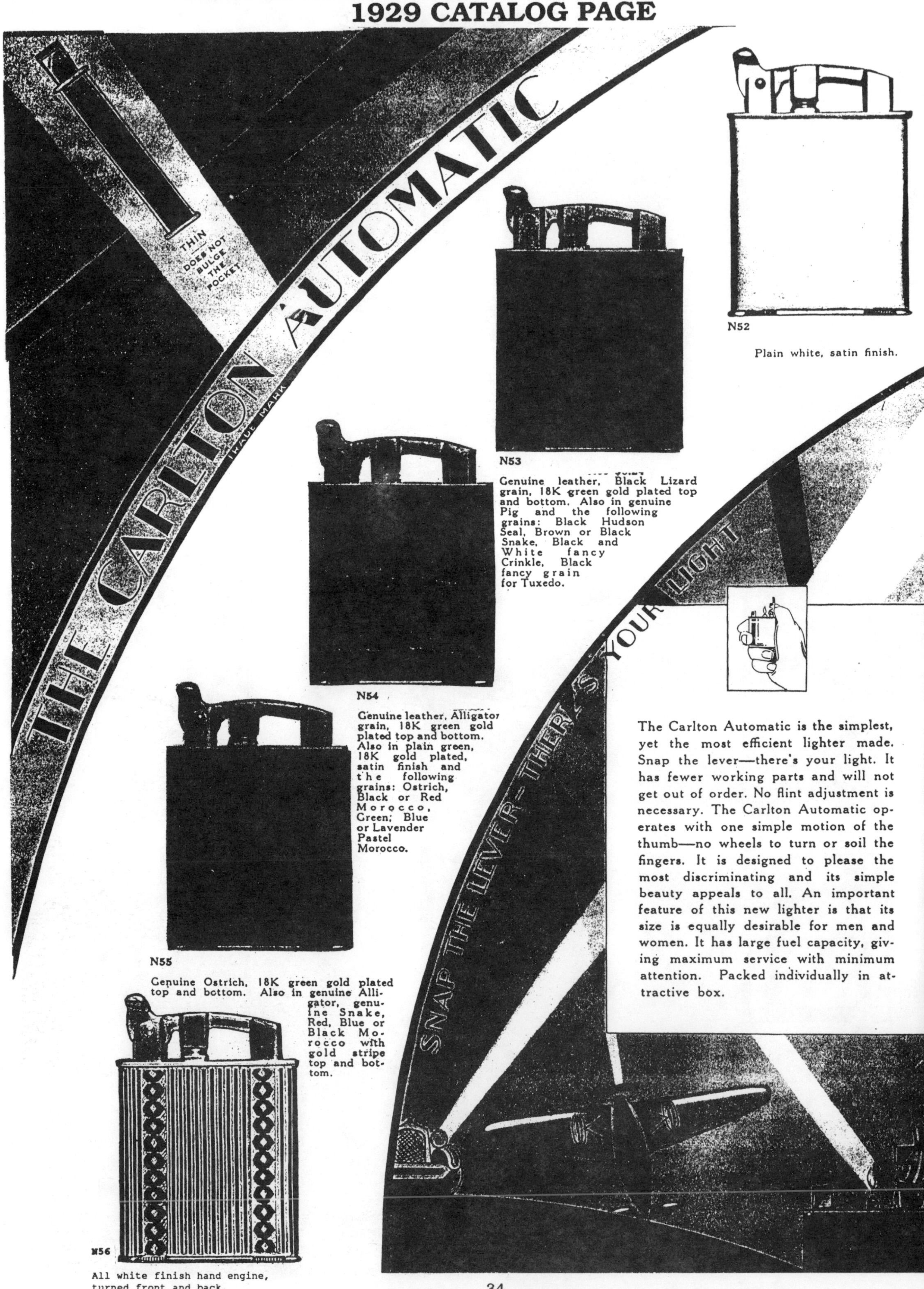
THE CARLTON AUTOMATIC
TRADE MARK
THIN
DOES NOT BULGE THE POCKET
SNAP THE LEVER—THERE'S YOUR LIGHT

N52

Plain white, satin finish.

N53

Genuine leather, Black Lizard grain, 18K green gold plated top and bottom. Also in genuine Pig and the following grains: Black Hudson Seal, Brown or Black Snake, Black and White fancy Crinkle, Black fancy grain for Tuxedo.

N54

Genuine leather, Alligator grain, 18K green gold plated top and bottom. Also in plain green, 18K gold plated, satin finish and the following grains: Ostrich, Black or Red Morocco, Green; Blue or Lavender Pastel Morocco.

N55

Genuine Ostrich, 18K green gold plated top and bottom. Also in genuine Alligator, genuine Snake, Red, Blue or Black Morocco with gold stripe top and bottom.

N56

All white finish hand engine, turned front and back.

The Carlton Automatic is the simplest, yet the most efficient lighter made. Snap the lever—there's your light. It has fewer working parts and will not get out of order. No flint adjustment is necessary. The Carlton Automatic operates with one simple motion of the thumb—no wheels to turn or soil the fingers. It is designed to please the most discriminating and its simple beauty appeals to all. An important feature of this new lighter is that its size is equally desirable for men and women. It has large fuel capacity, giving maximum service with minimum attention. Packed individually in attractive box.

1929 CATALOG PAGE

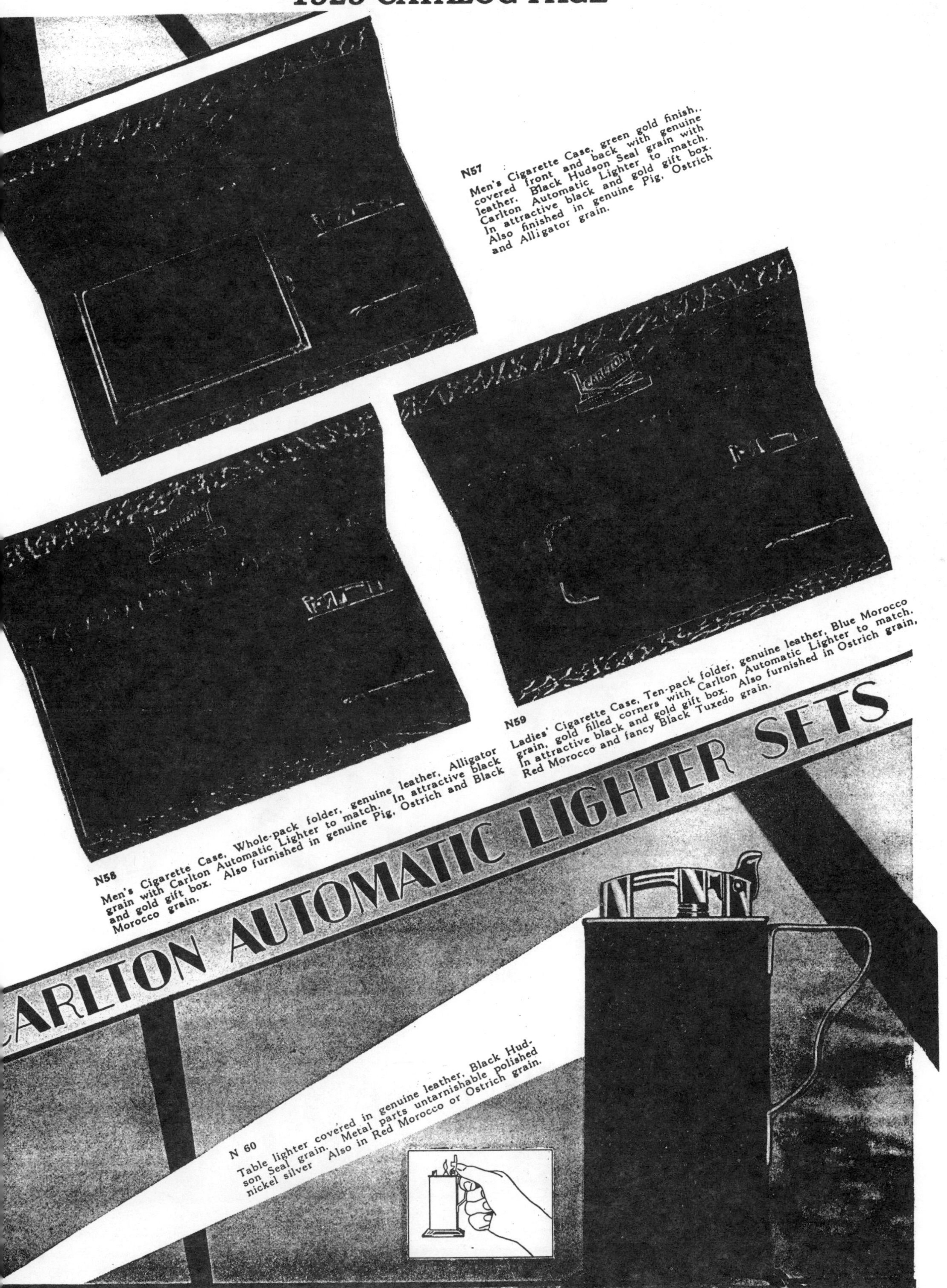

N57
Men's Cigarette Case, green gold finish, covered front and back with genuine leather. Black Hudson Seal grain with Carlton Automatic Lighter to match. In attractive black and gold gift box. Also finished in genuine Pig, Ostrich and Alligator grain.
N58
Men's Cigarette Case, Whole-pack folder, genuine leather, Alligator grain with Carlton Automatic Lighter to match. In attractive black and gold gift box. Also furnished in genuine Pig, Ostrich and Black Morocco grain.
N59
Ladies' Cigarette Case, Ten-pack folder, genuine leather, Blue Morocco grain, gold filled corners with Carlton Automatic Lighter to match. In attractive black and gold gift box. Also furnished in Ostrich grain, Red Morocco and fancy Black Tuxedo grain.
ARLTON AUTOMATIC LIGHTER SETS
N 60
Table lighter covered in genuine leather, Black Hudson Seal grain. Metal parts untarnishable polished nickel silver. Also in Red Morocco or Ostrich grain.

1930 CATALOG PAGE

CARLTON AUTOMATIC LIGHTER

FULLY AUTOMATIC

R 51

Genuine leather, black and silver.

A man with a Carlton Automatic Lighter never fights for fire. Just "Press the lever—there's your light," without fuss or two or three tries . . . a Carlton is sure-fire. And because a Carlton is the thinnest lighter made you're barely conscious of carrying it. Reliable action, smart appearance and extra slimness make Carltons popular with men and women.

R 52

Genuine leather, alligator grain.

R 53

Red and black enamel both sides.
R 54 Green and black enamel both sides
Same price as above

R 55

Genuine leather, black Scotch grain
R 56
Same as above, without signet.

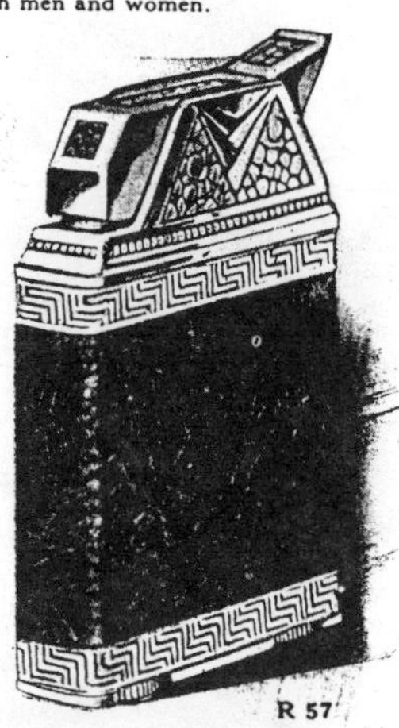

R 57

Genuine leather, ostrich grain.

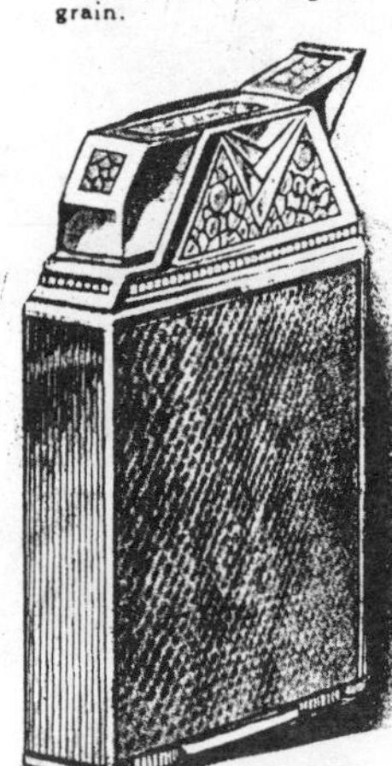

R 58

Genuine snake skin.

R 59

Enamel both sides with egg-shell design.

R 60

Hand engine-turned both sides.

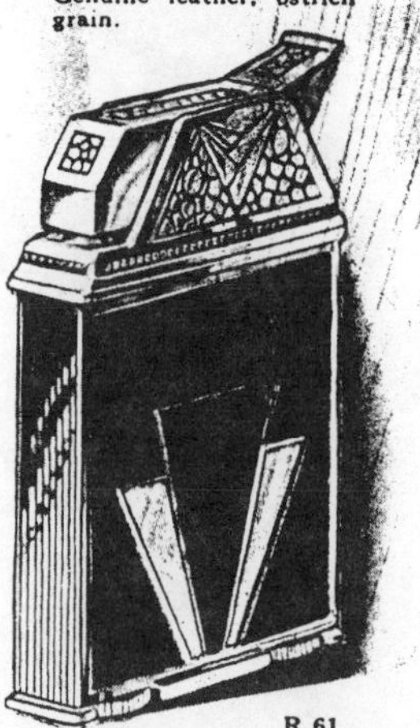

R 61

Genuine hard enamel.

R 62

Genuine pearl and black both sides.

1930 CATALOG PAGE

63

garette Case, covered both sides with nuine leather, black Scotch grain with Carlton Automatic Lighter to match. In attractive tan and gold gift box.

R 64

Cigarette Case, enamel, with Carlton Automatic Lighter to match. In attractive tan and gold gift box.

65

garette Case, enamel with egg-shell design; arlton Automatic Lighter to match. In attractive n and gold gift box.

R 66

Cigarette Case; enamel with egg-shell design; Carlton Automatic Lighter to match. In attractive tan and gold gift box.

1930 CATALOG PAGE

N1043

Whole-pack Cigarette Case, genuine leather. Blue pebble grain with Carlton Automatic Lighter to match. In attractive green and gold gift box.

N1044

Men's Cigarette Case; Whole-pack folder, genuine leather. Brown snake grain with Carlton Automatic Lighter to match. In attractive green and gold gift box.

igarette Case; green gold finish; covered both sides with leather, Black Scotch grain with Carlton Automatic Lighter . In attractive green and gold gift box.

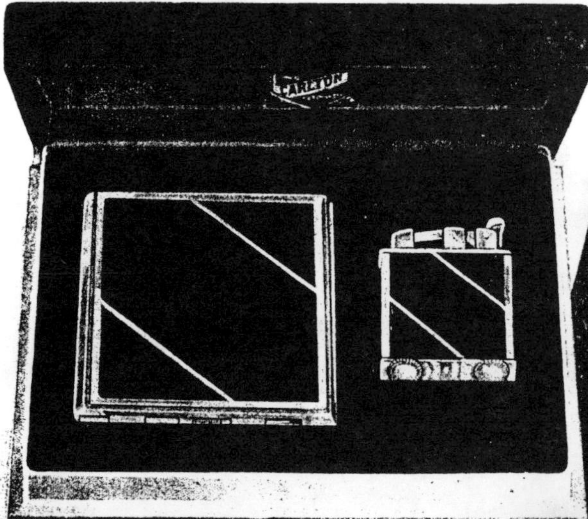

N1046

Men's Cigarette Case; green gold finish; Red and Black ena sides; with Carlton Automatic Lighter to match. In attrac and gold gift box.

CARLTON AUTOMATIC LIGHTER SETS

CARLTON TABLE AUTOMATIC LIGHTER

The Carlton Automatic Table Lighter works on the same sure, simple principle as the Carlton Automatic Pocket Lighter—*snap the lever —there's your light.*

SEE CARLTON AUTOMATIC LIGHTERS ON REVERSE SIDE.

N1047

Carlton Automatic Table Lighter; Red and Black enamel both sides; 18K green gold plated top and bottom.

1928 CATALOG PAGE

CLARK LIGHTERS

new Clark Wind-
r. Platinum elec-
te on nickel silver.
Each.......**$16.00**

ie as above in gold trim, covered with genuine h, alligator or k shark, skin er.
1a Each.....**$18.00**

Platinum electro-plate, nickel silver, engine turned in rich diamond cut design.
J16432 Each..**$13.50**

Same as above in small size.
J16432a Each..**$13.50**

Green gold top, covered with genuine alligator or water snake leather.
J16433 Each..**$11.50**

Same as above in small size.
J16433a Each..**$11.50**

Ladies' smoke set, green gold filled, pink enameled on both sides, sterling and enameled rose plaque; washable. Cigarette case holds six cigarettes. Set includes famous Clark Lighter, complete in presentation gift box.
J16434 Per set.................................**$23.60**

WALES LIGHTERS

een gold trim, er covered, genuine skin.
5 Each......**$8.25**

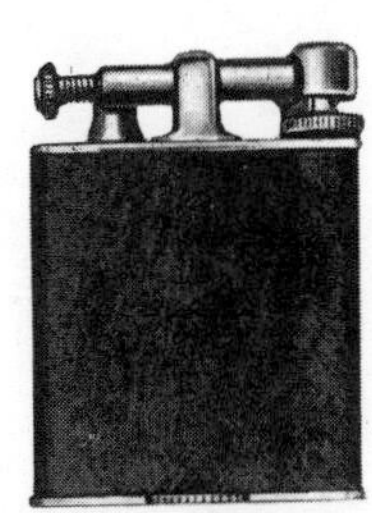

Green gold trim, leather covered, genuine ostrich.
J16436 Each.......**$8.25**

Green gold trim, leather covered, Florentine green calf skin.
J16437 Each.......**$8.25**

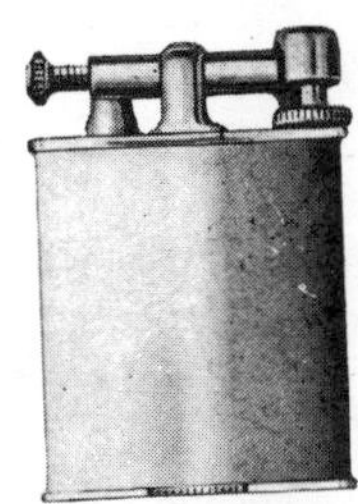

Silver plated on nickel silver. Plain.
J16438 Each......**$6.00**

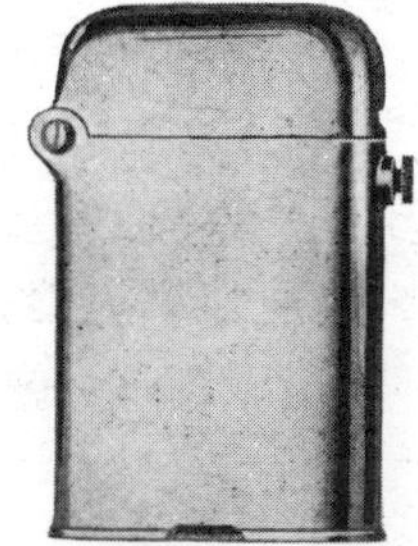

The Thorens Automatic Lighter, one of the most successful and reliable automatic lighters on the market, guaranteed to be fool proof. All parts interchangeable Has safety shutting and compartment for reserve flints.
J16439 Each **$3.60**
Same in engine turned.
J16439a Each **$6.00**

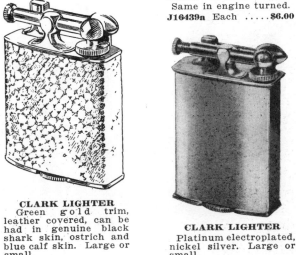

Men's smoke set, green gold filled, black enameled, guaranteed, case holds ten cigarettes, with the famous Clark Lighter, complete in gift presentation box.
J16440 Per set...**$22.80**

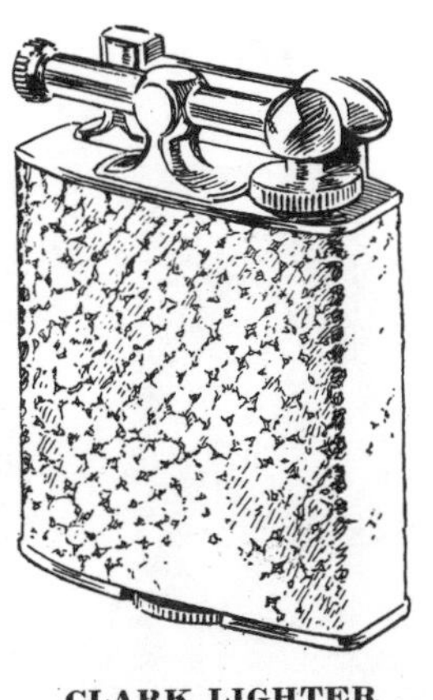

CLARK LIGHTER
Green gold trim, leather covered, can be had in genuine black shark skin, ostrich and blue calf skin. Large or small.
J16441 Each.....**$11.50**

CLARK LIGHTER
Platinum electroplated, nickel silver. Large or small.
J16442 Each......**$8.32**

The New Model Clark Lighter

No. 4153..................
Silver plated.
Satin finish.

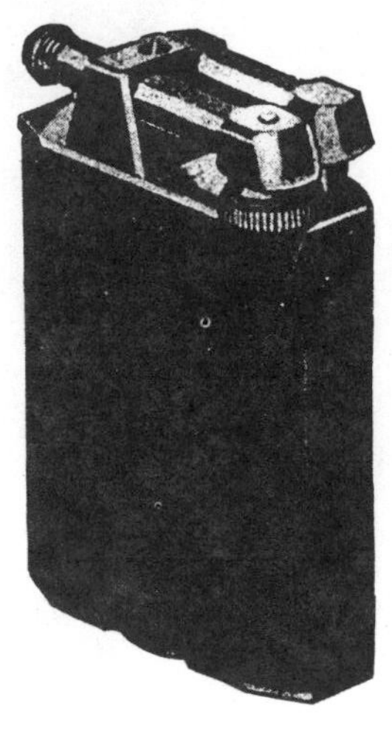

No. 4154..................
Real ostrich.
No. 4155..................
Green alligator.

No. 4156....................
Silver plated. Satin finish.
Junior size.

No. 4157..................
Green alligator.
No. 4158..................
Real ostrich. Junior siz

The Firefly-A Clark Lighter

No. 4159............
Silver plated.

No. 4160............
Engine turned.

No. 4161............
Signet.

No. 4162............
Ostrich.

No. 4163............
Tweed.

No. 4164............
Pin seal.

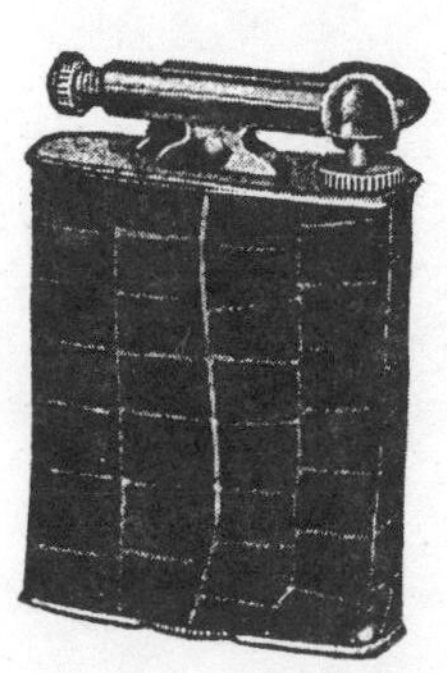

No. 4165............
Alligator.

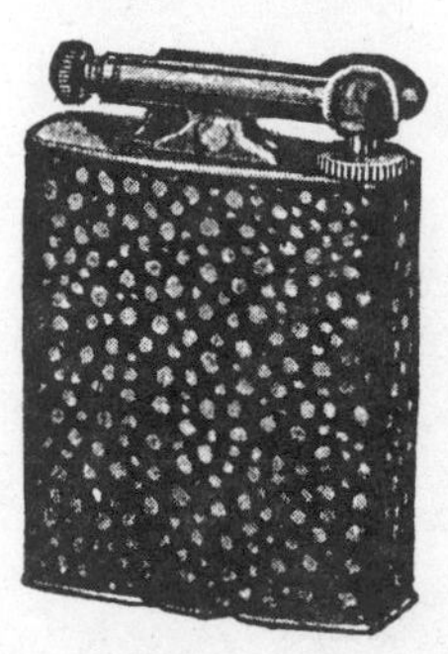

No. 4166............
Pebble.

No. 4167............
Black lizard.

No. 4168............
Tan Snake.

1930 CATALOG PAGE

Petite polished platinum engine turned. List $10.40. To retail at $7.50.
N 1005
signet. List
To retail at $8.50
N 1004
Modernistic ena
at $7.50.
N 1006
uine blue liz-
10.40. To retail
$7.50.
1003
Modernistic ena
List $10.40. To
at$7.50.
N 1007
Windodger genuine alligator. List $15.60. To retail at $12.50.
N 1008
To retail
Windodger genuine black lizard and 14 K. signet. List $17.70. To retail at $15.00
N 1010
Polished platinum finish engine turned. List
To retail at $8.50.
N 1011
Genuine ostrich paneled leather. List $15.60. To retail at $12.50.
Inlaid enamel. List $15.60. To retail at $12.50.
N 1013
Clark Smoking Set in genuine brown lizard. List $18.80. To retail at $15.00.

1930 CATALOG PAGE

ELGIN AMERICAN
SMOKER SETS
EA-245—Green Gold Plated, Elginite enamel Bridge Smoking Set, consisting of double ash tray and cigarette container . . . .
EA-244—Indestructib... ...sh, Elginite enamel mahogany-li... ...te humidor and automatic table ... set in handsome presentation box . . . .
EA-246 — In... ...tilbe whit... Elginite enamel, ...ernistic design large table li...
EA-247—Indestructible white finish, Elginite enamel mahogany-lined, double cigarette humidor and automatic lighter . . . .
EA-248—Indestructible white finish, Elginite enamel mahogany-lined, medium size, cigarette humidor . . . .
EA-249—Indestructible white finish, Elginite enamel mahogany-lined, large size, cigarette humidor . . . .

ELGIN AMERICAN
SMOKER SETS
EA-238—
Indestructible white
finish, Elginite enamel mahogany lined cigarette humidor and
automatic table lighter set, in hand-
some presentation box ..
EA-239 — Indestructible white finish, Elginite enamel automatic table lighter.
EA-241 — Indestructible white finish, Elginite enamel automatic table lighter.
EA-243 — Indestructible white finish, Elginite enamel automatic table lighter.
large tray, cigarette humidor, automatic table lighter and four individual
ash trays
ELGIN AMERICAN MFG. CO
ELGIN ILLINOIS U.S.A.

1930 CATALOG PAGE

THE CHARM OF ELEGANCE THAT COMPELS IMMEDIATE INTEREST

There's inherent beauty in the handcrafting of these new Elgin Craft lighter sets . . . refinement and good taste in design give them an undeniable charm. Put several sets in your windows . . . we know they'll delight your customers. Order from your jobber, or direct from us, today.

ELGIN AMERICAN MFG. CO.

FACTORY and GENERAL OFFICE at ELGIN, ILLINOIS

NEW YORK: 20 West Forty-seventh Street

CHICAGO: 35 Wacker Drive

MONTREAL: 209 St. Catherine Street, East LONDON: 65 Holborn Viaduct

1930 CATALOG PAGE

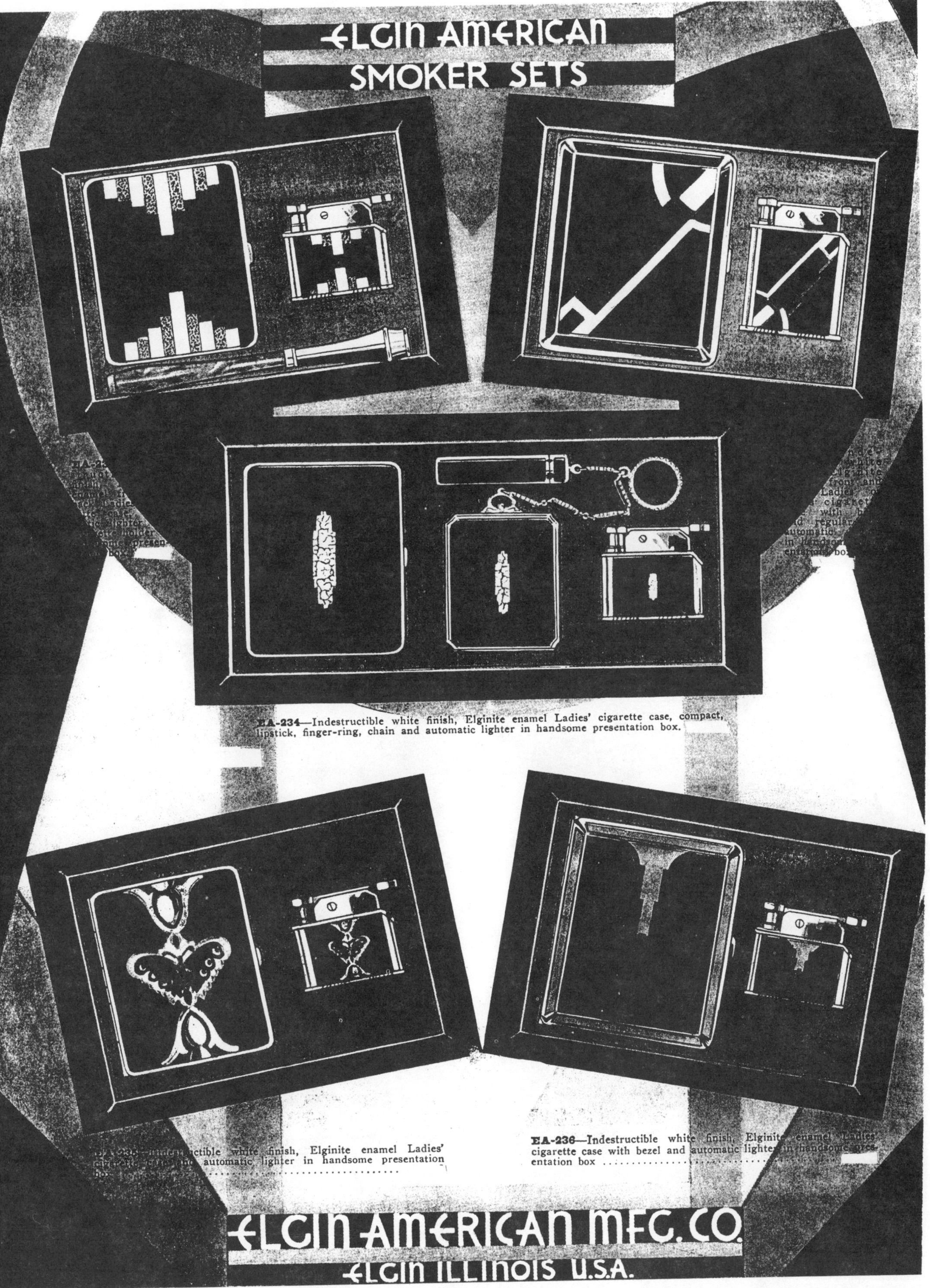

ELGIN AMERICAN
SMOKER SETS
EA-234—Indestructible white finish, Elginite enamel Ladies' cigarette case, compact, lipstick, finger-ring, chain and automatic lighter in handsome presentation box.
EA-236—Indestructible white finish, Elginite enamel Ladies' cigarette case with bezel and automatic lighter in handsome presentation box
ELGIN AMERICAN MFG. CO.
ELGIN ILLINOIS U.S.A.

1929 CATALOG PAGE

EVANS

The outstanding characteristic of the EVANS LIGHTER is its REFINEMENT of DESIGN and CONSTRUCTION—SMART ENGINE TURNED, BROCADE, ENAMEL SILHOUETTE and DRESDEN ENAMEL EFFECTS on a THIN KNIFE EDGE CASE, made and finished as a piece of JEWELRY that produces a PRIDE and SATISFACTION in ownership for PRACTICAL USE ON ALL OCCASIONS.

No. E1200.................$6.00
Pocket Lighter. Hammered design, polished top and bottom, white gold finish.

No. E1201.................$6.75
Pocket Lighter. In crystalized, black japanned effect, polished top and bottom.

No. E1202.................$7.50
Pocket Lighter. Engine turned and hammered design, chased border, with center shield, polished white gold finish.

No. E1203.................$8.25
Pocket Lighter. Hand brocade scroll design, with chased border, white gold finish.

Patent 72965

Licensed Patent 1022140

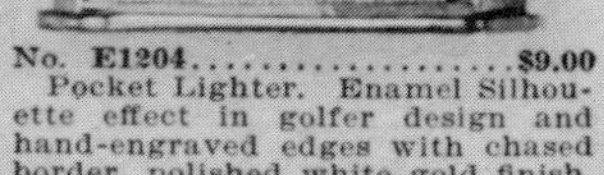

No. E1204.................$9.00
Pocket Lighter. Enamel Silhouette effect in golfer design and hand-engraved edges with chased border, polished white gold finish.

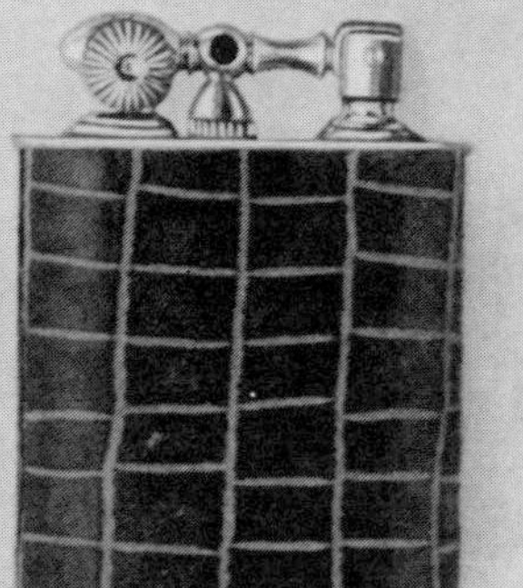

No. E1205.................$9.00
Pocket Lighter. Leather covered, as illustrated, in alligator or in assorted rose or blue ecrase, ostrich, pigskin and pin seal, polished white gold finish on top and bottom.

No. E1206.................$10.50
Pocket Lighter. Hand engraved enamel insert, checkerboard effect in assorted colors with chased border, polished white gold finish.

No. E1207.................$10.50
Pocket Lighter. With hand-engraved Dresden enamel insert in regimental stripe, assorted colors, blue and black, red and black, white and black, chased border, polished white gold finish.

No. E1208.................$11.25
Pocket Lighter. With hand-engraved, genuine hand-painted Dresden enamel in assorted colors, blue and white, yellow and white, black and white, with chased border, polished white gold finish.

No. E1209.................$15.00
Pocket Lighter. With double hand-engraved enamel insert, both sides, assorted colors in variegated mottled effects.

1930 CATALOG PAGE

INTERNATIONAL 

SILVERPLATE

TRADE MARK

TABLE LIGHTERS

(*EVANS UNIT*)

A series of novel and attractive designs and shapes that combine the general reliability and ease of performance of the EVANS lighter with the beauty and quality of International Silverplate by Wilcox.

No. 132
Table Lighter
Paisley Pattern
Height 6½ inches

No. 130
Table Lighter
Height 4¼ inches

No. 131
Table Lighter
Height 4¼ inches

No. 133
Table Lighter
Height 6¼ inches

No. 135
Table Lighter
Height 6½ inches
Light Jade
Enamel Pillar

No. 137
Table Lighter
Height 6½ inches

No. 129
Table Lighter
Height 3¾ inches

No. 134
Table Lighter
Height, 6 inches
With Bands of
Red Enamel

May also be had with Black or Light Jade Enamel

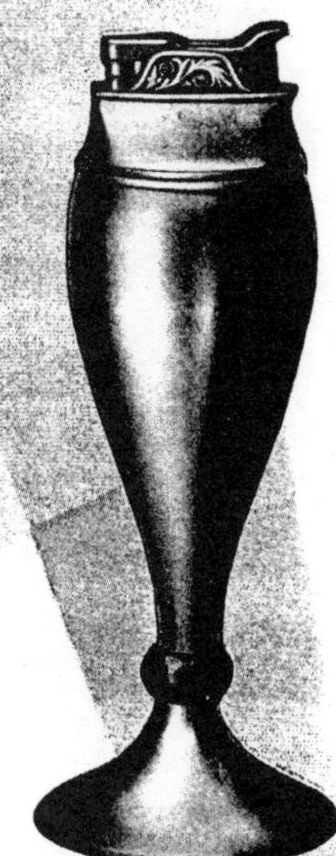

No. 136
Table Lighter
With Black
Enamel Pillar
Height 6 inches

Where several optional colors are offered please express your preference; otherwise, black will be sent.

All Table Lighters in International Silverplate are furnished in Butler Finish.

1930 CATALOG PAGE

TABLE LIGHTERS

(*EVANS UNIT*)

In presenting this series of Table Lighters and Combination Table Lighters and Cigarette Holders in International Silverplate, we believe that we offer an unbeatable combination. An ingenious article with a widespread popular appeal; sure action with the EVANS Roller Bearing unit and the exquisite design, workmanship and finish, and the fine quality of International Silverplate, join to form a most attractive and readily salable novelty.

Cross-lever, roller bearing action is a new principle in lighter-building—exclusively EVANS—exclusively INTERNATIONAL. It means smoother action, wider clearance between snuffer and wick, an almost complete revolution of the sparking wheel that spurts a veritable shower of sparks to insure ignition—not at one, but at several points in the revolution of the wheel, from just one pressure of the thumb.

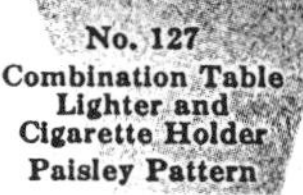

No. 127
Combination Table Lighter and Cigarette Holder
Paisley Pattern

This type of Combination Table Lighter and Cigarette Holder is 5 inches in height.

No. 138
Combination Table Lighter and Cigarette Holder
Genuine Brown Leather Snake Grain

May also be had in genuine Leather, Black Lizard or Red Morocco Grain

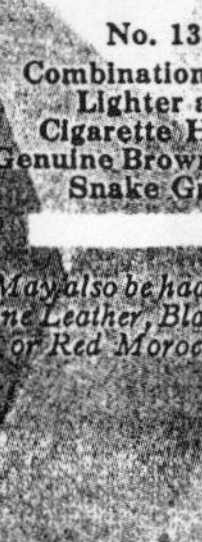

No. 128
Combination Table Lighter and Cigarette Holder
Ardsley Pattern

No. 126

Lighter top removed to show Cigarette Holder

No. 126
Combination Table Lighter and Cigarette Holder

No. 141
Combination Table Lighter and Cigarette Holder
Engine turned

No. 139
Combination Table Lighter and Cigarette Holder
Applied Design

This type of Combination Table Lighter and Cigarette Holder is 6 inches in height.

No. 142
Combination Table Lighter and Cigarette Holder
Genuine Red Leather Morocco Grain

May also be had in genuine Leather, Black Lizard or Brown Snake Grain

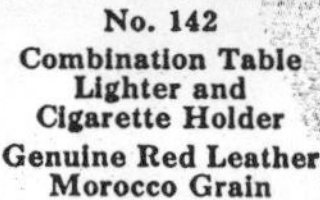

Opened to show Cigarette Holder and Lighter

No. 140
Combination Table Lighter and Cigarette Holder
Paisley Pattern

The charmingly colored leathers, the colorful inlaid enamels, the delicate tracery of the chasing offer to the consumer a wide selection, wider than in any other line—and all lighters are backed by the full guarantee of the makers, Wilcox Silver Plate Co., International Silver Company Successor.

1930 CATALOG PAGE

EVANS

N961—Combination paper weight and automatic Roller Bearing desk lighter in contrasting colors of French enamel, polished green finish..................

N962—The Alladin Lamp of Learning combination paper weight and automatic Roller Bearing desk lighter, antique green finish.

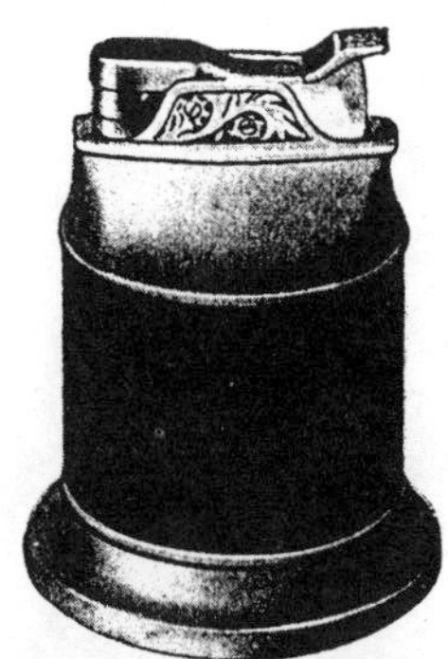

N963—Combination paper weight and automatic Roller Bearing desk lighter, genuine ostrich covered, polished green finish.......

N964—Automatic Roller Bearing desk or table lighter, genuine leather covered in Bombay reptile grain, polished green finish.

N965—Desk or table combination with removable automatic Roller Bearing lighter unit and ash receptacle in French enamel, polished green finish.........

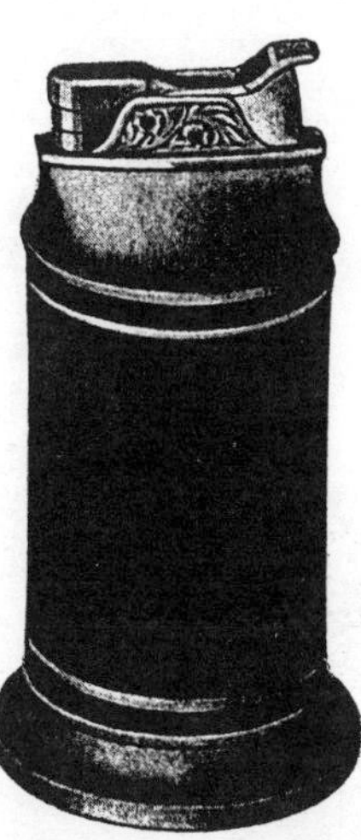

N966—Automatic Roller Bearing desk or table lighter in contrasting colors of French enamel, polished green finish...............

N967—Automatic Roller Bearing desk or table lighter, contrasting colors of French enamel, polished green finish.............

N968—Desk or table combination with removable automatic Roller Bearing lighter unit and ash receptacle in contrasting colors of French enamel, polished green finish..................

N969—Automatic novelty desk or table lighter in contrasting colors of French enamel, removable top serving as ash tray......

Illustrations two-third size.

1934 CATALOG PAGE

EC133—Combination Cigarette Case and Compact: Thin knife edge model, non-tarnishing chromium finish. French enamel front and back. Holds seven cigarettes. Fitted with patented Evans' tap-sift loose powder container large mirror, full size rouge.

Enamel Colors: Cream and Black

EC134—Combination Cigarette Case and Compact with Lighter, knife edge model in non-tarnishing chromium, French enamel front. Compact contains large mirror, patented Evans' tap-sift loose powder container, full-size rouge

Enamel Colors: Light and Dark Green

EC135—Combination Cigarette Case and Compact, thin knife edge model, non-tarnishing chromium finish, French enamel front and back with genuine hand-painted Cloisonne enamel compact cover. Holds seven cigarettes. Fitted with patented Evans' tap-sift loose powder container, full size rouge, and large mirror . . . .

Enamel Color: Pastel Yellow

EC136—Combination Cigarette Case and Compact with Lighter, thin knife edge model in non-tarnishing chromium finish. French enamel front. Compact contains large mirror, patented Evans' tap-sift loose powder container, full size rouge.

Enamel Color: Black

EC137—Combination Cigarette Case and Compact with Lighter. Very thin knife edge model, non-tarnishing chromium finish. French enamel front and back. Holds ten cigarettes, single row. Compact fitted with large mirror, patented Evans' tap-sift loose powder container and full size rouge. . . . .

Enamel Colors: Tortoise, Cream and Black

EC138—Combination Cigarette Case and Compact with Lighter, knife edge model, non-tarnishing chromium finish. French enamel front with hand-engraved Cloisonne enamel compact cover. Compact fitted with large mirror, patented Evans' tap-sift loose powder container, and full size rouge . . . . .

Enamel Colors: Pastel Yellow and Black

EC139—Combination Cigarette Case and Compact, very thin knife edge, single row model, holds thirteen cigarettes, French enamel front and back with genuine handpainted Cloisonne enamel compact cover. Fitted with large mirror, patented Evans' tap-sift loose powder container, full size rouge. . . . .

Enamel Colors: White and Black

EC140—Combination Cigarette Case and Compact, very thin knife edge, single row model, holds thirteen cigarettes, French enamel front and back. Compact contains large mirror, patented Evans' tap-sift loose powder container, full size rouge . . . .

Enamel Colors: Light and Dark Blue

1934 CATALOG PAGE

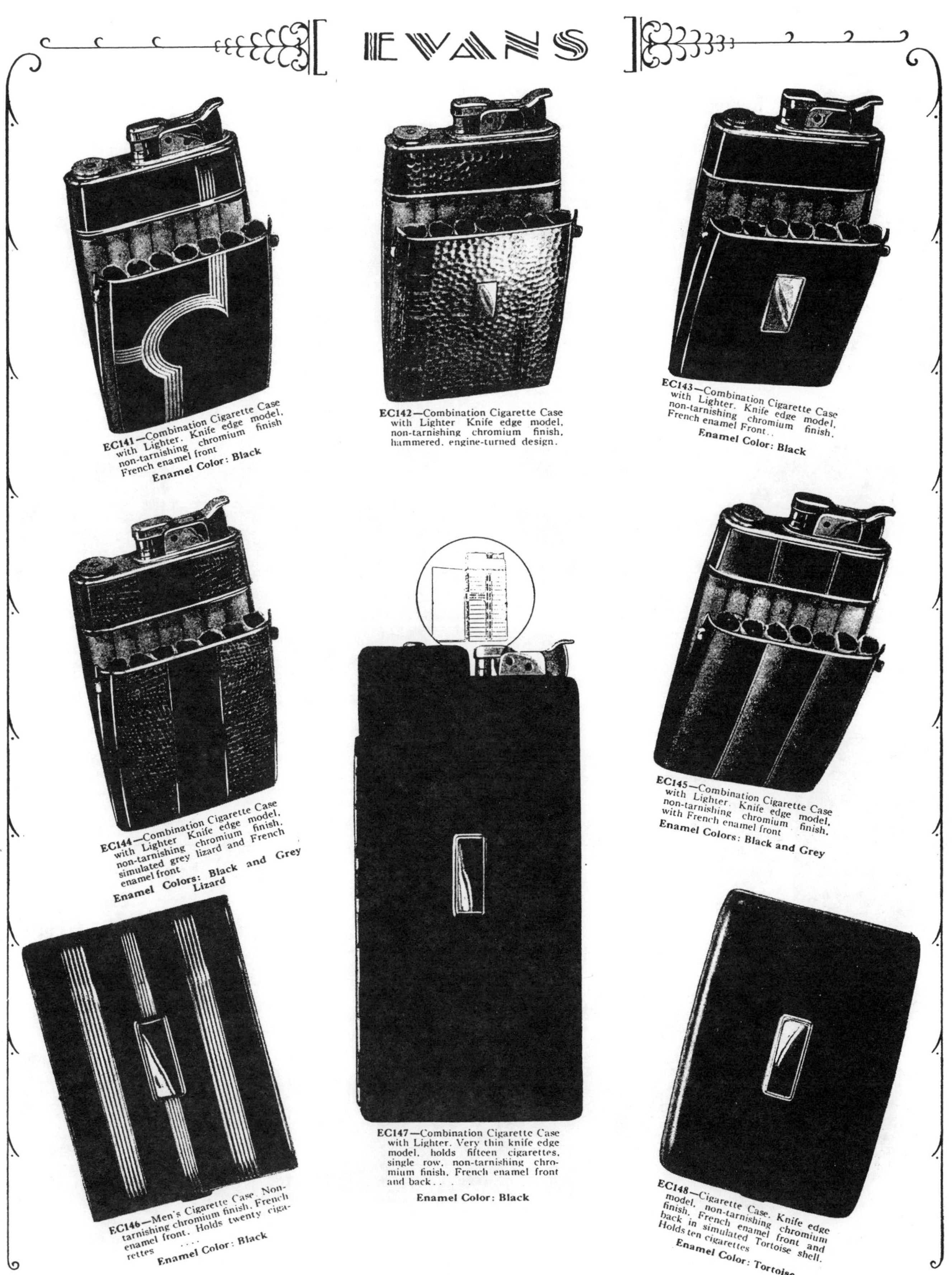

EC141—Combination Cigarette Case with Lighter. Knife edge model, non-tarnishing chromium finish French enamel front
Enamel Color: Black

EC142—Combination Cigarette Case with Lighter Knife edge model, non-tarnishing chromium finish, hammered, engine-turned design.

EC143—Combination Cigarette Case with Lighter. Knife edge model, non-tarnishing chromium finish, French enamel Front..
Enamel Color: Black

EC144—Combination Cigarette Case with Lighter Knife edge model, non-tarnishing chromium finish, simulated grey lizard and French enamel front
Enamel Colors: Black and Grey Lizard

EC145—Combination Cigarette Case with Lighter. Knife edge model, non-tarnishing chromium finish, with French enamel front
Enamel Colors: Black and Grey

EC146—Men's Cigarette Case. Non-tarnishing chromium finish. French enamel front. Holds twenty cigarettes ....
Enamel Color: Black

EC147—Combination Cigarette Case with Lighter. Very thin knife edge model, holds fifteen cigarettes, single row, non-tarnishing chromium finish. French enamel front and back.. . .
Enamel Color: Black

EC148—Cigarette Case. Knife edge model, non-tarnishing chromium finish, French enamel front and back in simulated Tortoise shell. Holds ten cigarettes
Enamel Color: Tortoise

1941 CATALOG PAGE

EVANS SPITFIRE AUTOMATIC LIGHTERS and CASE COMBINATIONS

SPITFIRE Automatic Pocket LIGHTERS

The "Windbreaker"

Paneled design, with streamlined top. Nickel finish. Monogram shield. Positive "Spitfire" action—simply press to light and release to extinguish. LIST,
No. 3Q-E4134. Each,
3, ea.,
Less 2%,
net........

Positive "Spitfire" action, windbreaker top—lights even in a high wind. Nickel finish with "turned-down" corner; monogram shield on black enamel background. LIST,
No. 3Q-E4150. Each,
3, each,
Less 2%,
net..........

Favored for evening and all dress occasions. Rich black enamel with nickel trim. Smart oval monogram shield. Positive "Spitfire" lighting action. LIST,
No. 3Q-E4139. Each,
3, each,
Less 2%,
net............

An overwhelming favorite. Evans "Spitfire" lighter with U.S. army insignia in green gold effect emblazoned on black enamel background. Green gold effect trim. LIST,
No. 3Q-E4143. Each,
3, each, Less 2%, net..

Same as above, less army insignia. LIST,
No. 3Q-E4145. Each,
3, each, Less 2%, net.

Tortoise shell enamel finish, with green gold effect trim and monogram shield. LIST,
No. 3Q-E4160. Each,
3, each, Less 2%, net.

Same as above, in Black with green gold effect trim. LIST,
No. 3Q-E58-1. Each,
3, each,
Less 2%, net.............

CIGARETTE CASE-and-LIGHTER

Combinations—with Automatic Lighter Action

A striking design in nickel finish, black enamel stripes, and monogram shield. Holds 14 cigarettes. LIST,
No. 3Q-E4113. Each,
3, each,
Less 2%, net....
No. 3Q-E4114. Same, in all-over green gold effect. LIST,
Each,
3, each,
Less 2%, net.....

Immensely popular Case - and - "Spitfire" Lighter with U.S. Army insignia on field of navy blue enamel. Nickel trim. Case holds 14 cigarettes. LIST,
No. 3Q-E4126. Each,
3, each,
Less 2%, net.....

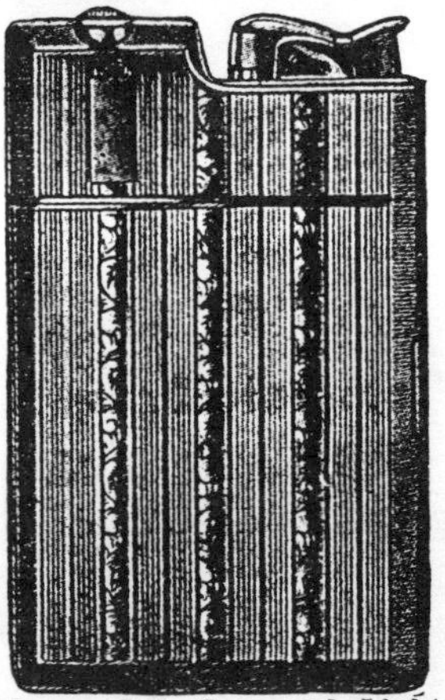

Thin model Case-and-Lighter with engraved and engine turned design, in nickel finish. Monogram shield. Holds 9 king size or 11 regular cigarettes. LIST,
No. 3Q-E4122. Each,
3, each, Less 2%, net..
No. 3Q-E36-3. Same, green gold effect with black enamel trim. LIST,
Each, 3, each,
Less 2%, net................

For the Ladies

Lighter-Case-Vanity

For the feminine smoker—combines famous "Spitfire" action Lighter-Case-and-loose powder Vanity. Holds 7 regular or king size cigarettes. Vanity lid has hand-painted colored flower on white Dresden enamel, black enamel borders. LIST,
No. 3Q-E4119. Each,
3, each, Less 2%, net.

EVANS

Smokers' Accessories *For Table and Desk*

Automatic Lighter

A real convenience in the home or office—always ready with a light. Positive "Spitfire" action. Top and base richly finished in a green gold effect, with body in contrasting jet black enamel. LIST, 4.20.
No. 3Q-E4145. Each, 2.10. 3, each,
Less 2%, net.............

Cigarette Box and Automatic Lighter

Genuine Pigskin Bronze Trim

Luxurious 2-in-1 Case and "Spitfire" Lighter. Top and bottom of case are **Genuine Pigskin.** All metal trim is bronze finish. Bronze lighter rests in well, is instantly removable for use. Case holds over a full pack of cigarettes. LIST,
No. 3Q-E4123. Each.

- EVANS -
World's Largest Manufacturers of STYLE Accessories

EVANS CLIPPER Lighter — Cases

Automatic Lighter Action

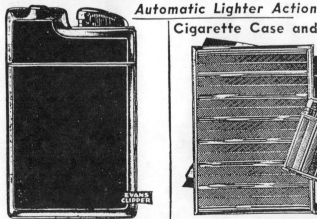

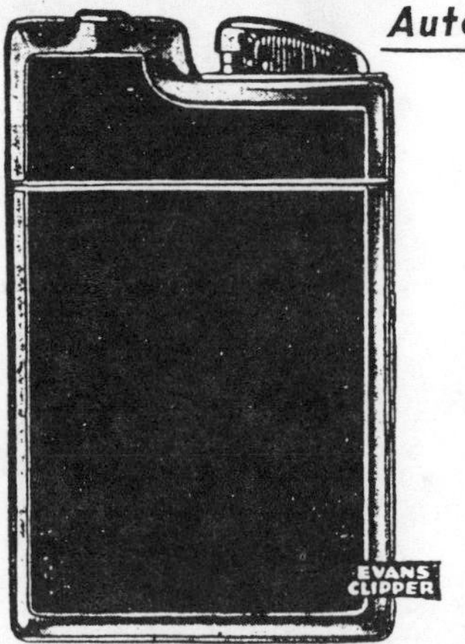

Smart black and gold model, suitable for any and all occasions. Case holds 10 regular or 9 king size cigarettes. Evans positive lighter action. Rich black enamel sides, with yellow gold trim. LIST,
No. 3Q-E3412. Each,
3, each, Less 2%, net......

Cigarette Case and Lighter Set

Golden Bronze

Set includes vest pocket Evans Lighter, and Evans Verithin Cigarette Case—holds 13 cigarettes. Distinctive engine-turned design, both Lighter and Case finished in rich Golden Bronze. In Gift Box. LIST,
No. 3Q-E4041. Pet set,
3, sets, per set,
Less 2%, net.......................

1941 CATALOG PAGE

Evans' New Automatic "Spitfire" Lighters

The new fully automatic lighter head permits the lighter to work with one simple operation. A flick of the finger and there's the flame! Simply press the thumb lever down to light and release to extinguish. Styled by Evans for economy and efficiency of performance.

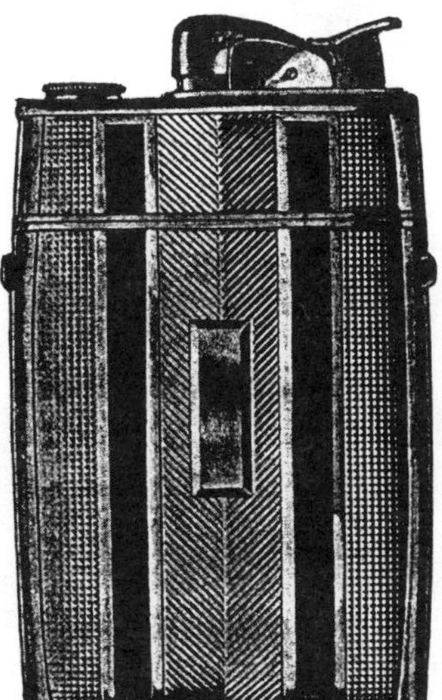

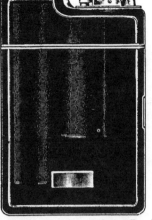

Combination Cigarette Case. Combined with the new Evans automatic lighter head, this lighter and cigarette case is one of the smokers' favorites. Non-tarnishing nickel-finish, black enamel trim. Holds 14 cigarettes. Ill. 2/3 actual size.
No. 232J87N—Each ....
Assortment of 4 in display box. Two designs. Per assortment.......

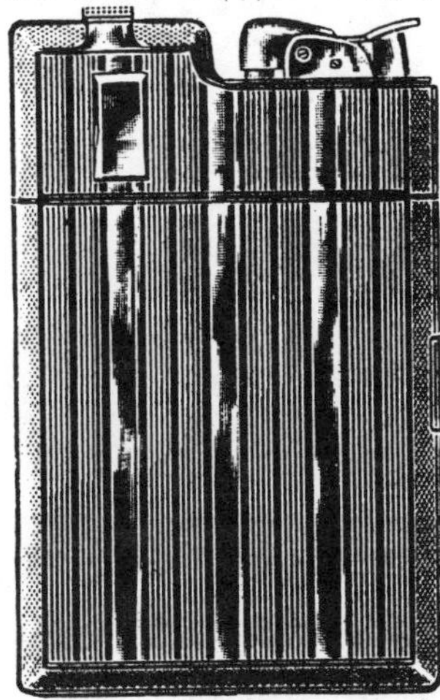

Case and Lighter Combination. Guaranteed by the manufacturer to give full satisfaction. Holds 12 King size or regular size cigarettes. Has non-tarnishing nickel finish with attractive engine-turned design. New flat type. Equipped with new "Spitfire" lighter head. Special while limited quantity lasts. Ill. approx. 1/2 actual size.
No. 232J91—
Each ....

Combination Lighter and Case. Fitted with the new "Spitfire" automatic lighter head, this handsome case has a 24K gold finish with French enamel front and back in black. New flat type for easy carrying. Holds 12 cigarettes. Illus. approx. 1/2 actual size. Styled to please the most discriminating smoker, it is two practical units in one.
No. 232J86N—
Each ....

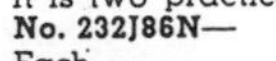

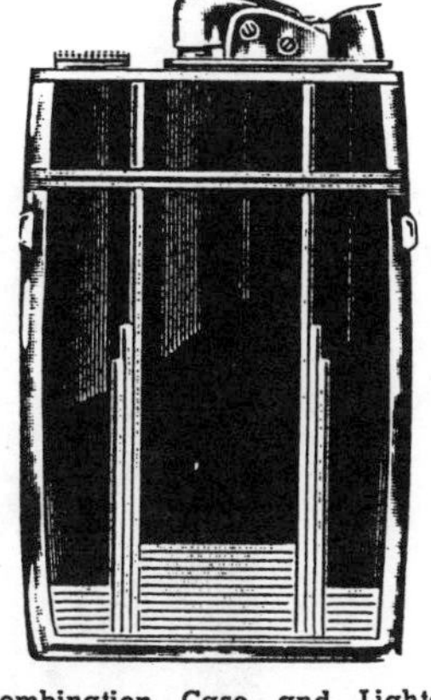

Combination Case and Lighter. Has non-tarnishing nickel finish with French black enamel front. Holds 14 cigarettes. Illustrated approx. 1/2 actual size.
No. 232J69N—Each .....
4-pc. assortment in display box; two designs. Per assortment.

Evans Assortment. Equipped with automatic head that permits the lighter to work with one simple operation. Has non-tarnishing nickel finish. Embossed and engine-turned patterns. Individually boxed and packaged 12 assorted in display box.
No. 218J161N—Each ......
Per assortment of 12.........

Pocket Lighter. Has golden bronze finish with English grosgrain engine-turned design. Bright polish trim. Illus. approx. 1/2 actual size. Guaranteed to give perfect satisfaction.
No. 218J159N—
Each ......

Nickel Finish. Has engine-turned design. French black enamel trim. Illus. approx. 1/2 actual size.
No. 218J156—
Each ....
Same lighter as above in golden bronze finish. Automatic "Spitfire" lighter head.
No. 218J157—
Each ....

Pocket Lighter. Has lustrous non-tarnishing nickel finish with French enamel front in black. English grosgrain engine-turned back. Illus. approx. 1/2 actual size. Order yours today!
No. 218J158N—
Each ......

Engine-turned. Has lovely non-tarnishing green finish with pink finish trim. Engine-turned tear drop design. Automatic "Spitfire" lighter head. Illustrated approx. 1/2 actual size.
No. 218J178N—
Each .....

Nickel Finish. Non-tarnishing, stainless. Has French enamel front and back in glistening black. Available in the popular large size only. Illustrated approx. 1/2 actual size.
No. 218J155N—
Each .....

Clipper Models Created by Evans

Case and Lighter Combination. Has lustrous nickel finish with black French enamel back and front. Guaranteed to give full satisfaction.
No. 232J84—Each ...

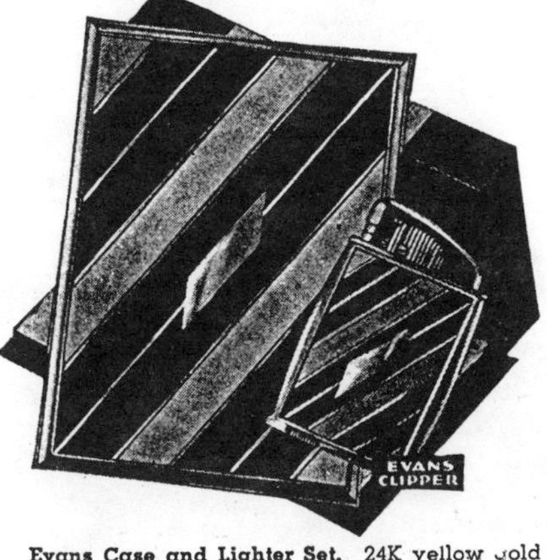

Evans Case and Lighter Set. 24K yellow gold electroplate. Cream and shell enamel top. Has engraving signet. Engine-turned backs. Case holds 13 cigarettes. Size: 4 1/4 x 3 1/8 in. Large size lighter. In gift box.
No. 213J43—Per set................

Lighter and Case Set. Golden bronze finish. Chevron design engine-turned front and back. Holds 13 cigarettes. 4 1/4 x 3 1/8 in. Boxed.
No. 213J44—Per set....................$5.10
As above. Non-tarnishing white metal.
No. 213J145—Per set ....

Case, Lighter and Vanity. Has rich nickel finish. Black enamel; cloisonne cover. Large mirror and powder container. Ill. 1/2 actual size.
No. 232J73—Each

1930 CATALOG PAGE

GOLDEN WHEEL SPIN-TYPE AUTOMATIC *Lighters*

N 1061

Automatic. Engine-turned and hand-engraved Platichrome—

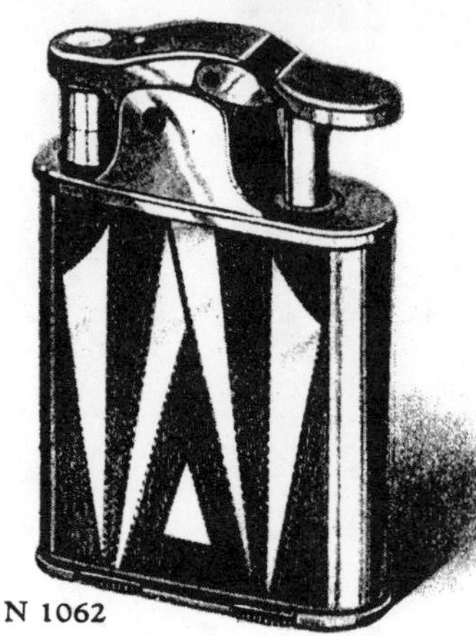

N 1062

Automatic. Engine-turned Platichrome—modernistic design—

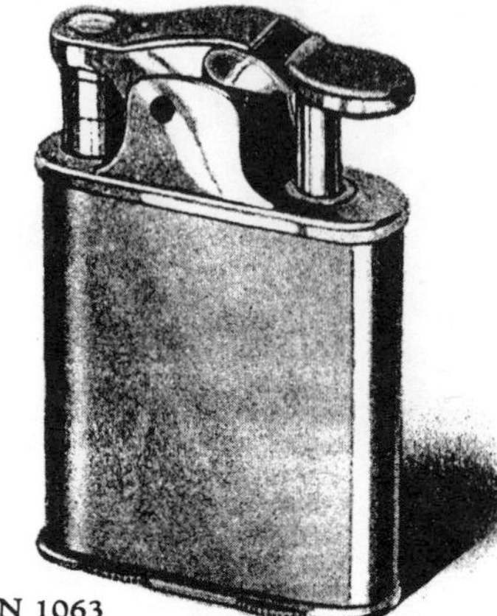

N 1063

Automatic in the exclusive, lasting Platichrome finish—

N 1064

Automatic in genuine leather, ostrich grain. With Platichrome signet—

N 1065

Automatic in polished enamel combination, red and black. Platichrome signet and trim.

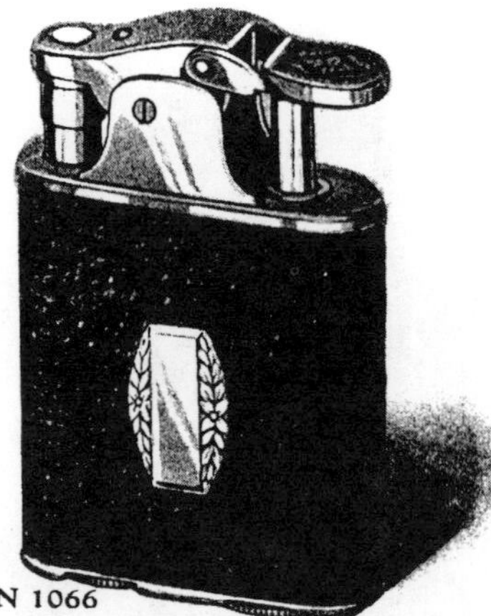

N 1066

Automatic in genuine leather, black morocco. Platichrome signet—

N 1067

Spin-type with Cigarette Case in genuine leather, ostrich grain, to match. Signets of Platichrome. In de luxe box

Lifetime Guarantee.

N 1068

Spin-type with flat Cigarette Case in genuine leather, black morocco, to match. Signet and corners of Platichrome

Lifetime Guarantee.

1930 CATALOG PAGE

GOLDEN WHEEL
SPIN·TYPE AUTOMATIC
Lighters

N 1052

-Spin-type Watch Lighter. Engine-turned and hand-engraved. 42-hour movement— *Lifetime Guarantee.*

N 1053

-Spin-type, junior size. Genuine ostrich— *Lifetime Guarantee.*

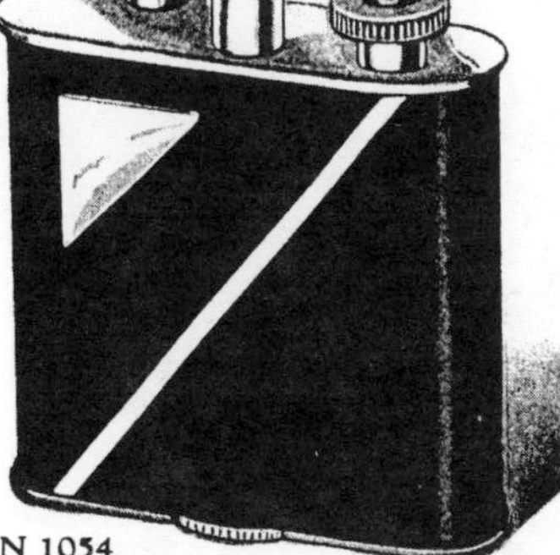

N 1054

-Spin-type, standard size. Full dress lighter, onyx black enamel, Platichrome signet and trim. *Lifetime Guarantee.*

N 1055

-Spin-type, standard size. Genuine alligator— *Lifetime Guarantee.*

N 1056

-Spin-type, junior size. In exclusive, durable Platichrome finish— *Lifetime Guarantee.*

N 1057

-Spin-type, standard size. Engine-turned and hand-engraved Platichrome — *Lifetime Guarantee.*

N 1058

-Spin-type, junior size. Engine-turned Platichrome — *Lifetime Guarantee.*

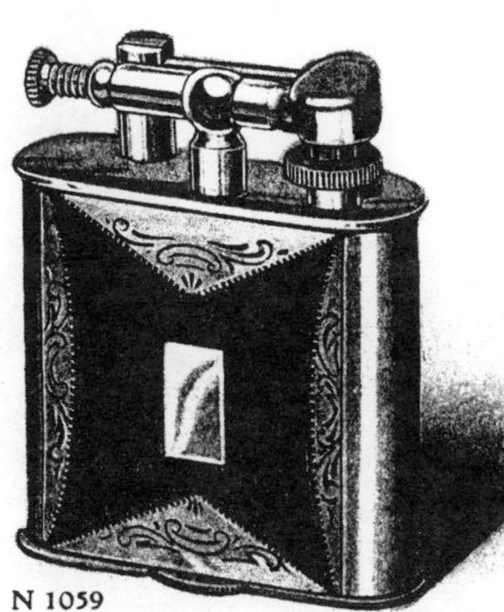

N 1059

-Spin-type, standard size. Engine-turned and hand-engraved Platichrome — *Lifetime Guarantee.*

N 1060

Spin-type, junior size. Combination black, abalone and white genuine pearl— *Lifetime Guarantee.*

1930 CATALOG PAGE

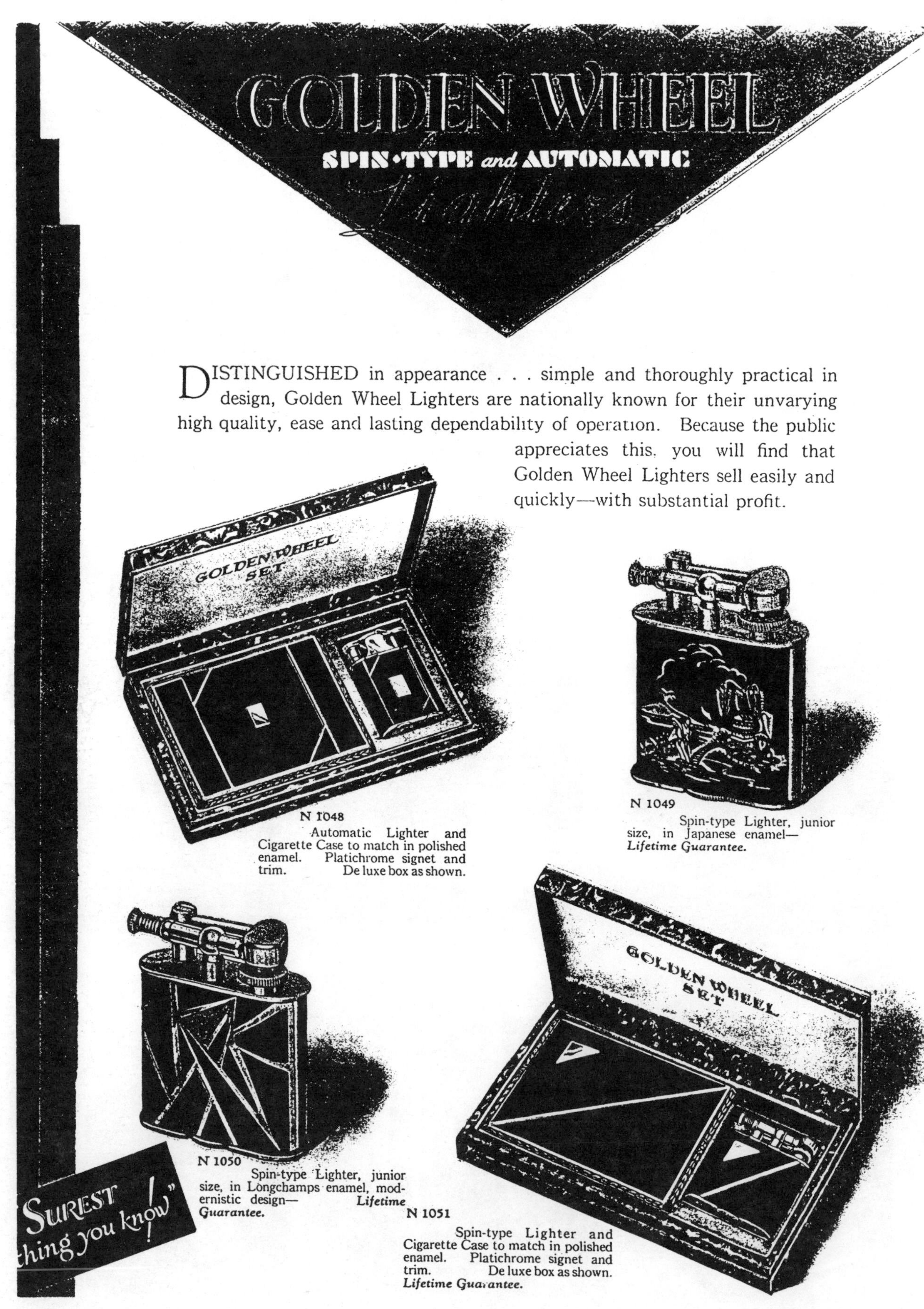

GOLDEN WHEEL
SPIN·TYPE and AUTOMATIC
Lighters
DISTINGUISHED in appearance . . . simple and thoroughly practical in design, Golden Wheel Lighters are nationally known for their unvarying high quality, ease and lasting dependability of operation. Because the public appreciates this, you will find that Golden Wheel Lighters sell easily and quickly—with substantial profit.
GOLDEN WHEEL SET
N 1048
Automatic Lighter and Cigarette Case to match in polished enamel. Platichrome signet and trim. De luxe box as shown.
N 1049
Spin-type Lighter, junior size, in Japanese enamel—Lifetime Guarantee.
N 1050
Spin-type Lighter, junior size, in Longchamps enamel, modernistic design— Lifetime Guarantee.
"Surest thing you know!"
GOLDEN WHEEL SET
N 1051
Spin-type Lighter and Cigarette Case to match in polished enamel. Platichrome signet and trim. De luxe box as shown. Lifetime Guarantee.

1931 CATALOG PAGE

Golden Wheel Pocket Lighter Sets

ILLUSTRATIONS FULL SIZE—MAKES AN IDEAL GIFT—PRICES PER SET

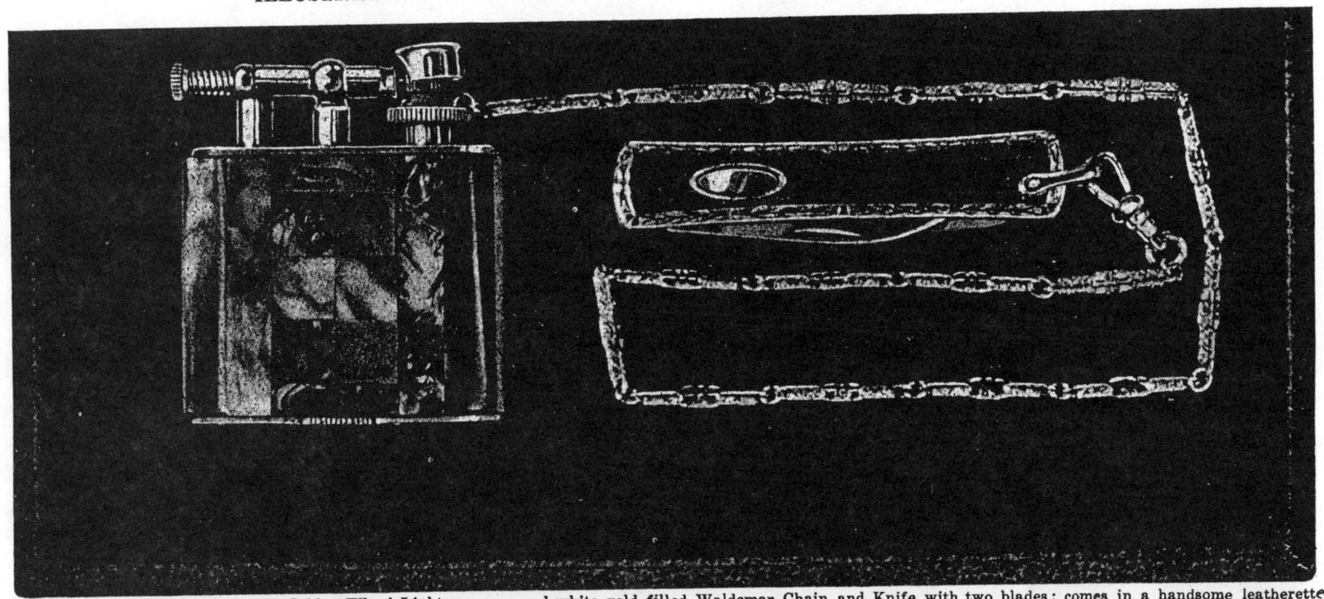

No. T18801—Genuine pearl inlaid Golden Wheel Lighter, green and white gold filled Waldemar Chain and Knife with two blades; comes in a handsome leatherette plush-lined gift case.

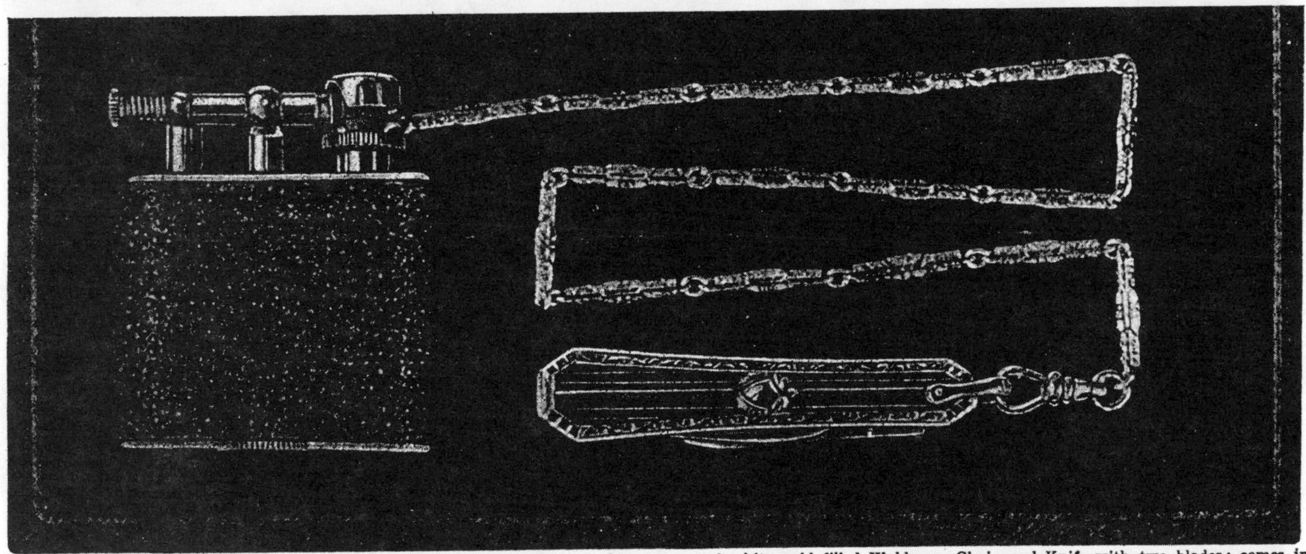

No. T18802—Genuine shark skin Golden Wheel Pocket Lighter, fancy design green and white gold filled Waldemar Chain and Knife with two blades; comes in a beautiful leatherette, plush-lined gift case.

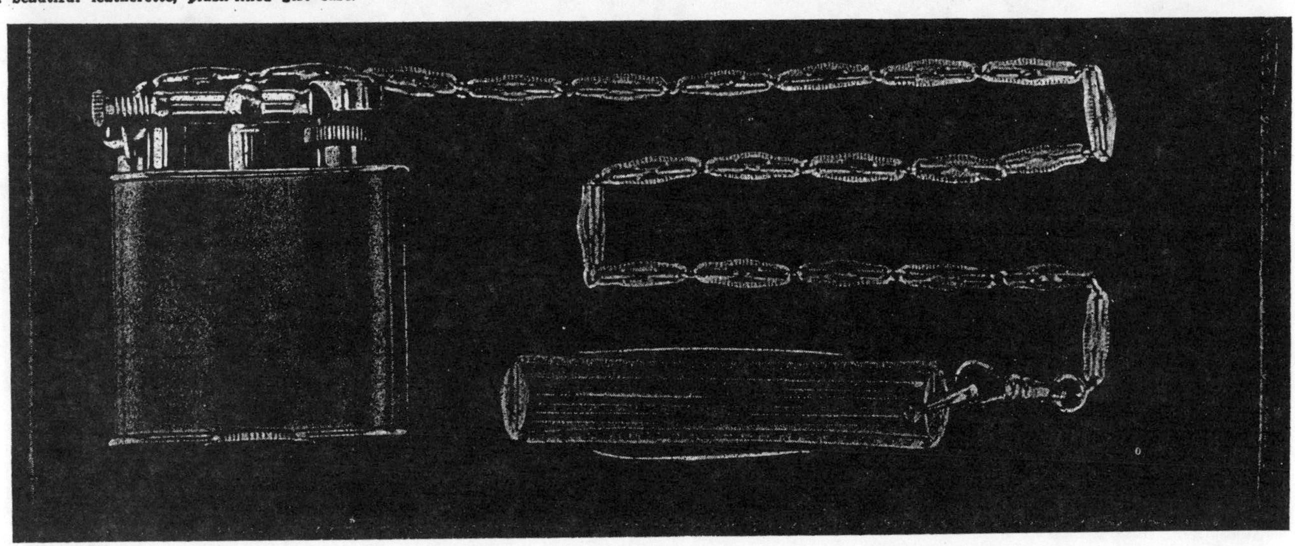

1931 CATALOG PAGE

Golden Wheel Pocket Lighter Sets

ILLUSTRATIONS FULL SIZE—VERY PRACTICAL—PRICES PER SET

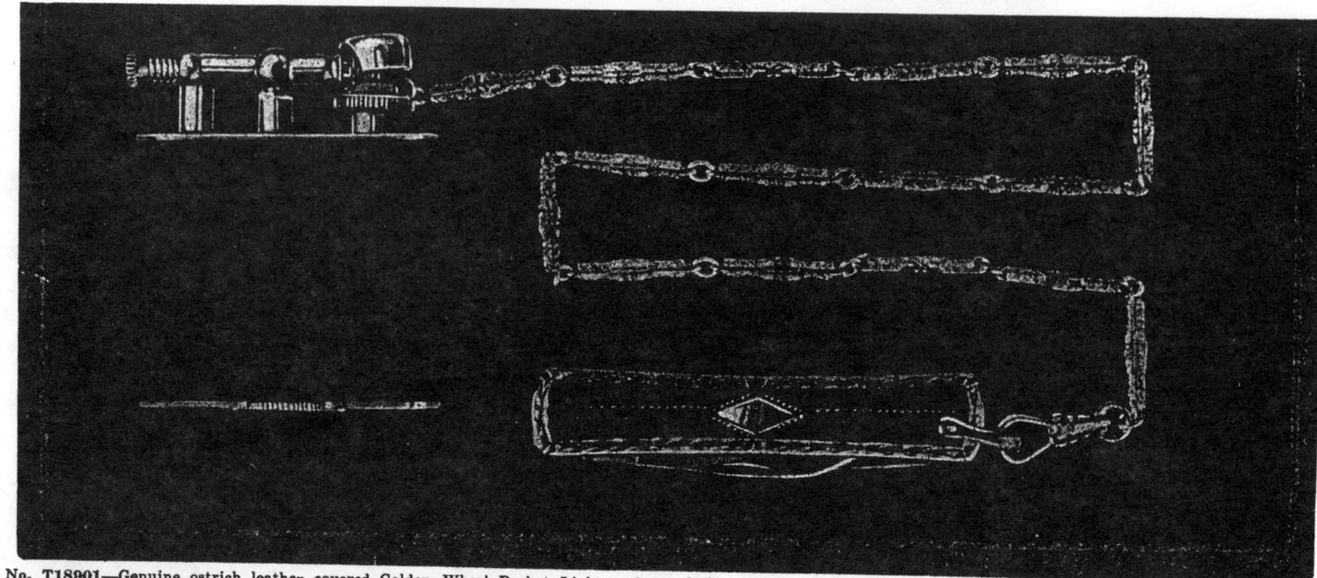

No. T18901—Genuine ostrich leather covered Golden Wheel Pocket Lighter, fancy design green and white golld filled Waldemar Chain and Knife with two blades; comes in a leatherette gift case, plush lined.

No. T18902—Platichrome plated Golden Wheel Pocket Lighter, fancy engine-turned white gold filled Waldemar Chain and Knife with one blade and file; comes in a leatherette gift case, plush lined.

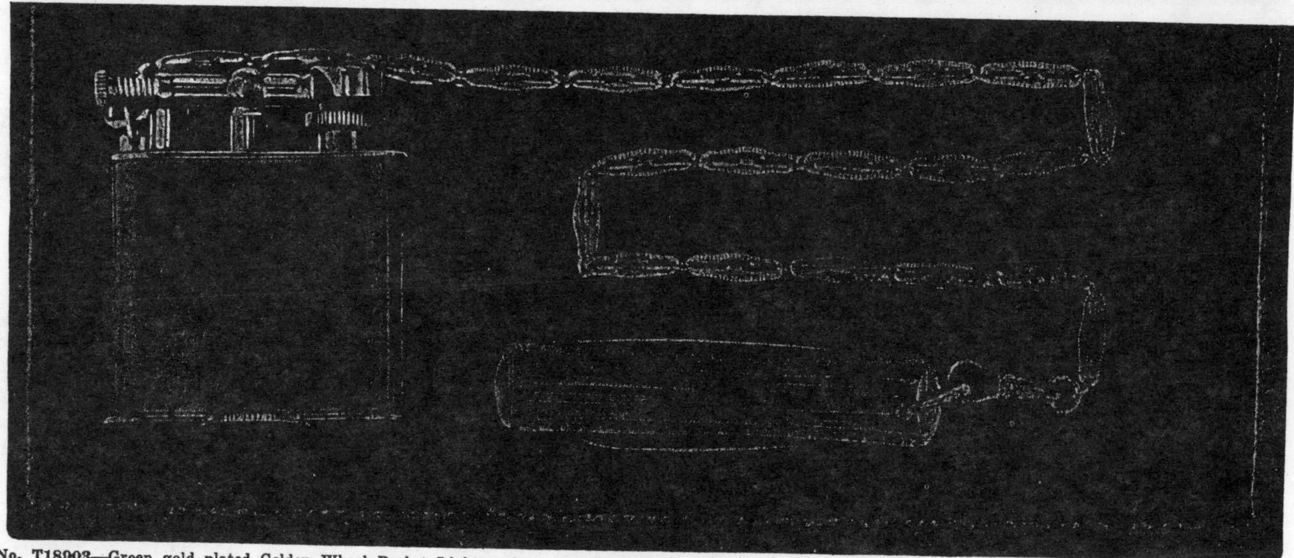

No. T18903—Green gold plated Golden Wheel Pocket Lighter, fancy green gold filled Waldemar Chain and Knife with two blades; comes in a leatherette gift case, plush lined.

1931 CATALOG PAGE

GOLDEN WHEEL

Lighter Sets

SPIN TYPE ONLY

STYLES FOR BOTH LADIES AND GENTLEMEN

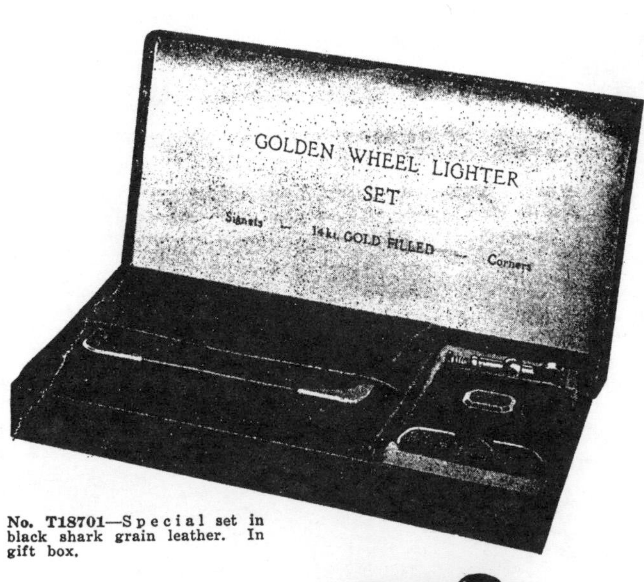

No. T18701—Special set in black shark grain leather. In gift box.

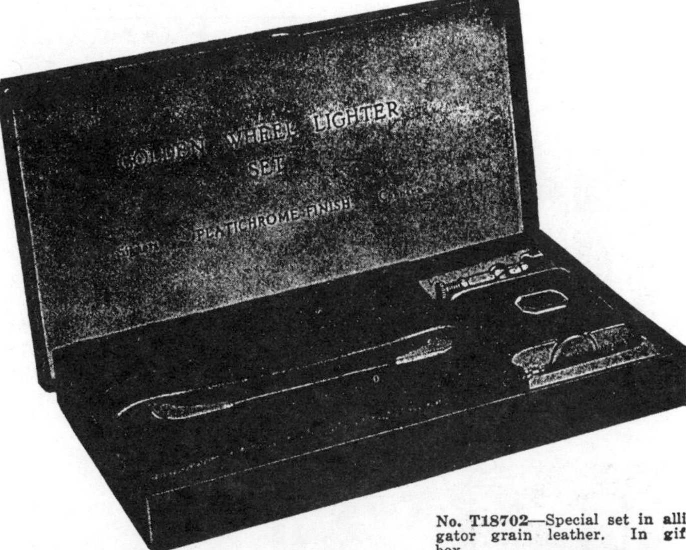

No. T18702—Special set in alligator grain leather. In gift box.

All Sets on this page furnished with Spin Type Lighters only.

No. T18703—Red and black polished enamel set. Regimental stripe and signet of Platichrome. With automatic lighter.

No. T18704—Similar to above, with black, green and red polished enamel.

No. T18705—Similar to above, with yellow center panel and two shades of green polished enamel.

Each Set packed in Handsome Gift Box.

No. T18706—Ultra Marine blue and yellow polished enamel set. Regimental stripe and signet of Platichrome.

No. T18707—Same as above, in maroon and gold enamel.

No. T18708—Special set in ostrich grain leather. Case is made to take full pack of cigarettes. In gift box.

No. T18709—Special set in alligator grain. Cigarette case made to take full pack of cigarettes. In gift box.

THE WORLD'S GREATEST LIGHTER

"A Flip -and it's lit!"

RONSON *De-light*

"Release -and it's out!"

PATENTED. OTHER PAT'S. P'D'G. TRADE MARKS REGISTERED

HOMELIGHTERS

RONSON "BRIDGE" LIGHTER
Chromium, Leather Covered

No.
12968 Blue Leather - - -

RONSON "BOGEY" LIGHTER
Reproduction of Regulation Golf Ball

No.
13007 Old Ivory - - - - - - - - -
13007 Polished Chromium - - - - -

RONSON "NEW YORKER"
Chromium Lighter

No. 12790
Mottled Orange Base

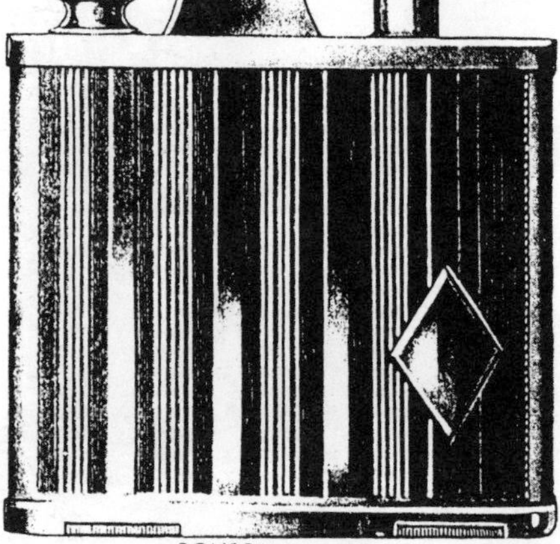

RONSON "JUMBO"
Chromium Plate

No.
817 Engine Turned - - - - - - - - -
801 Black Leather - - - - - - - - - -

"RONDELIGHT"
Combination Paper Weight and Lighter

No.
12875 Polished Chromium

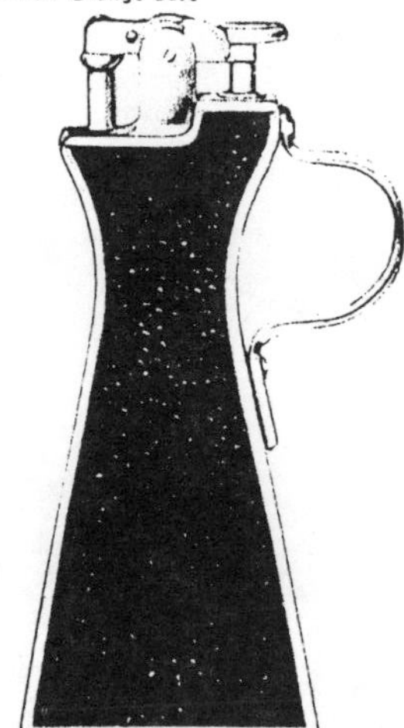

RONSON TABLELIGHTER
(Height 4½")

No.
12099 Green Leather

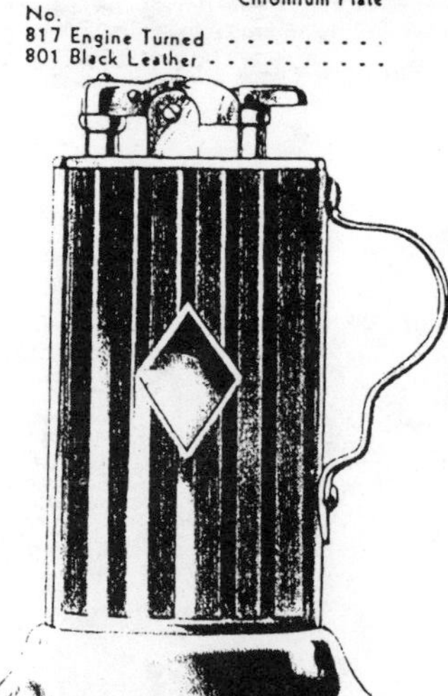

RONSON TABOURETTE
(Height 4½")

No.
12417 Chromium, E. T.
12280 Black Leather

RONSON SMOKER SET
With removable Tabourette Lighter and Pottery Bowl on Marbleized Base

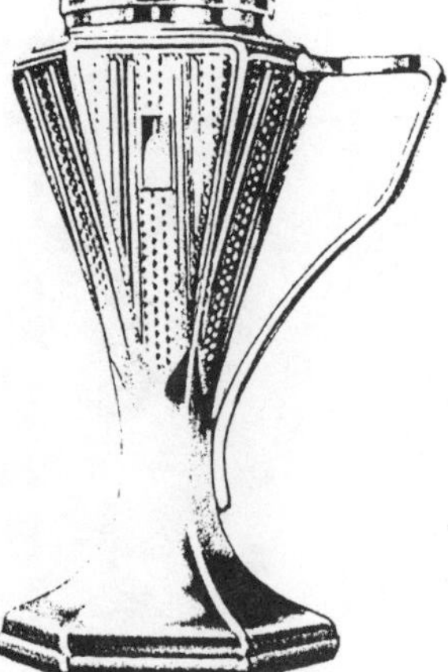

RONSON SUPERBA
(Height 5")

No. 12773
Chrom. Plate, E. T.

1934 CATALOG PAGE

RONSON POCKET LIGHTERS
Richly Enameled in Black, Tortoise or White
No.
01151 Princess...
1151 Standard..

RONSON "JUNIOR" MODEL
Chromium "Butler" and "Engine Turned" Designs
No.
153 Butler......
151 Eng. Turned.

RONSON POCKET LIGHTERS
Chromium "Butler".
No.
021 Princess....
21 Standard....

RONSON POCKET LIGHTERS
Richly Enameled in Black or Maroon with Chromium
No.
1936 Princess....

RONSON POCKET LIGHTERS
Richly Enameled in Black with Chromium or Black and White
No.
1944 Princess....

RONSON POCKET LIGHTERS
Richly Enameled in Black and Ivory or Black and Red
No.
14312 Princess...

RONSON POCKET LIGHTERS
Richly Enameled in Black and Green or Black and White
No.
1948 Princess....

RONSON POCKET LIGHTERS
Richly Enameled in Black, Tortoise or White. Raised Shield
No.
1934 Princess....
1933 Standard...

RONSON POCKET LIGHTERS
Richly Enameled in Black and White or Black and Chromium
No.
1946 Princess....

RONSON "PRINCESS" GEM
Black with Brilliant Vari-Colored Gemmed Effects
No.
1940 Ronson Gem

RONSON POCKET LIGHTERS
New Rich "Cloisonette" in Blue or Amber. Raised Shield.
No.
1938 Princess....

RONSON "TWIN BAR" MODEL
Chromium Bars and Monogram Shield with Rich Black Enamel
No.
1102 Standard...

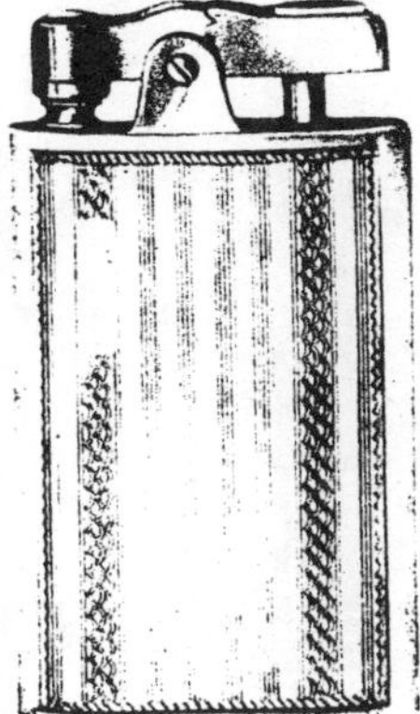

RONSON
"JR. SPORT"
Chromium
'Engine Turned"
Design.
Monogram
Shield.
No. 100
Eng. Turned

RONSON POCKET LIGHTERS
Chromium "Engine Turned" Design. Monogram Shield
No.
12351 Princess...
17 Standard..

Illustrations on this Page Are Almost Actual Size

RONSON "IMPERIAL" LIGHTERS
Ultra-fine Chromium "Engine Turned" Design, Richly Enameled in Black
No.
01152 Princess...
1152 Standard..

RONSON
"JR. SPORT"
Rich Two-Tone Enamels:
Black and Ivory or Black and Green with Chromium
No. 14319

RONSON LIGHTERS AND COMBINATIONS

Ronson De-light—The World's Greatest Lighter. "A Flip—and it's lit—Release—and it's out." Ronson lighters are renowned for their performance, quality and appearance. Illustrations show reduced size.

Prices Subject to Wholesale Discounts. See Page 2.

RONSON LIGHTERS
CJ3217 Princess Size...
CJ3218 Standard Size..

Smart black enamel; enduring chromium finish shield, stripes and exposed parts. For actual sizes see note to right.

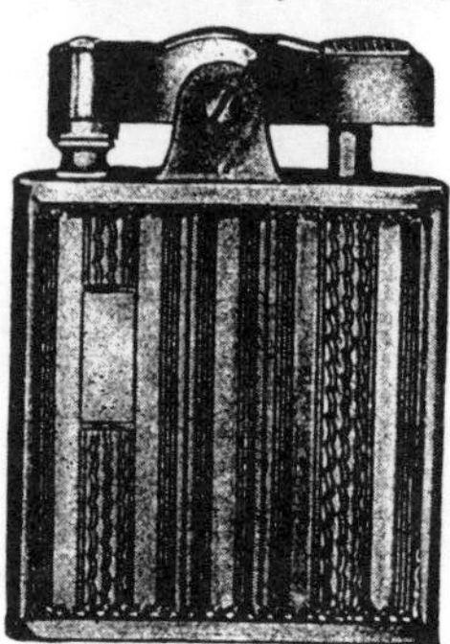

RONSON LIGHTERS
CJ3219 Princess Size...
CJ3220 Standard Size..

The popular engine turned effect; enduring chromium finish, monogram shield. For actual sizes, see below.

RONSON LIGHTERS
CJ3221 Princess Size...
CJ3222 Standard Size..

A popular chromium plain satin finish design; bright monogram shield. For actual sizes, see below.

RONSON LIGHTERS
CJ3223 Princess Size...
CJ3224 Standard Size..

Stylish brown tortoise enamel; enduring chromium finish shield, stripes and exposed parts. For actual sizes, see note to left.

ACTUAL DIMENSIONS OF RONSON LIGHTERS
Standard, or men's size 2 x 1¾ in.
Princess, or ladies' size, 1¾ x 1⅜ in.

NUMBER CJ3229

RONSON LIGHTERS
CJ3225 Brown Alligator Leather ....
CJ3226 Grey Snake Leather...
Above are Standard Size
CJ3227 Brown Alligator Leather ....
CJ3228 Brown Morocco Leather
Above are Princess Size
Retail Price $4.50
The most popular models of Ronson Lighters. Genuine leather. Raised monogram shield and all exposed parts enduring chromium finish. Illustration shows actual size of Standard Model.

NUMBER CJ3230

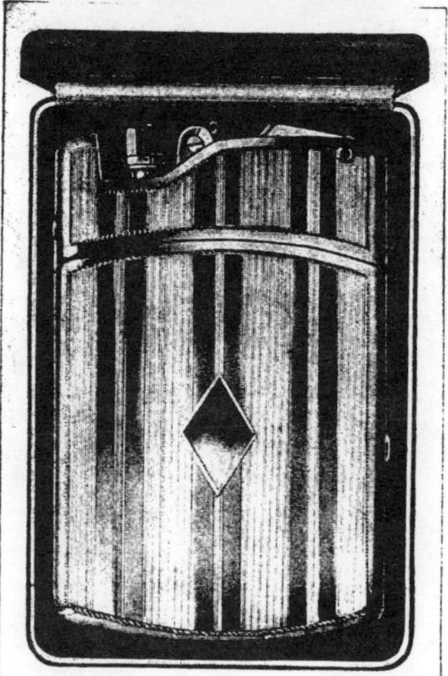

NUMBERS CJ3231 AND CJ3232

CJ3229 Ronson Super Case...........................

A refined Ronson lighter and cigarette case combination. Height, 4⅛ inches; width, 2½ inches. Effective design, richly enameled in black, white, and snake with enduring chromium monogram shield, edges and exposed parts. Holds 14 cigarettes.

CJ3230 Ronson Master Case ....

The popular priced combination Ronson lighter and cigarette case. Size 4⅛ x 2½ inches. Richly enameled in black and smoked pearl; enduring chromium finished shield, stripes and exposed parts; holds 14 cigarettes.

RONSON TUXEDO LYTA-CASE SETS

The highest grade, finest quality combination Ronson Lighter and Cigarette Case. Though compact in size, the case holds 14 cigarettes. Length, 4 inches; width, 2½ inches. Furnished in handsome velvet lined gift box.
CJ3231 Chromium finish; engine turned; stylish satin monogram shield ....
CJ3232 Chromium finish; plain design; bright shield..
CJ3233 Rich black enamel; enduring chromium finish stripes, monogram shield and exposed parts.........

NUMBER CJ3233

1934 CATALOG PAGE

THE WORLD'S GREATEST LIGHTER
RONSON
DeLight
"A FLIP—AND IT'S LIT!"
PATENTED. OTHER PATS. PDG. TRADE MARKS REGISTERED
"RELEASE—AND IT'S OUT!"

RONSON SETS—Cigarette Case (14 Cigarettes) and "Princess" Lighter. Richly Enameled in Black or Tortoise with Chromium

No.
14364 Ronson Set. . . . .

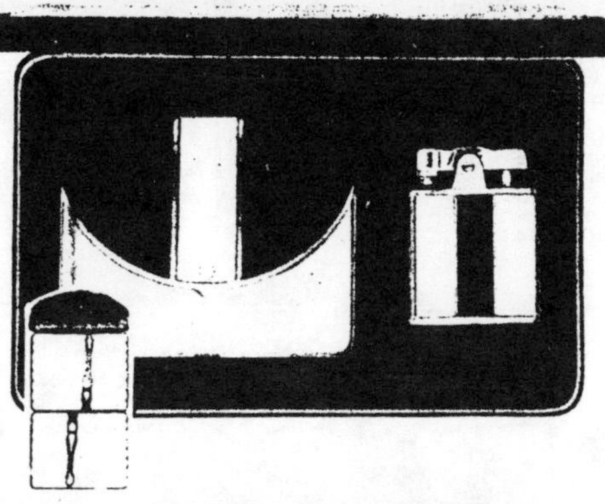

RONSON WOMEN'S SETS—Cigarette Case (14 Cigarettes) and "Princess" Lighter. Chromium Plate with Rich Two-Tone Enamels: Black and White or White and Red

No.
14363 Ronson Set. . . . .

RONSON SETS—Cigarette Case (14 Cigarettes) and "Princess" Lighter. Richly Enameled in Black and Ivory with Chromium or Black with Chromium

No.
14359 Ronson Set. . . . .

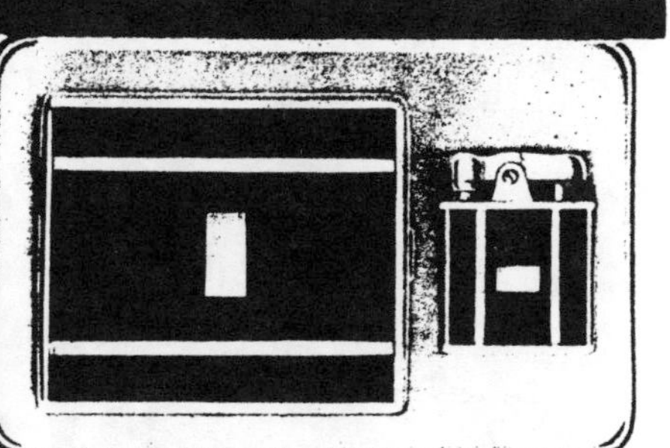

RONSON SETS—Cigarette Case (20 Cigarettes) and Lighter. Richly Enameled in Black with Chromium. Monogram Shield

No.
14453 "Princess". . . . .
14452 "Standard". . . . .

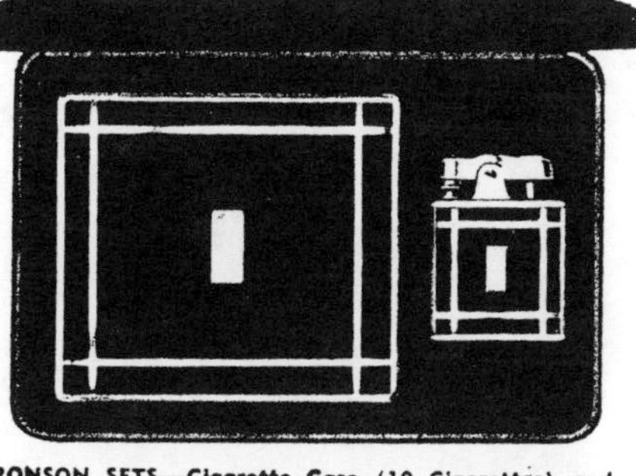

RONSON SETS—Cigarette Case (10 Cigarettes) and "Princess" Lighter. Richly Enameled in Black or Tortoise with Chromium. Monogram Shield

No.
14619 Ronson Set. . . . .

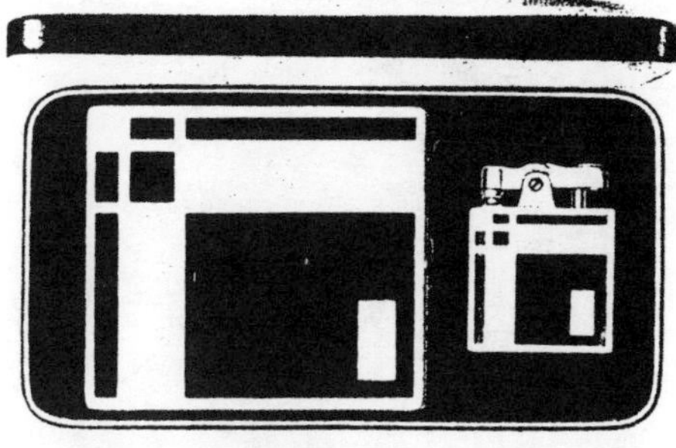

RONSON SETS—Cigarette Case (20 Cigarettes) and Lighter. Richly Enameled in Black and Ivory with Chromium or Black with Chromium. Monogram Shield

No.
14454 "Standard". . . . .
14455 "Princess". . . . .

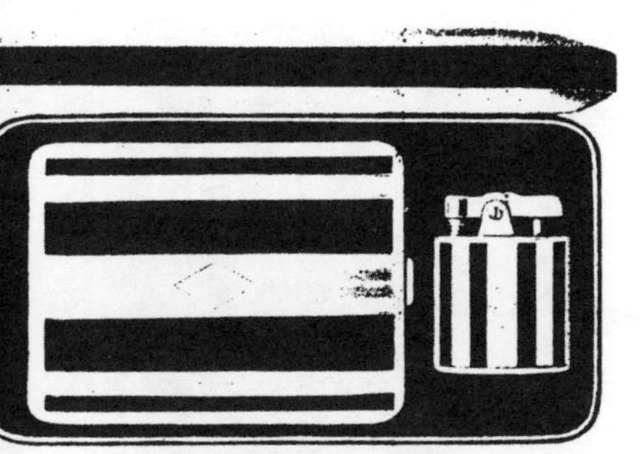

SPECIAL "IMPERIAL" MODEL

RONSON "IMPERIAL" SETS—Cigarette Case (10 Cigarettes) and Lighter. Ultra-Fine Chromium "Engine Turned" Design. Richly Enameled in Black

No.
14304 "Princess". . . . .
14305 "Standard". . . . .

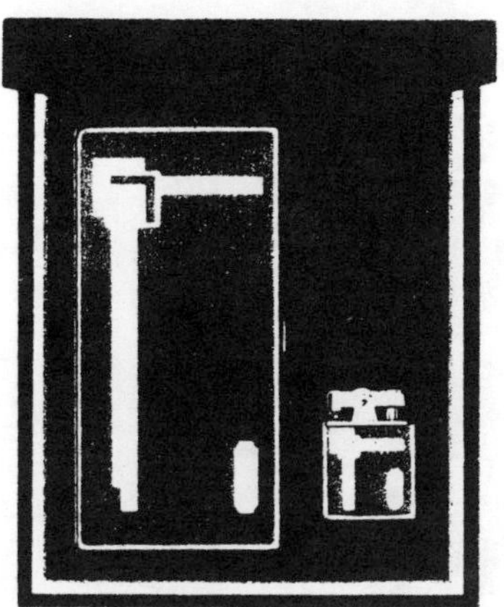

RONSON SETS—Cigarette Case (20 Cigarettes) and "Princess" Lighter. Richly Enameled in Black and White or Black and Gray. Monogram Shield

No.
14612 Ronson Set. . . . .

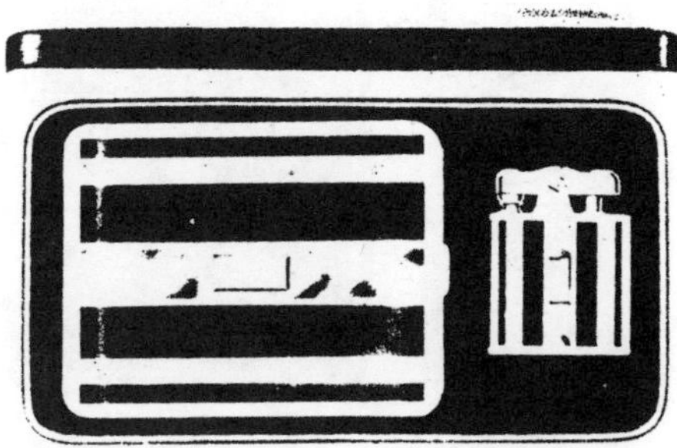

RONSON SETS—Cigarette Case (10 Cigarettes) and "Princess" Lighter. Richly Enameled in Black and Smoked Pearl or Black and Tortoise,—with Chromium. Monogram Shield

No.
14615 Ronson Set. . . . .

1941 CATALOG PAGE

Lights the Smokes of the World
One Finger — One Motion
RONSON
WORLD'S GREATEST LIGHTER

RONSON RONDETTE LIGHTER

Extremely attractive hand engraved and engine-turned chrome trim case richly enameled in Black or Tortoise and with polished shield for monogram. RONSON excellence—a flip and it's lit. Release and it's out. Simple to use—light, compact—**Specify Color.**

No. 3Q-R6603

RONSON Whirlwind with DISAPPEARING WINDSHIELD

WORLD'S GREATEST LIGHTER

Lights Up Anywhere

Exclusive new RONSON —gives lighter service anywhere under any kind of condition—indoors — outdoors. Disappearing windshield telescopes within case and is hidden from view when not needed to protect flame in windy weather. Butler finish chrome plate case with engine turned design and polished monogram shield.

No. 3Q-R6414.

RONSON PRINCESS LIGHTER

Pocket type lighter—original RONSON made famous by its amazing performance—never fails to light. Famous RONSON action—a single easy flip and it's lit, similar action and it's out! Butler finish with polished shield for initials or monogram.

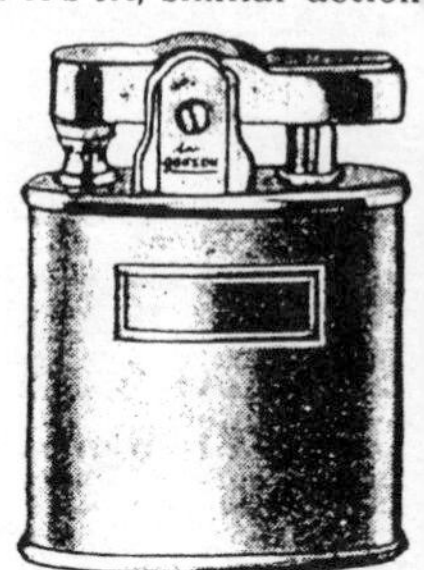

No. 3Q-R6048. Princess Model.

RONSON PAL LIGHTER-CIGARETTE CASE

WORLD'S GREATEST LIGHTER

to retail at a new low price — NEW STYLE CASE

RONSON Streamlined flame-shielded combination cigarette lighter and cigarette case. Large fuel capacity—effective instantaneous light by simple RONSON method. Holds 10 cigarettes in special compartment. Quality built case of Dureum, a gold-color thru and thru metal alloy with deep grooved diamond pattern, bordered by striped bands. Polished shield for initials or monogram. Inside view to left shows compactness of the "Pal."

No. 3Q-R7070.

RONSON PENCILITER Pocket Lighter

Two-Purpose Lighter and Pencil

Operates on Same Famous RONSON Principle

Handy—Light Efficient

RONSON offers in this exceptional number the facilities of both lighter and pencil — two daily needs supplied from one compact unit. Here is a genuine RONSON lighter cleverly built into a super-fine, propel-repel pencil and designed for the millions of busy folk who write while they smoke and smoke while they write. The appealing point to this new RONSON is that it takes no extra room and the pencil costs no extra money. Finished in polished chrome with engine-turned design and polished shield for initials or monogram. Pearl green or Black writing grip. Has eraser and arsenal of extra leads.

No. 3Q-R15252.

RONSON NEW MASTERCASE COMBINATION LIGHTER-CIGARETTE CASE

This RONSON, the new Mastercase is liked by both men and women—its features appeal, its snappy style and finish catches the eye. The double utility idea "clicks." Holds 14 cigarettes and the ever-ready lighter in a single compact handsome hand engraved and engine turned case, richly enameled in Black and Pearl or Tortoise and Ivory. Polished monogram shield. Embodies the lighting efficiency that makes RONSON the finest lighter. **Specify Color.**

No. 3Q-R6723.

RONSON LADY-PACT COMBINATION Cigarette Lighter and Vanity

- *Smart—Graceful Streamlined*
- *A Real Compact*
- *A Real Lighter*

Dainty enough to appeal to the most fastidious modern Miss and practical enough for everyone. Small, compact size fitting snugly into the handbag—Streamlined, slim; handsomely finished and decorated. Engine turned and hand engraved pattern, richly enameled **Tortoise or Black.** Polished monogram shield. **Specify color.**

No. 3Q-R7496.

RONSON Ten and Twenty Cases Combination Cigarette Lighter

Engine-Turned Enameled Cases

RONSON Monogram Shields

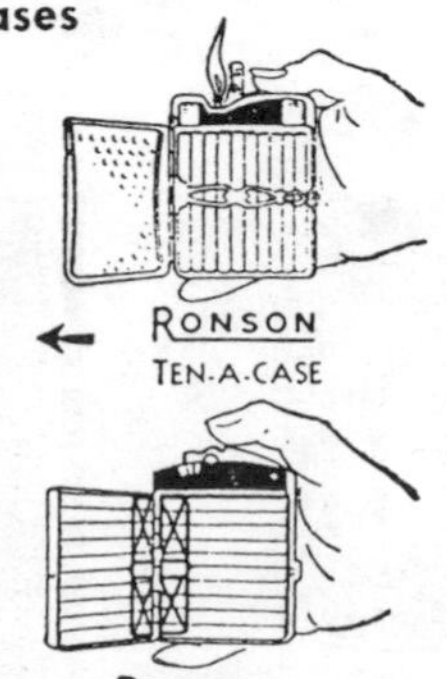

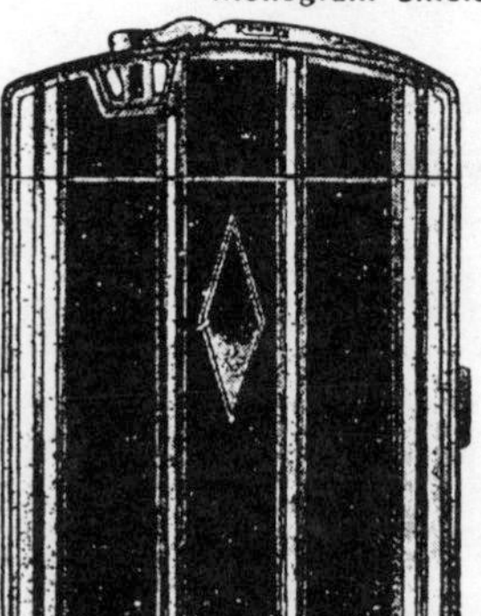

RONSON Latest TEN-A-CASE

Smart, thin model for "all occasion" use. So slim it slips in tuxedo pocket or fancy handbag without conspicuous bulge—yet holds ten cigarettes and lighter. Chrome plated engine-turned design, black-and-white enamel, or Two-Tone Tortoise. Monogram shield. **Specify Color.**

No. 3Q-R5232.

HANDSOME TWENTYCASE

Holds a full pack of twenty cigarettes. A real smoker's adequate supply and a sure-fire light for every "smoke." Smart, in chrome plated case with engine-turned stripe design with panels of black and white or Two-Tone Tortoise. Polished shield for initials. **Specify Color.**

No. 3Q-R6939.

1954 CATALOG PAGE

RONSON "WINDSOR"

Gracefully contoured in a choice of rich, gleaming Gem-Tone finishes. Initials, signatures, emblems, etc. can be inscribed in color with New Hermes Engravograph, for extra gift appeal.

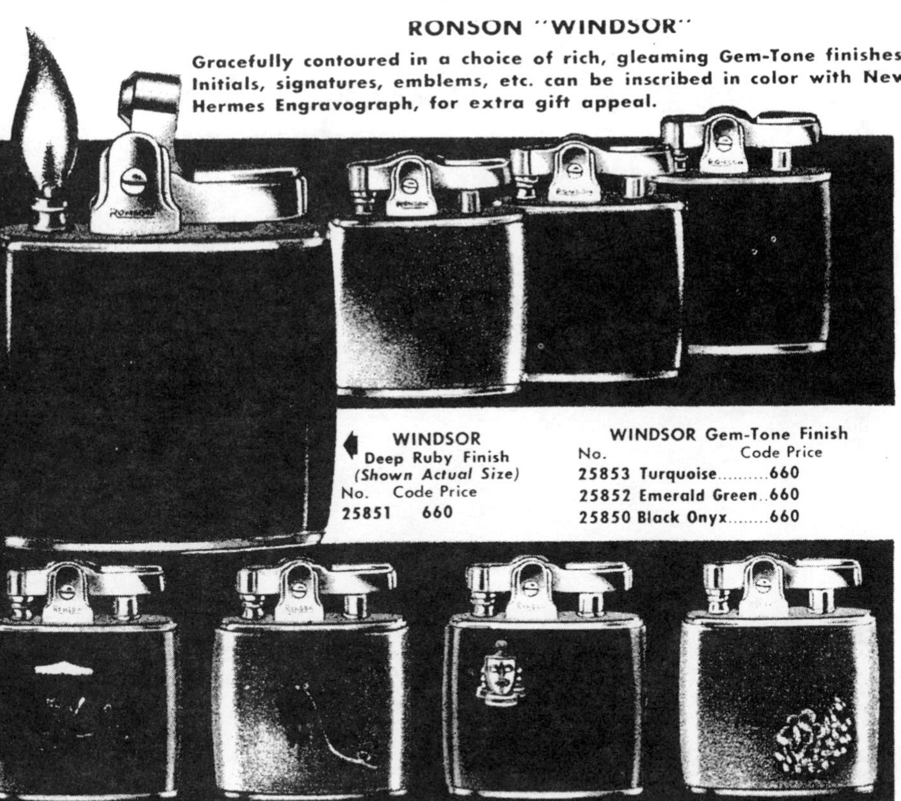

◀ **WINDSOR**
Deep Ruby Finish
(Shown Actual Size)
No. Code Price
25851 660

WINDSOR Gem-Tone Finish

No.		Code Price
25853	Turquoise	660
25852	Emerald Green	660
25850	Black Onyx	660

WINDSOR
Black Onyx Finish
with Early Auto Design
No. Code Price
25854.....780

WINDSOR
Turquoise Finish
with Poodle Design
No. Code Price
25855.....780

WINDSOR
Black Onyx Finish with
Applied Heraldic Crest
No. Code Price
25856.....834

WINDSOR
Turquoise Finish
with Applied
Jeweled Decoration
No. Code Price
25857.....900

All RONSONs listed are in chromium plate. Attractively boxed.

RONSON

WORLD'S GREATEST LIGHTER

On this and the seven following pages you'll find illustrations and descriptions of current RONSON products. All RONSONs are crafted to finest precision jewelry standards, for years of dependable service.

Consistent RONSON advertising continues to urge the trade and the public to look for the RONSON trademark on the product itself, as a mark of the highest quality and performance and as a safeguard against inferior imitations.

Keep an adequate stock of RONSONs on hand and on display at all times and enjoy greater year round sales.

Over 56 million RONSONs have been sold.

Important notice regarding retail prices and Federal retail taxes:—

The RONSON retail prices listed on this page and the seven RONSON pages following are subject to Fair Trade Laws of all states in which such legislation is in force and are subject to change without notice. The Federal retail tax (currently 20%) is to be added to those prices earmarked "plus tax".

RONSON Art Metal Works, Inc.

PRESS, it's lit!
RELEASE, it's out!

Safely out the instant you lift your finger.

RONSON "STANDARD"

Trim RONSON Standards for men and women are practical, beautiful, present-day gifts. All with polished monogram shield.

◀ **STANDARD**
Satin Finish, Engine-turned
(Shown Actual Size)
No. Code Price
15179 924

STANDARD Glow-Enamel Finish

No.		Code Price
15518	Golden-Tan	834
15517	Silver-Blue	834
15516	Silver-Gray	834

STANDARD
Engine-turned
No. Code Price
15104 1008

STANDARD
Engine-turned
No. Code Price
15166 1008

STANDARD
Tortoise Enamel Finish
Engine-turned
No. Code Price
15535 1008

STANDARD
Tortoise Enamel Finish
Engine-turned
No. Code Price
15534 1152

STANDARD
Genuine Alligator
No. Code Price
15806 1152

Lighters shown in reduced sizes unless otherwise indicated.

1954 CATALOG PAGE

RONSON® Lighter Necessities

World's Finest • Most Advertised • In Greatest Demand

Because the smoking public has learned that RONSON Lighter Necessities are the finest produced and give the best results, the demand for them is constantly reaching new highs.

Gain valuable repeat patronage by having on hand at all times an ample supply of the items illustrated and described on this p Order them from your RONSON distributor and display them so you can get an increasing share of valuable store traffic, sales, customer goodwill.

RONSONOL LIGHTER FUEL
(Super-Life Formula)

This improved fuel lasts longer and gives more lights per filling with less frequent refills, and has a pleasant aroma. Because of its high quality and costlier ingredients, and considering how much further it will go, RONSONOL actually costs your customer less — with greater profit to YOU.

Per case of 24 cans

No.		Code Price	Retail
99009	RONSONOL	720	

RONSON BU-TANK

Disposable (blue) Cartridges—Style E, made exclusively for fueling all RONSON Gas Lighters equipped with the blue screw cap at the bottom plate of lighter or reservoir. A single cartridge loading gives thousands of lights.

Per carton of 12 packages of 2 Bu-Tanks each

No.		Code Price	Retail
99050	BU-TANK	1080	

RONSON LITERKIT

This handsome, sturdy, compact and convenient compartment-case of solid plastic with hinged transparent lid holds the following necessities for long-term lighter service:

5 Extra-length RONSON 'Flints'
1 High Absorption RONSON Wick
1 Wick Inserter
1 Cleaning Brush

Shipped in display carton of 24 kits. Carton forms neat, compact counter dispenser.

Per carton of 24 Kits

No.		Code Price	Retail
99025	LITERKIT	720	

RONSON PENCILITER ACCESSORY KIT

Contains:

24 Special Quality Thin Leads
2 Metal-mounted Erasers
2 Special Penciliter Wicks
3 RONSON 'Flints'
Wick Inserter
Cleaning Brush
Instruction Folder

No.		Code Price	Retail
99029	PENCILITER ACCESSORY KIT (per dozen)	720	

RONSON PENCILITER WICKS

Envelope contains 2 Special Wicks and Inserter.

Packed six dozen per carton.

No.		Code Price	Retail
99027	PENCILITER WICK ENVELOPE (per dozen)	144	

RONSON PENCILITER ERASERS

Envelope contains 2 metal-mounted erasers.

Packed 2 dozen per carton.

No.		Code Price	Retail
99026	PENCILITER ERASER ENVELOPE (per dozen)	144	

RONSON PENCILITER THIN LEADS

Wooden tube contains 24 Special Quality Black Thin Leads for use in the RONSON Penciliter.

Packed 2 dozen tubes per carton

No.		Code Price	Retail
99028	PENCILITER LEADS (per carton)	432	

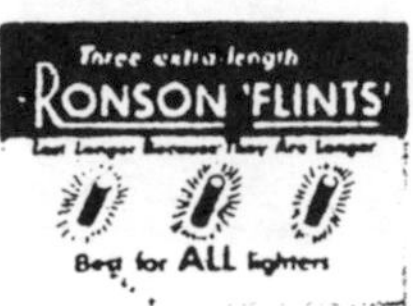

RONSON 'FLINTS'
Uncarded Envelopes

Contains 3 extra-length genuine RONSON 'Flints.'

Per dozen envelopes

No.		Code Price	Retail
99013	'FLINT' ENV.	144	

RONSON SYNDICATE STORE 'FLINT' CARD

For stores equipped with self-service open compartment counters and bins. Each display card holds one RONSON 'Flint' envelope.

Per carton of 48 cards

No.
99047 SYNDICATE STORE 'FLINT' CARD
Code Price: 576 Retail:

RONSON "FIVE-FLINTER"

Clever "Safe-Deposit" packet with compartment slide holding 5 extra-length RONSON 'Flints.' Packed in cartons of 24 "FIVE-FLINTERS.

Per carton of 24 packets

No.		Code Price	Retail
99008	"FIVE-FLINTER"	432	

RONSON "FIVE-FLINTER" SELF-SERVICE CARTON

Striking display unit contains 24 RONSON "Five-Flinters" each mounted on $3\frac{3}{4}$" x $4\frac{1}{2}$" card.

Per carton of 24 cards

No.		Code Price	Retail
99002	"FIVE-FLINTER" SELF SERVICE CARTON	432	

RONSON WICK CARD

Display card holds 24 envelopes: each containing 1 genuine RONSON Wick and Inserter.

Per card of 24 envelopes

No.		Code Price	Retail
99021	WICK CARD	288	

RONSON 'FLINT' CARD

Dislay card holds 24 envelopes e containing 3 extra-length gen RONSON 'Flints.'

Per card of 24 envelopes

No.		Code Price	Re
99001	'FLINT' CARD	288	

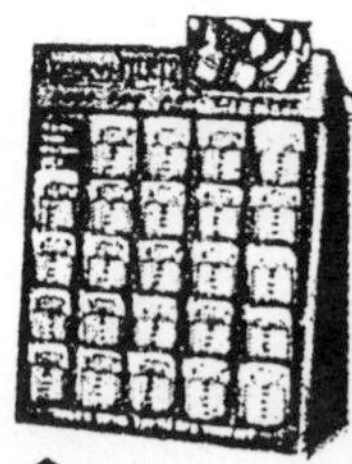

RONSON "FIVE-FLINTER" CA

Each card contains 24 "FI FLINTERS" each holding 5 ex length, genuine RONSON 'Flint

Per card of 24 packets

No.		Code Price	Re
99046	"FIVE-FLINTER" CARD	432	

RONSON WICKS
Uncarded Envelopes

Envelope contains 1 genu RONSON Wick and Inserter. Ret at 10c per envelope.

Per dozen envelopes

No.		Code Price	Re
99014	WICK ENVELOPE	144	

RONSON TOUCH-TIP WICK UNITS

Made exclusively for the torch of the RONSON Touch-Tip to lighter and all combinati thereof. Each envelope contain RONSON Wick Units.

No.
99004 TOUCH-TIP WICK ENVEL
Code Price: 30 Retail:

See note re retail prices and Federal retail taxes on first page of this RONSON section.

1954 CATALOG PAGE

RONSON
WORLD'S GREATEST LIGHTER

RONSON "PRINCESS"

Ladies' dainty lighters, smartly styled for practical gift appeal. She'll use her slender RONSON Princess more often than she uses her lipstick.

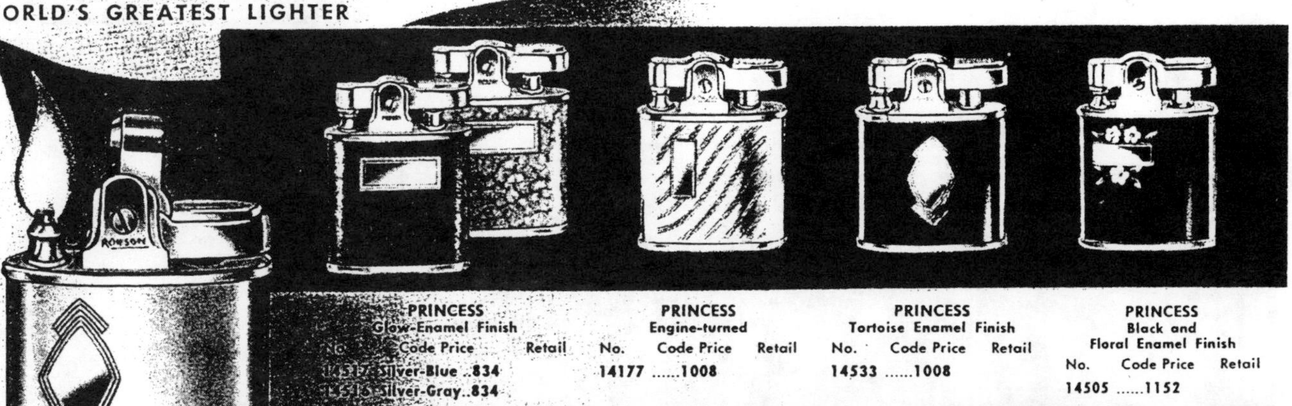

PRINCESS
[illegible]

PRINCESS
Glow-Enamel Finish

No.	Code Price	Retail
14517 Silver-Blue	..834	
14516 Silver-Gray	..834	

PRINCESS
Engine-turned

No.	Code Price	Retail
14177	1008	

PRINCESS
Tortoise Enamel Finish

No.	Code Price	Retail
14533	1008	

PRINCESS
Black and Floral Enamel Finish

No.	Code Price	Retail
14505	1152	

PRINCESS
Black and Floral Enamel Finish

No.	Code Price	Retail
14547	1152	

PRINCESS — Blue and Gold
Enamel Finish, Fleur-de-Lis Design

No.	Code Price	Retail
14532	1152	

PRINCESS
Genuine Alligator

No.	Code Price	Retail
14806	1152	

PRINCESS
Heavy Silver Plate comb. with Engine-turned Gold-toned Metal

No.	Code Price	Retail
14609	1080	

RONSON "TRIUMPH"

RONSON pocket lighter with new "Easy-fill" bottom. Just flip it . . . and fill it. You can see as you fuel, for the whole bottom swings wide open. No cap to unscrew. Helps to prevent under-fueling and over-fueling. New modern taper shape.

TRIUMPH — Engine-turned
(Shown Actual Size)

No.	Code Price	Retail
82162	1020	

RONSON

See note re retail prices and Federal retail taxes on first page of this RONSON section.

RONSON "GEM"

This slim lighter for ladies is a welcome accessory for any handbag. Compact in size, smart in appearance.

GEM — Satin Finish
(Shown Actual Size)

No.	Code Price	Retail
13100	924	

GEM
Tortoise Enamel Finish

No.	Code Price
13541	1008

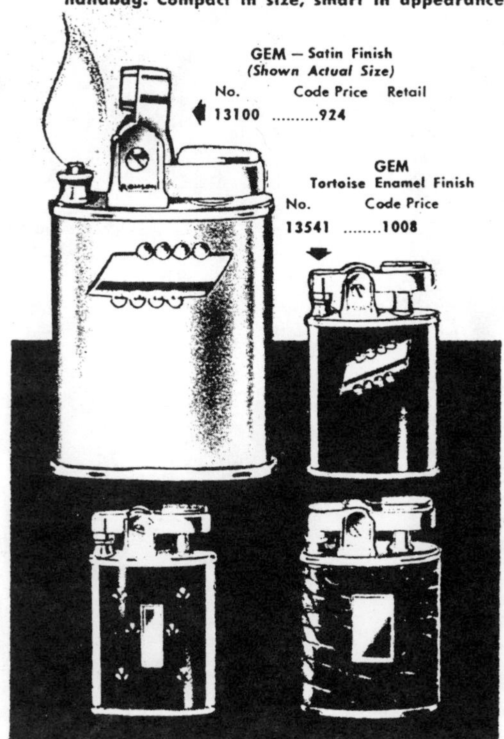

GEM
Black and Gold Enamel Finish

No.	Code Price	Retail
13540	1152	

GEM
Genuine Alligator

No.	Code Price	Retail
13806	1152	

RONSON "BANKER"

A precious personal accessory men will treasure for a lifetime. Tall, sleek body holds enough fuel to serve for weeks.

BANKER
14K Gold, Engine-turned
(Shown Actual Size)

No.	Code Price	Retail
11951	18000	

All RONSONs listed (except gold Banker and silver plated Princess) are in chromium plate. All with polished monogram shield. Attractively boxed.

1954 CATALOG PAGE

RONSON GAS POCKET LIGHTERS

RONSON "MAXIMUS"

This graceful, tapered edge pocket lighter is fueled from a RONSON Bu-Tank disposable cartridge (Style E). Each fueling supplies thousands of lights with both REGULAR Flame and PIN-POINT Flame.

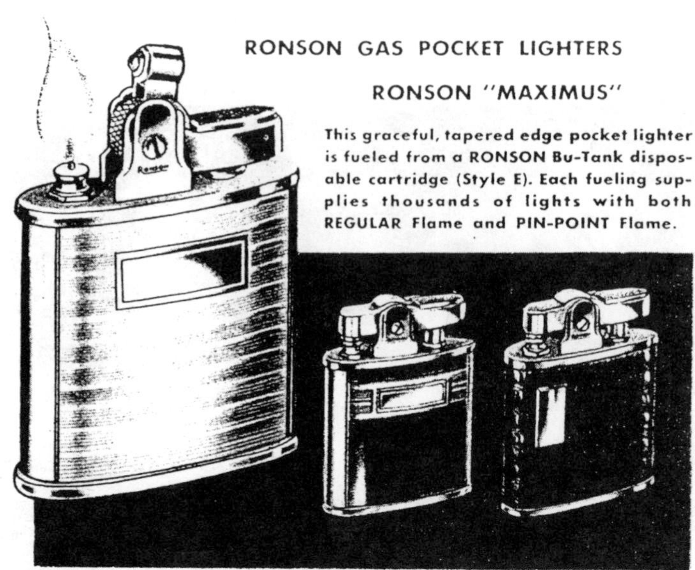

MAXIMUS Engine-turned *(Shown Actual Size)*	MAXIMUS Tortoise Enamel, Engine-turned	MAXIMUS Genuine Alligator — Lizard
No. Code Price Retail	No. Code Price Retail	No. Code Price Retail
95170 1500	95522..1620	95815..1740

All RONSON pocket lighters listed are in chromium plate with polished monogram shield. Attractively boxed.

RONSON

WORLD'S GREATEST LIGHTER

RONSON GAS LIGHTERS with "THROW-AWAY" CARTRIDGE FUELING and NEW, 2-WAY LIGHTING

This new and distinctly different type of RONSON Lighter combines the following features:

1. Uses a clean burning gas as fuel.
2. Uses no wick.
3. Is fueled from a single "throw-away" cartridge, supplying thousands of lights.
4. No finger acrobatics, thanks to famous one-finger, one-motion safety action "Press, it's lit! Release, it's out!"

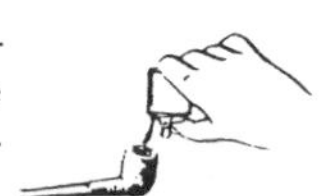

5. REGULAR Flame ideal for lighting cigarettes and cigars, can be changed instantly to a PIN-POINT Flame for pipes.

NOTE: All prices of gas lighters on this page include two RONSON Bu-Tank disposable cartridges (Style E).

RONSON *Penciliter* Writes — Lights

For every smoker who writes and every writer who smokes! The World's Greatest Lighter and a superb mechanical pencil are combined in the handsome RONSON Penciliter. Always at hand to write with . . . to light with. Gift boxed.

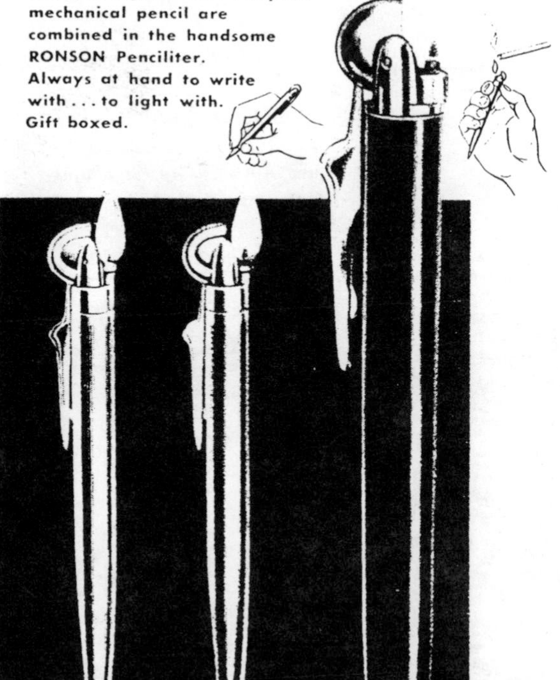

PENCILITER	PENCILITER	PENCILITER
Plated with Rhodium, a Precious Non-tarnishing Metal of the Platinum Group Engine-turned	1/20 14K Gold-Filled, Engine-turned	Ebony Enamel and Gold Finish *(Shown Actual Size)*
No. 48701	**No. 48902**	No. 53753
Code Price: 1392	Code Price: 1800	Code Price: 1392
Retail:	Retail:	Retail:

RONSON GAS TABLE LIGHTERS

All table models shown here are fueled from a single RONSON Bu-Tank disposable cartridge (Style E) and have new 2-way lighting feature.

The styling, colors and finishes of these models lend themselves effectively to a wide variety of decorative schemes in home or office.

All table lighters shown in reduced size.

VICEROY Chromium Plate, Genuine Walnut	VERNON Chromium Plate, Birch Wood, Maple Finish	VERA Silver Plate, Floral Porcelain, with Rhodium Plate Fitment
No. Code Price Retail	No. Code Price Retail	No. Code Price Retail
12230 1884	12231 1884	12571 1740

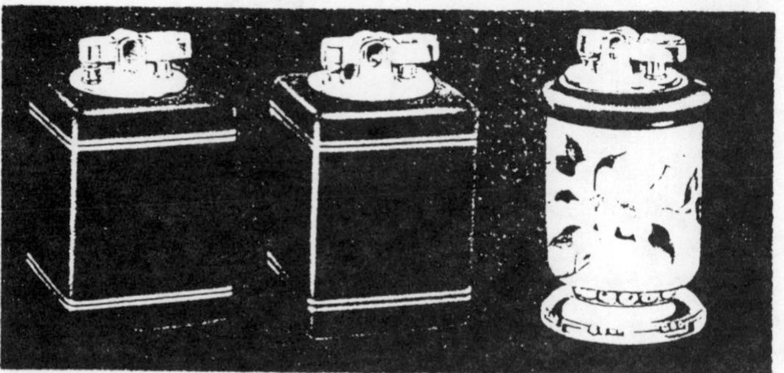

VICTOR Chromium Plate, Genuine Leather, 24K Gold-Tooled	VIOLA Silver Plate, Floral Porcelain, with Rhodium Plate Fitment
No Code Price Retail	No. Code Price Retail
12840 Green 1884	12570 1800
12841 Tan 1884	

See note re retail prices and Federal retail taxes on first page of this RONSON section

RONSON®

VORLD'S GREATEST LIGHTER

Ronson Table Lighters

Table RONSONs are always smart to own, smart to give. Designs appropriate for every room in the home and for any decorative scheme, each ready with swift, sure lights. The famous safety action of a RONSON protects fine furnishings from accidental burns. A single fueling serves for months.

MINERVA
Heavy Silver Plate and Porcelain with Floral Design
No. Code Price Retail
19572 1500

LEONA — Gold Finish and Emerald Isle Enamel
No. Code Price Retail
58783 1536

LEONA — Gold Finish, Ivory and Floral Enamel
No. Code Price Retail
58784 1884

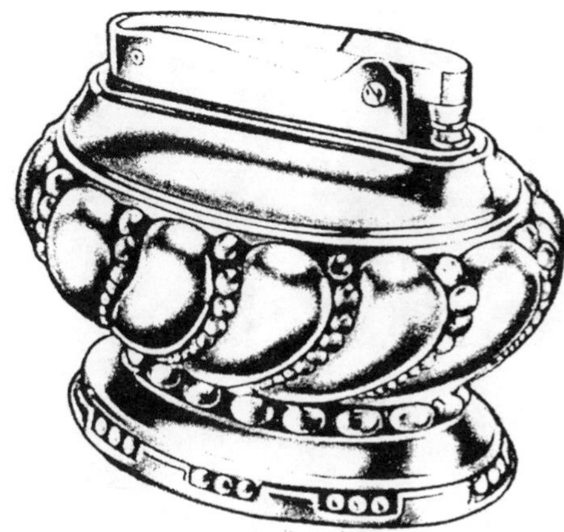

CROWN — Heavy Silver Plate
(Shown Actual Size)
No. Code Price Retail
30600 1470

MELROSE
Satin and Bright Heavy Silver Plate
No. Code Price Retail
24611 1320

LOTUS
Satin and Bright Heavy Silver Plate
No. Code Price Retail
37610 1320

LOTUS
Heavy 24K Gold Plate and Black Enamel
No. Code Price Retail
37759 1860

See note re retail prices and Federal retail taxes on first page of this RONSON section.

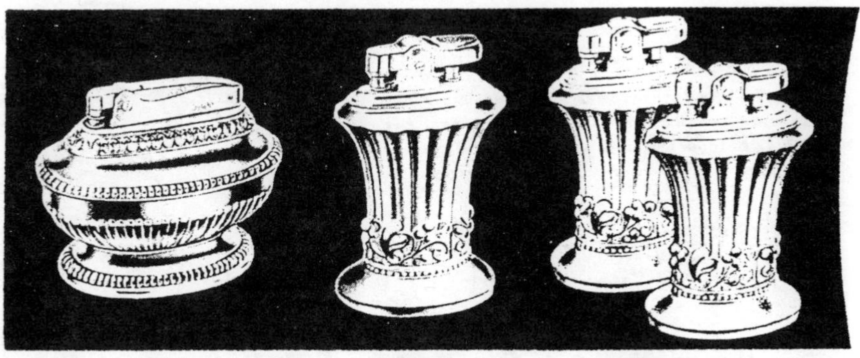

QUEEN ANNE—Heavy Silver Plate
No. Code Price Retail
56600 1470

NEWPORT
Heavy Silver Plate
No. Code Price Retail
51600......1200

NEWPORT PAIR
Heavy 24K Gold Plate
No. Code Price Retail
51762 3300

In distinctive presentation box.

DIANA — Satin and Bright Heavy Silver Plate, Sterling Silver Monogram Shield
No. Code Price Retail
55601 1140

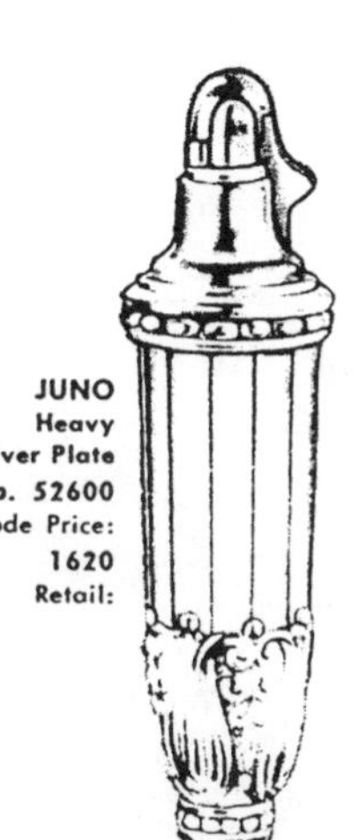

JUNO
Heavy Silver Plate
No. 52600
Code Price: 1620
Retail:

GLORIA — Satin and Bright Heavy Silver Plate
No. Code Price Retail
80601 1470

DECANTER — Heavy Silver Plate
No. Code Price Retail
31600 1920

SAVOY — Heavy 24K Gold Plate
No. Code Price Retail
22761 2340

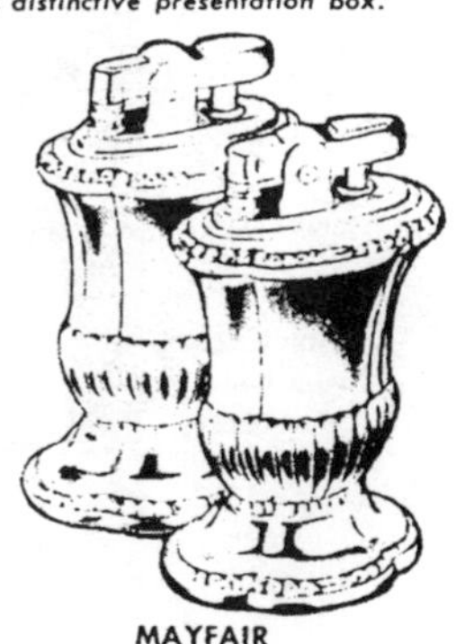

MAYFAIR
Heavy Silver Plate
No. Code Price Retail
54600 2190

In distinctive presentation box.

RONSON "ADONIS"

Slim as a fine watch . . . graceful in design . . . a possession to treasure with finest personal jewelry. Modern, sweeping lines appeal to both men and women.

RONSON
WORLD'S GREATEST LIGHTER

ADONIS
Glow-Enamel Finish

No.	Code Price	Retail
18516 Silver-Gray	1314	
18517 Silver-Blue	1314	

ADONIS
Satin and Bright Finish, Engine-turned

No.	Code Price	Retail
18184	1392	

ADONIS
Black and Floral Enamel Finish

No.	Code Price	Retail
18538	1740	

ADONIS
Engine-turned
(Shown Actual Size)

No.	Code Price	Retail
18185	1392	

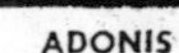

ADONIS
Tortoise Enamel Finish, Engine-turned

No.	Code Price	Retail
18539	1740	

ADONIS
Genuine Alligator

No.	Code Price	Retail
18806	1740	

ADONIS — Sterling Silver

No.	Code Price	Retail
18928	3000	

Also available with matching cigarette case (See next page).

ADONIS
14K Gold, Engine-turned

No.	Code Price	Retail
18950	24000	

14K Gold, Plain

No.	Code Price	Retail
18955	24000	

RONSON "WHIRLWIND"

Two-in-one lighter with disappearing windshield. Great outdoors, smart indoors. For windy outdoors, simply slide the shield up. For indoors, just slide the shield down. Large fuel capacity.

All RONSONs listed (except Gold Adonis and Sterling Adonis) are in chromium plate, with polished monogram shield. Attractively boxed.

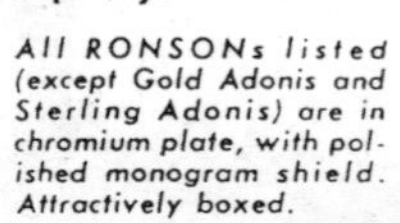

WHIRLWIND
Glow-Enamel Finish
No. 16518
Golden-Tan
Code Price: 1074
Retail:
No. 16519
Gunmetal
Code Price: 1074
Retail:

WHIRLWIND
Satin and Bright Finish, Engine-turned
(Shown Actual Size)
No. 16182
Code Price: 1152
Retail:

WHIRLWIND
Engine-turned
No. 16183
Code Price: 1290
Retail:

WHIRLWIND
Genuine Alligator
No. 16806
Code Price: 1392
Retail:

See note re retail prices and Federal retail taxes on first page of this RONSON section.

WHIRLWIND
Tortoise Enamel Finish, Engine-turned

No.	Code Price	Retail
16537	1320	

WHIRLWIND
Tortoise Enamel Finish, Engine-turned

No.	Code Price	Retail
16536	1392	

1969 CATALOG PAGE

RONSON®

VARAFLAME® BUTANE

LIGHTERS

RONSON® VARAFLAME TABLE LIGHTERS

Styles for every taste, for every home and office decor. Adjustable flame for cigars, cigarettes, pipes. They light up to three years on a single fueling from the Ronson Multi-Fill® Injector . . . available everywhere.

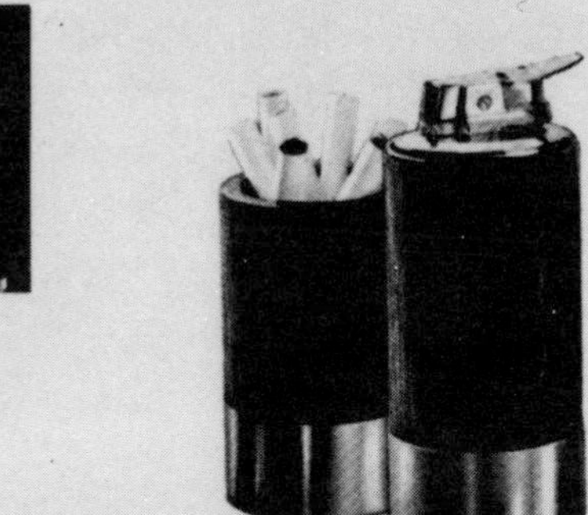

Varaflame NORSEMAN SET
8880J1750—Table lighter with matching cigarette urn. Walnut and stainless steel, chrome plate fitment.
8880/3J1625

Varaflame PATHFINDER SET
8867J1750—Table lighter, matching ash tray and cigarette urn. Olive water buffalo leather, gold plate fitment.
8867/3J1625

Varaflame WEIGHT
8870J1925—Antiqued brass finish, rosewood base, gold plate fitment.
8870/3J1788

Varaflame ERIC
8881J1750—Rosewood and satin finish aluminum, chrome plate fitment.
8881/3J1625

Varaflame LURALITE
8902J1575—Gold-tone mosaic finish, gold plate action.
8902/3J1463

Varaflame LA RONDE
8879J907—Walnut and white, chrome plate fitment.
8879/3J842

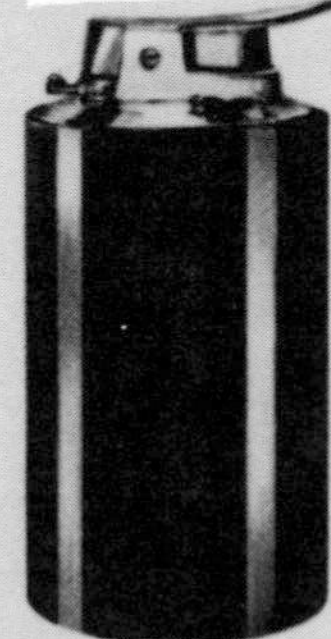

Varaflame SKOAL
8813J1750—Rosewood and satin finish aluminum, chrome plate fitment.
8813/3J1625

Varaflame CROWN
8651J1750—Genuine silver plate, chrome and silver-plate fitment.
8651/3J1625

Varaflame OPTIC
8903J1225—Cut grooved aluminum band and black satin-finish base, chrome plated fitment.
8903/3J1138

Varaflame OSLO
8904J1750—Rosewood and satin finish stainless steel, chrome plate fitment.
8904/3J1625

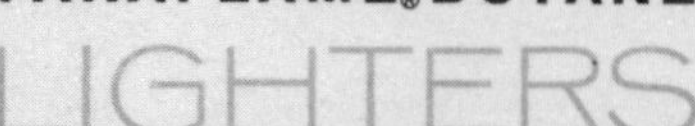

VARAFLAME® BUTANE
LIGHTERS

Fuel in seconds . . . light for months on clean odorless, smokeless, tasteless Ronson butane fuel . . . available everywhere. Ronson® quality plus Ronson dependability back up the Ronson guarantee and Lifetime Free Service Policy.

Varaflame
WINDLITE SLIMLINE
8905J907 — Bright chrome plate, engraved, engraveable shield.
8905/3J842

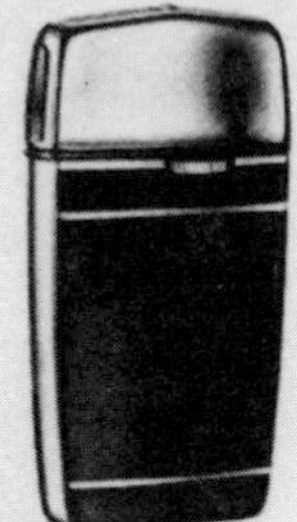

Varaflame
WINDLITE SLIMLINE
8906J977—Bright chrome plate, gun metal satin enamel.
8906/3J907

Varaflame
WINDLITE
8888J627—Satin chrome plate, bright cover, engraved.
8888/3J582

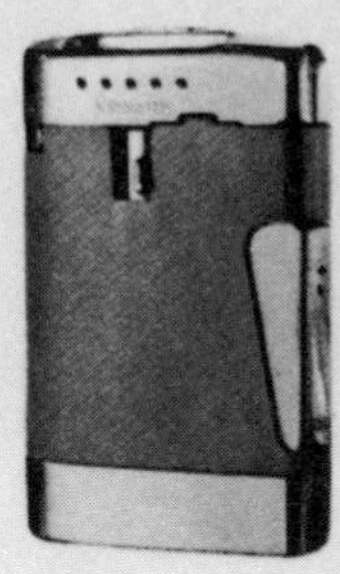

Varaflame **COMET**
8889J697—Bright gold plate, gray satin finish.
8889/3J647

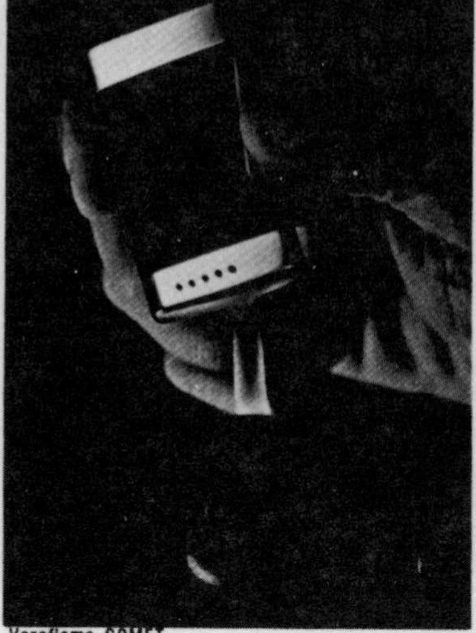

Varaflame **COMET**
8866J487—Bright chrome plate, black satin finish.
8866/3J452

Varaflame **PREMIER**
8907J977—Bright chrome plate, black sable finish.
8907/3J907

Varaflame **PREMIER**
8908J1117—Bright chrome plate, engraved, tortoise enamel, engraveable shield.
8908/3J1037

Varaflame **WHIRLWIND**
8909J907 — Silver-tone, bright finish, engine-turned.
8909/3J842

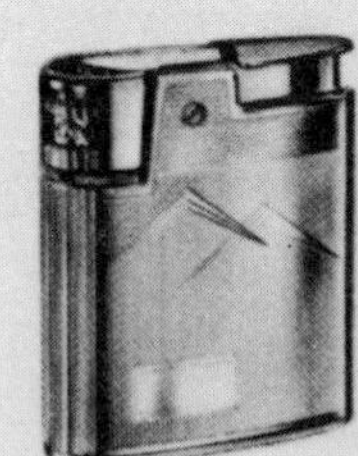

Varaflame **LITEGUARD**
8893J837 — Silver-tone, bright finish, engraved, engraveable shield.
8893/3J777

Varaflame **PRINCESS**
8901J1117—Gold-tone, charcoal satin finish, deep engraved.
8901/3J1037

Varaflame **ADONIS**
8910J1295—Bright chrome plate, engine-turned, tortoise enamel, gold emblem.
8910/3J1203

Varaflame **ADONIS**
8911J1047—Bright chrome plate, engine-turned, gold emblem.
8911/3J972

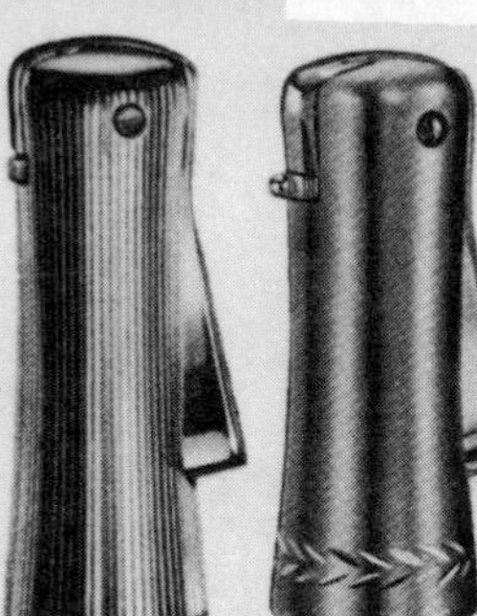

Varaflame
LADYLITE
8912J1155—Gold-tone, bright finish, engraved.
8912/3J1073—

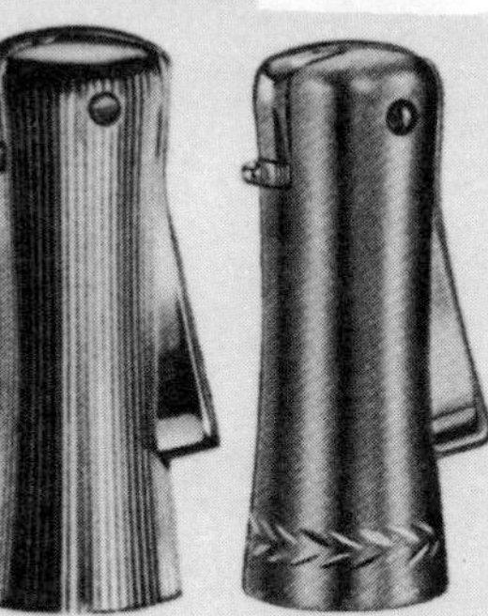

Varaflame
LADYLITE
8913J1155—Gold-tone, satin finish, deep engraved.
8913/3J1073—

Varaflame **PETITE**
8914J1047—Gold-tone, bright finish, engine turned.
8914/3J972

Varaflame **PETITE**
8897J907—Gold-tone, blue sable finish, deep engraved.
8897/3J842

Varaflame **STARFIRE**
8915J1047—Gold-tone, charcoal satin finish, deep engraved.
8915/3J972

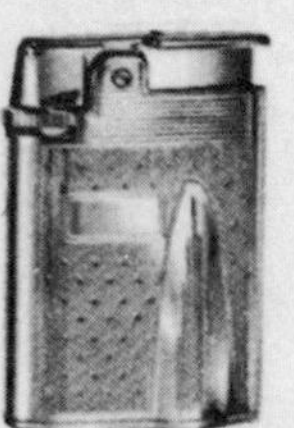

Varaflame **STARFIRE**
8899J837—Silver-tone, bright finish, engraved, engraveable shield.
8899/3J777

Varaflame **STANDARD**
8916J767—Gold-tone, bright finish, engraved, engraveable shield.
8916/3J712
more.

Retail Prices Are Suggested Only and May Vary in Different Trading Areas 123

RONSON®

WORLD'S GREATEST LIGHTER

Ronson Desk & Library Lighters

These new table RONSONs are styled especially for use in the office, the den and the library. They are tailor-made to harmonize with office and study accessories and to take the wear and tear of heavy business service.

SPARTAN — Chromium Plate, indented bands in Black Enamel Finish

No.	Code Price	Retail
37	1710	

SENATOR — Chromium Plate, Genuine Walnut Wood Veneer, Monogram Shield

No.	Code Price	Retail
76992	1848	

SENATOR — Chromium Plate, nuine Mahogany Wood Veneer, Monogram Shield

No.	Code Price	Retail
994	1848	

SENATOR — Chromium Plate, Genuine Blond Prima Vera Wood Veneer, Monogram Shield

No.	Code Price	Retail
76993	1848	

SENATOR — Chromium Plate, nuine Pigskin, Monogram Shield

No.	Code Price	Retail
801	1710	

SENATOR — Chromium Plate, Genuine Alligator, Monogram Shield

No.	Code Price	Retail
76807	1920	

1954 Magazine Ad

RONSON
introduces new Varaflame!
Lights for months!
Adjustable flame!
Fuels in seconds!
NEW!
NEW!
NEW!
RONSON
maker of the world's greatest lighters and electric shavers

1958 Magazine Ad

RONSON LIGHTERS NOW INCREASINGLY AVAILABLE
PRESS . . . it's lit. RELEASE . . . it's out. The famous patented one-finger one-motion Ronson action.
"Whirlwind" with Disappearing Windshield
"Standard"
7 BIG FEATURES
THAT MAKE RONSON "THE WORLD'S GREATEST LIGHTER"
SIMPLICITY . . . Press—it's lit; Release—it's out! RONSON'S famous patented one-finger, one-motion action. Fully automatic! No smudged fingers! No trick spin! No fumbling with lids!
DEPENDABILITY . . . Precision-made to light every time.
VERSATILITY . . . Equally useful for cigars, cigarettes or pipes—and wherever flame is needed.
DURABILITY . . . Scientifically hardened and tempered parts stand up under a long life of hard use.
SERVICE . . . Hermetic sealing conserves big fuel supply. Refilling is needed less often.
SMARTNESS . . . Handsomely styled with quiet dignity.
SAFETY . . . Snuffer cap puts out flame automatically, preventing accidental fires.
Ronson, Newark 2, N. J.
For Cigarettes, Cigars and Pipes
RONSON
WORLD'S GREATEST LIGHTER
Over 14 million RONSONS have been sold
★ BUILD YOUR FUTURE—HOLD YOUR WAR BONDS ★

1945 Magazine Ad

1949 Magazine Ad

1954 Magazine Ad

1954 Magazine Ad

1949 Magazine Ad

May, 1939
165
Before starting our tour of the RONSON Exhibit*, remember that the smart, modern way to light-up is with a lighter. (Particularly with a RONSON.) That it's the convenient, safe, clean and "proper" thing to do. For smartness, look at this RONSON Monarch Combination-Lighter-Cigarette Case. What a personal possession. What a gift.
"...AND HERE, FOLKS, IS RONSON—
WORLD'S GREATEST LIGHTER"
In front of you is Touch-Tip De Luxe. A masterpiece of Lighter craftsmanship. Note the modern lines and the superb enamel and chromium finish. One filling serves for months. An admiration-compelling table appointment. Let's get along, folks.
I now point to the RONSON Litepact. An open sesame to feminine favor, gentlemen. A genuine RONSON Lighter combined with powder compact, complete with sifter, puff and mirror.
Below us is something to interest both ladies and gentlemen. Either for themselves or for a friend. The RONSON Standard. It offers a lifetime of beauty, service and convenience.
On my right is RONSON Touch-Tip Lighter-Cigarette Box Combination. Note the roomy cedar-lined compartments and faithful walnut finish. At my left is the famous RONSON PenciLiter—the most modern and useful pencil ever made. When you smoke, it's a quick way to get "lit up"—when you write, the propel-repel action's as easy as butter. A real sensation.
SMART TO OWN
SMART TO GIVE
Mother's Day
Father's Day
Graduation
RONSON
WORLD'S GREATEST LIGHTER

1939 Magazine Ad

RONSON WORLD'S GREATEST LIGHTER

makes *light* of your *gift* problems!

CROWN Table Lighter, in heavy silver plate, $11.00 (plus tax).

RONSON PENCILITER

All models shown in reduced size. See these and other handsome Ronsons at your favorite dealer.

FOR POCKET OR HANDBAG • FOR EVERY TABLE AND DESK • FOR EVERY SMOKER WHO *writes*

Ronsons are indeed *present*-day gifts—practical, beautiful! From the trim pocket models to the gleaming, silver-plated table lighters and the sleek, new Penciliter (which lights *and* writes) . . . each is precision-made for a lifetime of use—perfect to give or receive.

PRESS IT'S LIT! . . . RELEASE, IT'S OUT!
Safely out the instant you lift your finger!

RONSON *means* WORLD'S GREATEST LIGHTER

NEWARK, N. J.
TORONTO, ONT.
LONDON, ENG.

FUN . . . EXCITEMENT . . . Tune in on Ronson's "20 Questions" Saturday nights (Pacific Coast, Sunday nights), Mutual Network.

HEAR RONSON'S "JOHNNY DESMOND SHOW" with the songs you love, every Sunday night, Mutual Network.

RONSON now on TELEVISION in many principal cities.

1949 Magazine Ad

choose a RONSON
WORLD'S GREATEST LIGHTER
for everyone on your gift list
There's nothing like a Ronson—to make people happy at Christmas—and for a long, long time to come! Every Ronson, whether it costs $6 or $200, is built as precisely, as dependably, as a fine watch. Built to give years of faithful lights—every light a reminder of you. Among the many styles you'll find the right Ronsons for all the names on your list. And on every one of them, for your protection, there's the famous trade-mark, RONSON. Look for it!
Remember! All lighters work best with Ronsonol Fuel and Ronson Redskin 'Flints'.

1950 Magazine Ad

In nationwide independent survey, folks of all types were asked:
"What lighter do you want for Christmas?"...and 77% said,
"The lighter I want is a RONSON!"
WORLD'S GREATEST LIGHTER
When you give a Ronson, it's sure to make a hit. Independent surveys prove it! Students and sportsmen, executives and hostesses, dads and moms, folks in general, hither and thither and yon, told the survey people: "The lighter I want is a Ronson!"
So what are you waiting for? Choose Ronson...the genuine, the incomparable...the world's greatest lighter...and no other!
Look on the lighter for the trade-mark RONSON ...assuring years of dependable service. And remember ...all lighters work best with Ronsonol Fuel and extra-length Ronson Redskin 'Flints'.
Be sure it's a RONSON for every smoker on your gift list!

1951 Magazine Ad

T. W. A. BOARD CHAIRMAN, *Warren Lee Pierson*, says: "I consider a lighter really a necessity. And having a mighty high regard for precision and dependability, naturally I have a mighty high regard for my Ronson lighter."

NEW YORK AREA FORD DISTRIBUTOR, ***Horgan***, says: "I admire fine perforn in lighters as in automobiles – so natu Ronson's the lighter for me!"

Here is **RAYMOND LOEWY PARTN** ***A. Baker Barnhart***, who says: "Desig are always impressed by a quality be appearance – performance. Ronson is most dependable lighter I know."

TOP EXECUTIVES SAY:

"The lighter for me is a RONSON"

Yes, Ronson was preferred 4 to 1 over any other brand, among all executives interviewed!

"I wouldn't be without a lighter," said executives in this nation-wide independent survey. "It's a necessity these modern days!"

And other surveys reveal that Ronson is the far-and-away favorite among hostesses, sportsmen, students, brides-to-be – and among smokers in general!

Ronson is acknowledged 'tops' in design – precision craftsmanship – long-lived performance and dependability. *Acknowledged the world's greatest lighter!*

So when you're shopping for a gift, or for something for yourself, think of a Ronson. Look right on the lighter for the famous trademark RONSON. It means "world's finest."

And remember: any lighter puts its "best flame forward" with Ronsonol Fuel and extra-length Ronson Redskin 'Flints.'

1951 Fashion Academy Gold Medal

RONSON

WORLD'S GREATEST LIGHTE

Press, it's lit – Release, it's out!

Lighters shown in reduced size.

RONSON PENCILITER. Lights! Writes! In chromium plate.

RONSON SENATOR. Desk and library lighter in genuine alligator. Other desk lighters from

RONSON STANDARD. Trim pocket lighter, in chromium plate, satin finish.

RONSON WHIRLWIND. Disappearing windshield. Two-toned ribbed genuine brown calfskin.

RONSON MASTERCASE. Combination Lighter-Cigarette Case, chromium plate.

RONSON ADONIS. Slim as a fine w Smart pocket lighter in chro plate, engine-turned.

Enjoy Ronson's "Star of the Family," CBS-TV Network; and Ronson's new Network Radio Show. (Watch local paper for details) *Ronson, Newark, N. J., Toronto, Ont., London*

1951 Magazine Ad

ZIPPO IDENTIFICATION

<table>
<tr><th colspan="3">IDENTIFICATION CODES FOR ZIPPO LIGHTER BOTTOMS</th></tr>
<tr><th>YEAR</th><th>LEFT</th><th>RIGHT</th></tr>
<tr><td>1932</td><td colspan="2">Patent Pending</td></tr>
<tr><td>1937</td><td colspan="2">Patent #2032695</td></tr>
<tr><td>1953</td><td colspan="2">Patent #2517191</td></tr>
<tr><td>1957</td><td colspan="2">Full stamp with patent pending</td></tr>
<tr><td>1958</td><td colspan="2">Full stamp with no patent pending</td></tr>
<tr><td></td><td>••••</td><td>••••</td></tr>
<tr><td>1959</td><td>••••</td><td>•••</td></tr>
<tr><td>1960</td><td>•••</td><td>•••</td></tr>
<tr><td>1961</td><td>•••</td><td>••</td></tr>
<tr><td>1962</td><td>••</td><td>••</td></tr>
<tr><td>1963</td><td>••</td><td>•</td></tr>
<tr><td>1964</td><td>•</td><td>•</td></tr>
<tr><td>1965</td><td>•</td><td></td></tr>
<tr><td>1966</td><td>||||</td><td>||||</td></tr>
<tr><td>1967</td><td>||||</td><td>|||</td></tr>
<tr><td>1968</td><td>|||</td><td>|||</td></tr>
<tr><td>1969</td><td>|||</td><td>||</td></tr>
<tr><td>1970</td><td>||</td><td>||</td></tr>
<tr><td>1971</td><td>|</td><td>||</td></tr>
<tr><td>1972</td><td>|</td><td>|</td></tr>
<tr><td>1973</td><td>|</td><td></td></tr>
<tr><td>1974</td><td>////</td><td>////</td></tr>
<tr><td>1975</td><td>////</td><td>///</td></tr>
<tr><td>1976</td><td>///</td><td>///</td></tr>
<tr><td>1977</td><td>///</td><td>//</td></tr>
<tr><td>1978</td><td>//</td><td>//</td></tr>
<tr><td>1979</td><td>//</td><td>/</td></tr>
<tr><td>1980</td><td>/</td><td>/</td></tr>
<tr><td>1981</td><td>/</td><td></td></tr>
<tr><td>1982</td><td>\\\\</td><td>\\\\</td></tr>
<tr><td>1983</td><td>\\\\</td><td>\\\</td></tr>
<tr><td>1984</td><td>\\\</td><td>\\\</td></tr>
<tr><td>1985</td><td>\\\</td><td>\\</td></tr>
<tr><td>1986</td><td>\\</td><td>\\</td></tr>
<tr><td>1986</td><td>G to L</td><td>II</td></tr>
<tr><td>1987</td><td>A to L</td><td>III</td></tr>
<tr><td>1988</td><td>A to L</td><td>IV</td></tr>
<tr><td>1989</td><td>A to L</td><td>V</td></tr>
<tr><td>1990</td><td>A to L</td><td>VI</td></tr>
<tr><td>1991</td><td>A to L</td><td>VII</td></tr>
<tr><td>1992</td><td>A to L</td><td>VIII</td></tr>
</table>

ZIPPO MFG. CO. BRADFORD, PA.
ZIPPO
PAT. PENDING MADE IN U.S.A.

1936 and before

ZIPPO MFG. CO. BRADFORD, PA
ZIPPO
PAT. 2032695 MADE IN U.S.A.

1942 and before

ZIPPO MFG. CO. BRADFORD, PA.
ZIPPO
PAT. 2032695 MADE IN U.S.A.

1952 and before

ZIPPO MFG. CO. BRADFORD, PA.
MADE IN ZIPPO U.S.A.
PAT. 2517191 ® PAT. PEND

1957 and before

BRADFORD, PA.
.ZIPPO
PAT. 2517191

1965 and before

BRADFORD, PA.
| ZIPPO
®

1973 and before

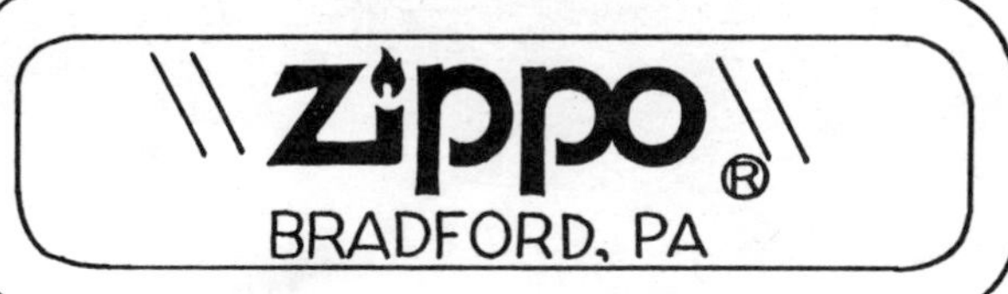

1986 and before

CATALOG CUTS

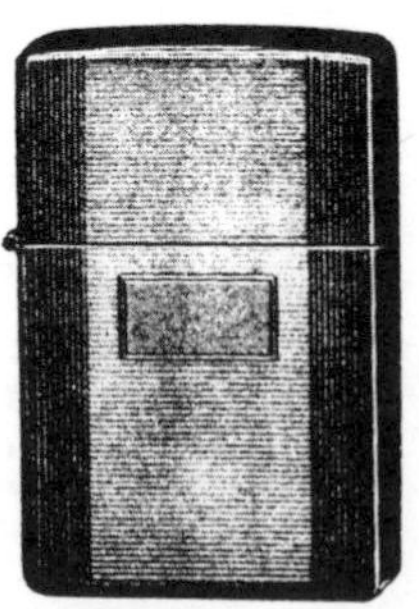

GG1085—

Sterling Silver Zippo lighter; engine turned design with plate for engraving.

GG1086—

14K Yellow Gold made up on special order only.

GG1083—

Zippo lighter with signature engraved in the case. Finished in highly buffed Chromium.

GG1084—

Same as above but plain.

GG1081—

The Zippo windproof lighter with your personal monogram on a black, red, blue, green, white or orange background on a chrome finish. Ten days are required to fill an order for this model.

ZIPPO Windproof Lighters

This lighter can be secured with emblems designating Masonic, Elk, Shrine, Rotary, K. of C. or F. of E. orders; Special designs for quantity orders submitted upon request.

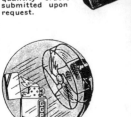

GG1080—

Zippo lighter made in a standard two-tone chrome over nickel on brass and will withstand hard usage.

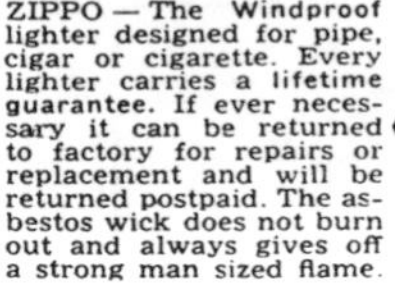

ZIPPO — The Windproof lighter designed for pipe, cigar or cigarette. Every lighter carries a lifetime guarantee. If ever necessary it can be returned to factory for repairs or replacement and will be returned postpaid. The asbestos wick does not burn out and always gives off a strong man sized flame.

Right—

GG1087—

NEW This Zippo table lighter of substantial weight stands 4¼" high and is 1⅞" x 1½" at the base. Finished in highly buffed chromium with a silver-like appearance.

1940

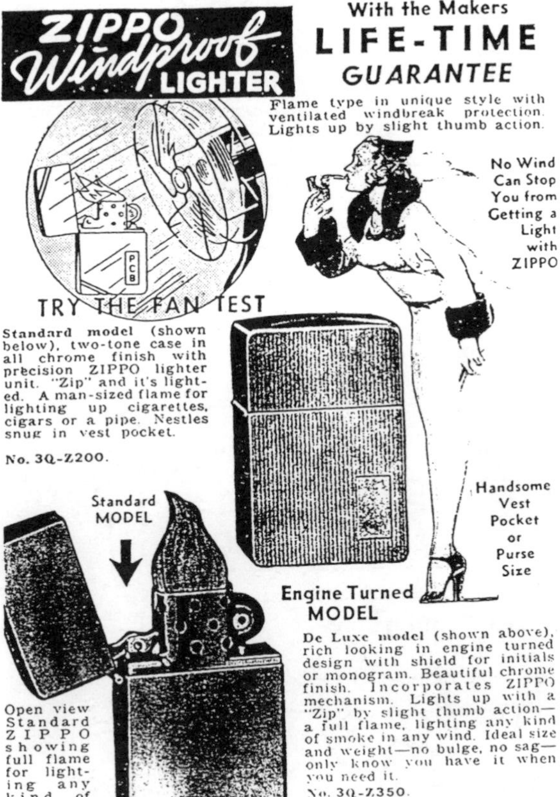

ZIPPO Windproof LIGHTER
With the Makers
LIFE-TIME
GUARANTEE
Flame type in unique style with ventilated windbreak protection. Lights up by slight thumb action.
No Wind Can Stop You from Getting a Light with ZIPPO
TRY THE FAN TEST
Standard model (shown below), two-tone case in all chrome finish with precision ZIPPO lighter unit. "Zip" and it's lighted. A man-sized flame for lighting up cigarettes, cigars or a pipe. Nestles snug in vest pocket.
No. 3Q-Z200.
Standard MODEL
Handsome Vest Pocket or Purse Size
Engine Turned MODEL
De Luxe model (shown above), rich looking in engine turned design with shield for initials or monogram. Beautiful chrome finish. Incorporates ZIPPO mechanism. Lights up with a "Zip" by slight thumb action—a full flame, lighting any kind of smoke in any wind. Ideal size and weight—no bulge, no sag—only know you have it when you need it.
No. 3Q-Z350.
Open view Standard ZIPPO showing full flame for lighting any kind of smoke anywhere.

1941

CIGARETTE LIGHTERS AND CASES

Practical and Popular Models. Made and Guaranteed by Foremost Manufacturers. Gift Boxes.

Prices Subject to Catalog Discounts.

AJ2571 Zippo Lighter...
Chromium plated; butler finish. Neatly striped corner decorations.
Usual Retail Price $2

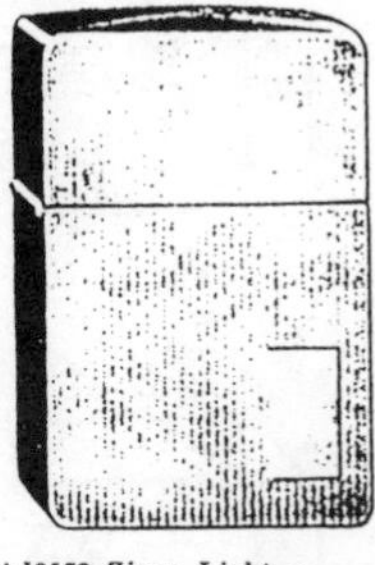

AJ2572 Zippo Lighter.
Chromium plated; engine turned design with shield for engraving.

AJ2573 Zippo Lighter.
Black enamel inlay; chromium plated trim. Shield for engraving.

AJ2574 Zippo Lighter.
Sterling Silver; engine turned design with shield for engraving.

Famous Zippo wind-proof lighters. The greater the wind, the larger the flame. Large fuel capacity; one hand control; dustproof case. Gives a man-sized flame—large and steady enough to light a pipe. Size closed 2 x 1¾ in. Unconditionally guaranteed. Neat gift boxes.

1939

1949 Magazine Ad

1949 Magazine Ad

1949 Magazine Ad

1951 Magazine Ad

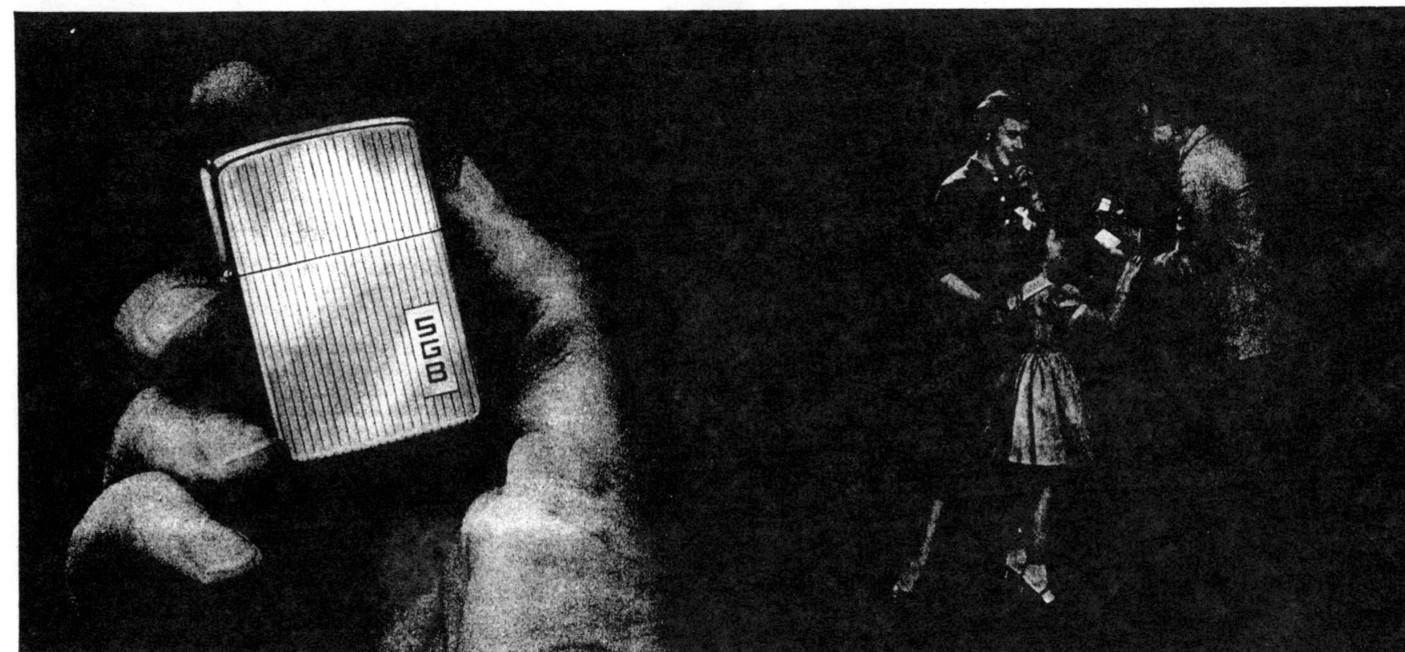

A gift as fine as Dad himself Zippos are so much better designed and built than other lighters that we promise Dad this—his Zippo will light easily, always, even in wind and rain . . . will never need coddling. He will treasure it over the years for its downright faithfulness—remembering the giver!

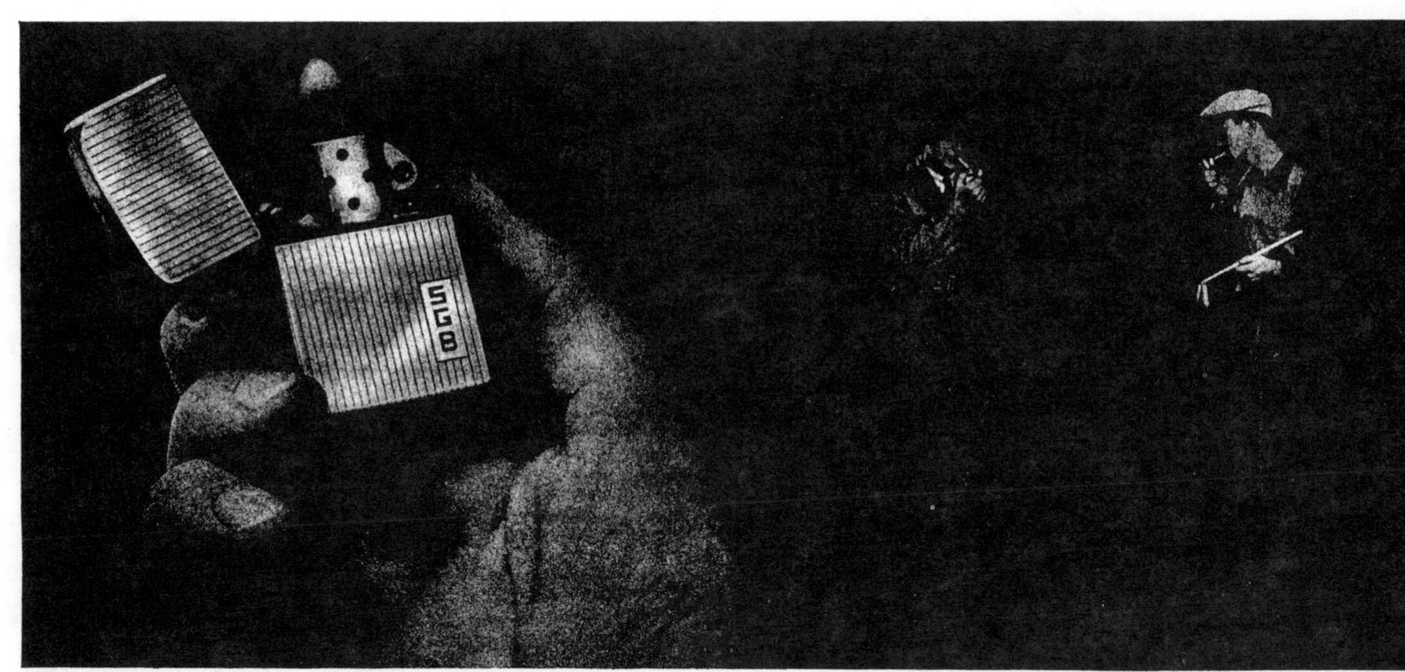

ZIPPO for Father's Day We further make this promise to Dad: that if ever—at any time—his Zippo fails to light perfectly, we will quickly put it into perfect working order free. No one has ever paid us a cent for the repair of a Zippo. The model shown above is gleaming, engine-turned heavy chrome.

Glowing colors on bright chrome. Choice of Trout, Mallard, Pheasant, Horse, Setter, Sailfish, Sloop.

Rich, genuine morocco, lizard or alligator. Black, blue, red, green, brown.

All prices include Federal tax

Lifetime-engraved in color. Choice of Bowler, Baseball Player, Fisherman, Golfer, Dog, Horse, Hunter, Sailboat.

ZIPPC

LIGHTS EASILY...ANYWHERE...ALW

Zippo Manufacturing Company, Bradfor

In Canada: Zippo Manufacturing Co., Canada Ltd., Niagara Fal

Genuine Zippo Fluid and Zippo Flints make all lighters work b

1954 Magazine Ad

1949 Magazine Ad

1955 Magazine Ad

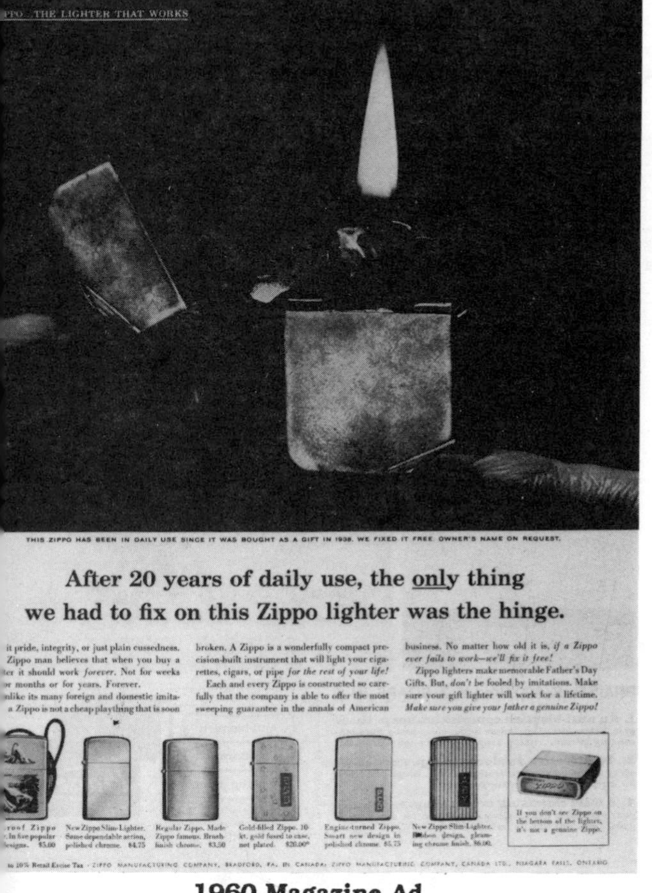

1960 Magazine Ad

1962 Magazine Ad

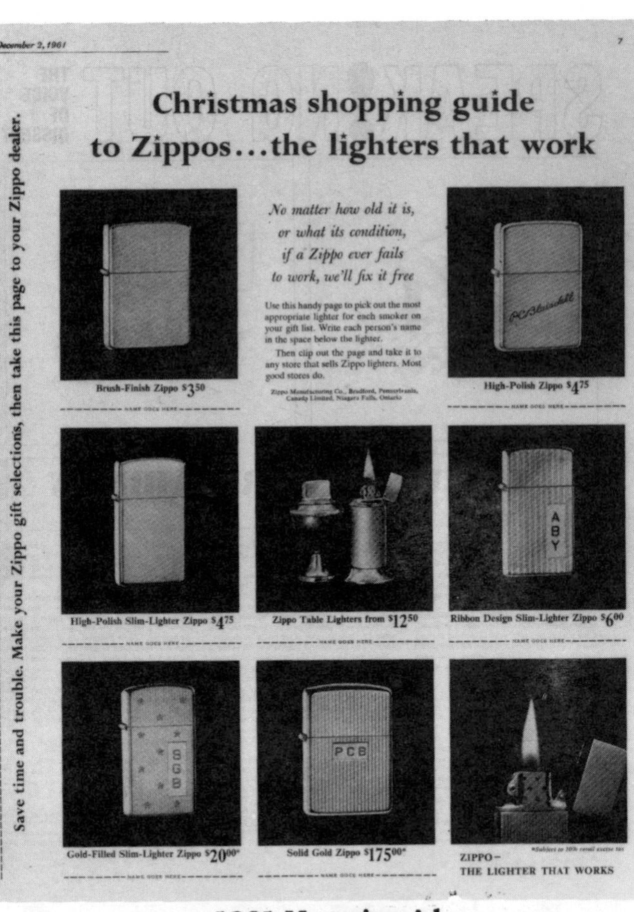

December 2, 1961 7

Save time and trouble. Make your Zippo gift selections, then take this page to your Zippo dealer.

Christmas shopping guide to Zippos...the lighters that work

No matter how old it is, or what its condition, if a Zippo ever fails to work, we'll fix it free

Use this handy page to pick out the most appropriate lighter for each smoker on your gift list. Write each person's name in the space below the lighter.

Then clip out the page and take it to any store that sells Zippo lighters. Most good stores do.

Zippo Manufacturing Co., Bradford, Pennsylvania. Canada Limited, Niagara Falls, Ontario

Brush-Finish Zippo $3.50

High-Polish Zippo $4.75

High-Polish Slim-Lighter Zippo $4.75

Zippo Table Lighters from $12.50

Ribbon Design Slim-Lighter Zippo $6.00

Gold-Filled Slim-Lighter Zippo $20.00*

Solid Gold Zippo $175.00*

*Subject to 10% retail excise tax

ZIPPO–
THE LIGHTER THAT WORKS

1961 Magazine Ad

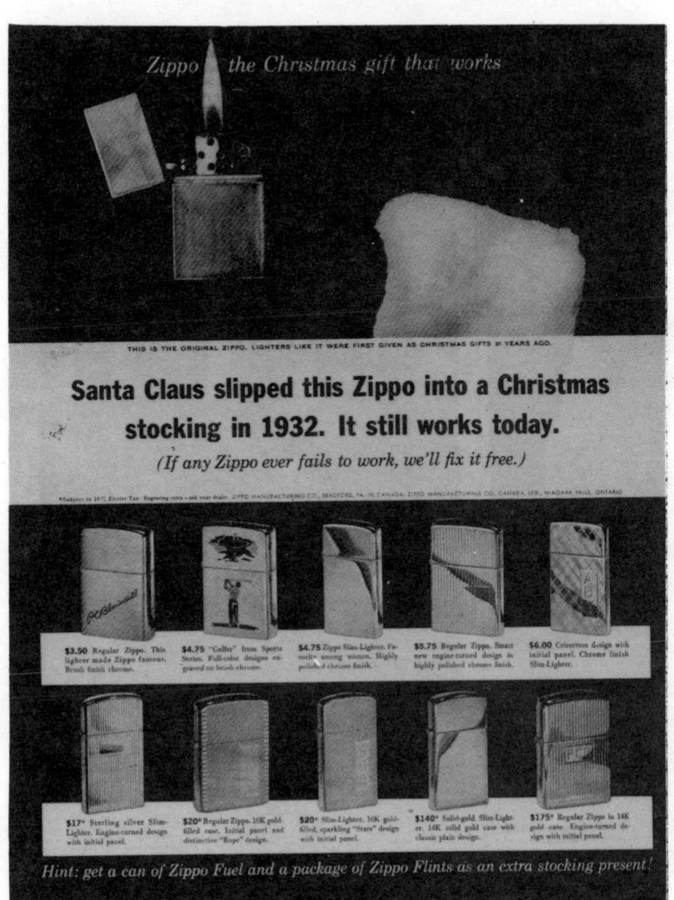

Zippo the Christmas gift that works

THIS IS THE ORIGINAL ZIPPO. LIGHTERS LIKE IT WERE FIRST GIVEN AS CHRISTMAS GIFTS 21 YEARS AGO.

Santa Claus slipped this Zippo into a Christmas stocking in 1932. It still works today.

(If any Zippo ever fails to work, we'll fix it free.)

$3.50 Regular Zippo. This lighter made Zippo famous. Brush finish chrome.

$4.75 "Golfer" from Sports Series. Full-color designs engraved on brush chrome.

$4.75 Zippo Slim-Lighter. Favorite among women. Highly polished chrome finish.

$5.75 Regular Zippo. Smart new engine-turned design in highly polished chrome finish.

$6.00 Crisscross design with initial panel. Chrome finish Slim-Lighter.

$17* Sterling silver Slim-Lighter. Engine-turned design with initial panel.

$20* Regular Zippo. 10K gold-filled case. Initial panel and distinctive "Rope" design.

$20* Slim-Lighter. 10K gold-filled, sparkling "Stars" design with initial panel.

$140* Solid-gold Slim-Lighter. 14K solid gold case with classic plain design.

$175* Regular Zippo in 14K gold case. Engine-turned design with initial panel.

Hint: get a can of Zippo Fuel and a package of Zippo Flints as an extra stocking present!

1932 Magazine Ad

Queen on HER day! Breakfast in bed . . . and a Zippo as a s

Mother's no mechanic!

Give her ZIPPO...it always li

Surprise and delight Mother with a different kind of gift—her own personal Zippo lighter.

She'll love it because it lights with wonderful ease, always. No triggers, buttons or latches to get out of order. Easy to fill. And Mother can change a flint easily without fracturing a finger nail.

Pick the Zippo that suits her best from a wide and beautiful variety—gleaming chrome, real leathers, sport and hobby designs.

Every Zippo carries this remarkable guarantee: if ever, at any time, a Zippo fails to light easily and perfectly, we will quickly put it into perfect working order absolutely free.

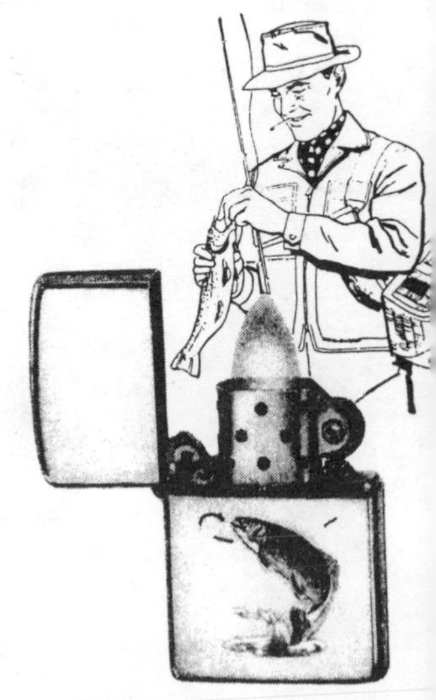

ZIPPO®

GUARANTEED TO WORK FOREVER

Zippo Manufacturing Company, Bradford, Pa.
In Canada: Zippo Manufacturing Co., Canada Ltd., Niagara Falls, Ontario

ZIPPOS ARE FOR EVERYONE

Father's Day is on the way, too. Suit hi hobby with this richly handsome model Choice of Trout, Mallard, Pheasant, H Setter, Sailfish, Sloop in rich ceramic colors on high-polish chrome.

1954 Magazine Ad

PEPSI-COLA ADVERTISING LIGHTERS

Metal and
Plastic Lighter
Circa 1970's
1" x 3"

Metal and
Plastic Lighter
Circa 1950's
1 1/2" x 2 1/2"

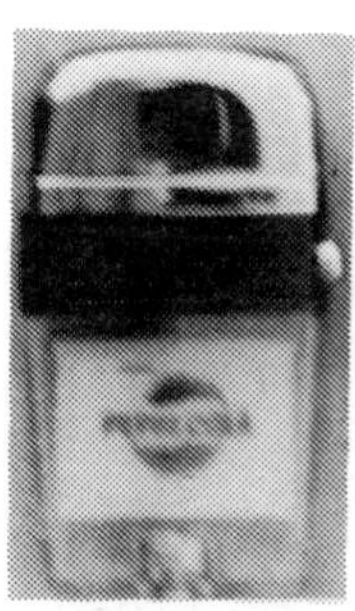

Plastic Lighter
Circa 1960's
1 1/2" x 2 1/2"

Metal Lighter
Circa 1960's
1 1/2" x 2 1/2"

Metal Lighter
Circa 1960's
1 1/2" x 2"

Metal Lighter
Circa 1960's
2" x 3"

Metal Lighter
(Pensacola, FL)
Circa 1960's
1 1/2" x 2 1/2"

Metal Lighter
Circa 1970's
1 1/2" x 2 1/2"

Metal Lighter
Circa 1960's
1 1/2" x 2 1/2"

Metal Lighter
with Enamel Insert
Circa 1960's
1 1/2" x 2 1/2"

Metal Lighter with
Enamel Insert
Circa 1950's
1 1/2" x 2 1/2"

Courtesy of Pepsi-Cola Collectibles, Vehling & Hunt

PEPSI-COLA ADVERTISING LIGHTERS

Metal Lighter
Circa 1950's
2 1/2" x 1 1/2"

Metal Lighter
Circa 1950's
2 1/2" x 1 1/2"

Metal Lighter
Circa 1970's
2" x 2"

Metal Lighter
Circa 1950's
2 1/2" x 1 1/2"

Metal Lighter
Circa 1950's
2 1/2" x 1 1/2"

Metal Lighter
Circa 1970's
2" x 2"

Metal Lighter
Circa 1950's
2 1/2" x 1 1/2"

Metal Lighter with
Enamel Insert
Circa 1960's
1 1/2" x 2 1/2"

Musical Lighter
(Two Views)
Circa 1950's
2" x 2"

Musical Lighter
(Two Views)
Circa 1950's
1 1/2" x 2 1/2"

Musical Lighter (Two Views)
Circa 1950's
2" x 3"

Musical Lighter/Box
(Three Views)
Circa 1950's
2" x 3"

Courtesy of Pepsi-Cola Collectibles, Vehling & Hunt

PEPSI-COLA ADVERTISING LIGHTERS

Metal Lighter
Circa 1950's
2" x 1"

Desk Lighter (Lucite)
Circa 1940's
5" x 5"

Can Lighter
Circa 1940's
12 oz. Can

Metal Lighter
Circa 1940's
2"

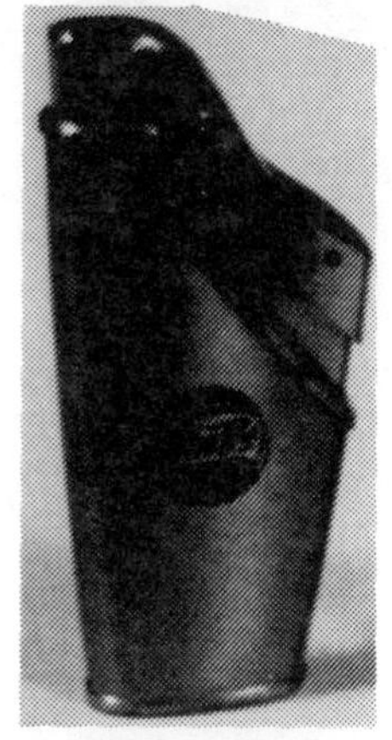

Metal Lighter
Circa 1950's
1" x 4"

Metal Lighter with
Enamel Insert
Circa 1940's
1 1/2" x 2 1/2"

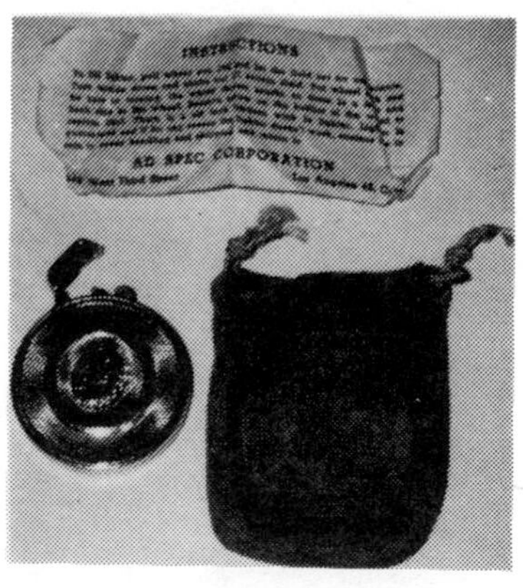

Lighter with Original Bag
Circa 1950's
2" Diameter

Metal Lighter
Circa 1950's
2 1/4" x 1 1/2"

Metal Lighter
Circa 1950's
1 1/2" x 3"

Courtesy of Pepsi-Cola Collectibles, Vehling & Hunt

Japan

VAT 69 Bottle – Lighter in Cap
Bottom is a Cigarette Holder

Marble Base Glass Riser – Early Japan

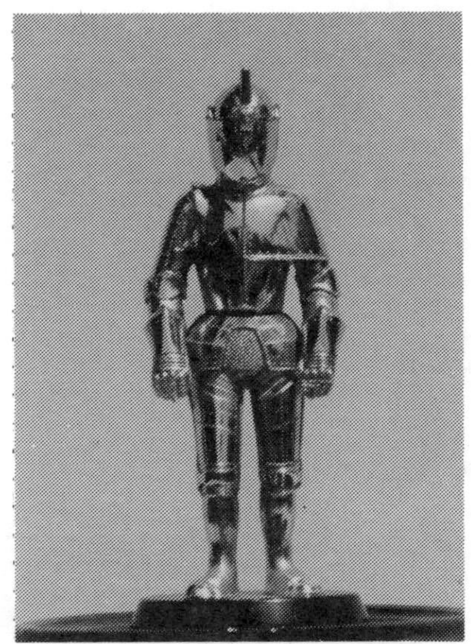
Knight with Music Box

left: Japan
right: Colibri – Kreisler W. Germany

left: Ronson Varaflame – Gas Lighter
right: Japan

Electric Lighter – Germany

Elephant & Donkey – Japan

Round Ball Lighter - Japan

Japan

Left: Golf Bag
Right: Carved Face

Japan

All Ronson

1. Crown
2. Regal
3. Georgian
4. Newport

1. Diana
2. Newport
3. Tempo

Sterling Silver

American Safety Razor "A.S.R"

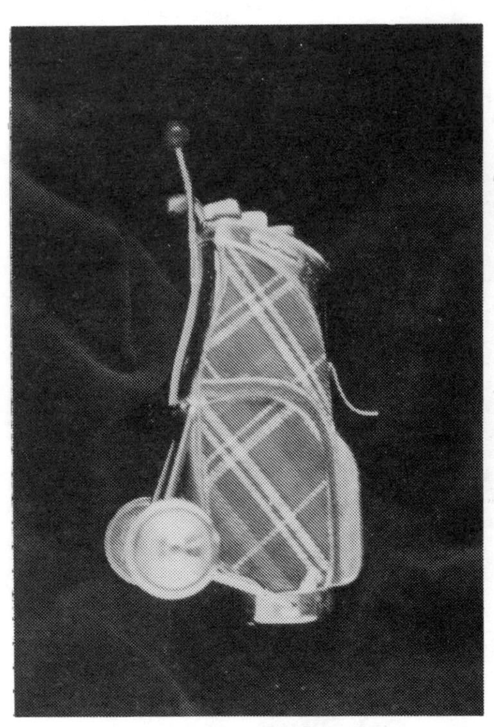

Golf Clubs – Gas Lighter
Japan

Gun – Japan
marked (Colt Government)

Dragon – Gas Lighter
Japan

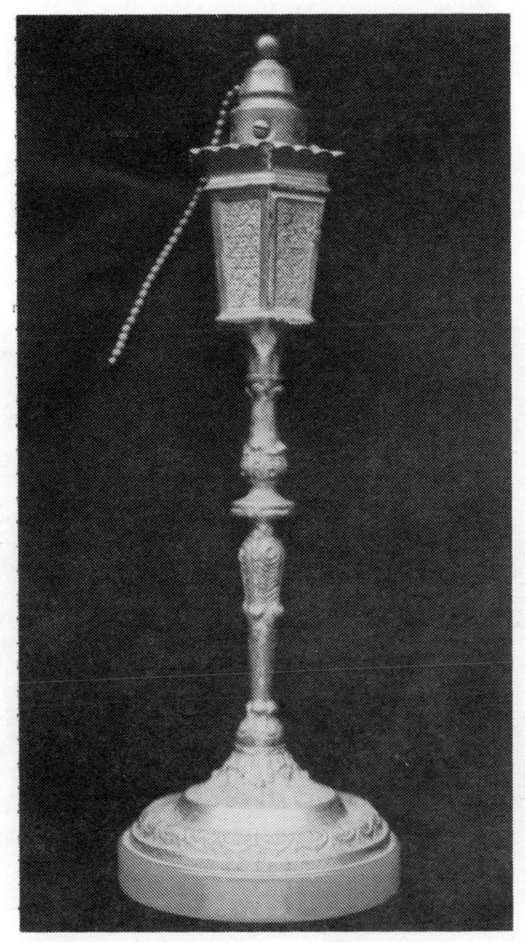

Lamp Post – USA

Made in Occupied Japan

Store Cigar Lighter

50 Caliber Bullet - hand made
Grenade – visa brass

Both made in Occupied Japan

John Anderson & Co.
Cigar Cutter & Lighter
Iron – 6" x 6" x 23"

Reciprocity Cigar Cutter & Lighter
Iron -7" x 10" x 14"

Poet Cigars Cutter & Lighters
Iron -5" x 12" x 14"

Dexter, Flotilla and Nerve Cigar Cutters & Lighters
Iron -4" x 8" x 10"

Courtesy of Antique Advertising Encyclopedia – Ray Klug

Cinco Cigar Lighter
Iron – 7" x 5" x 12"

Charles Denby Cigar Lighter
Iron – 5" x 4" x 11"

Punch Gas Cigar Lighter
Iron -5" x 8"

Betsy Ross Cigar Lighter
Iron – 7" x 12"

Lillian Russel Cigar Lighter
Iron -7" x 7" x 12"

Courtesy of Antique Advertising Encyclopedia – Ray Klug

1945 Ronson WWII Magazine Ad

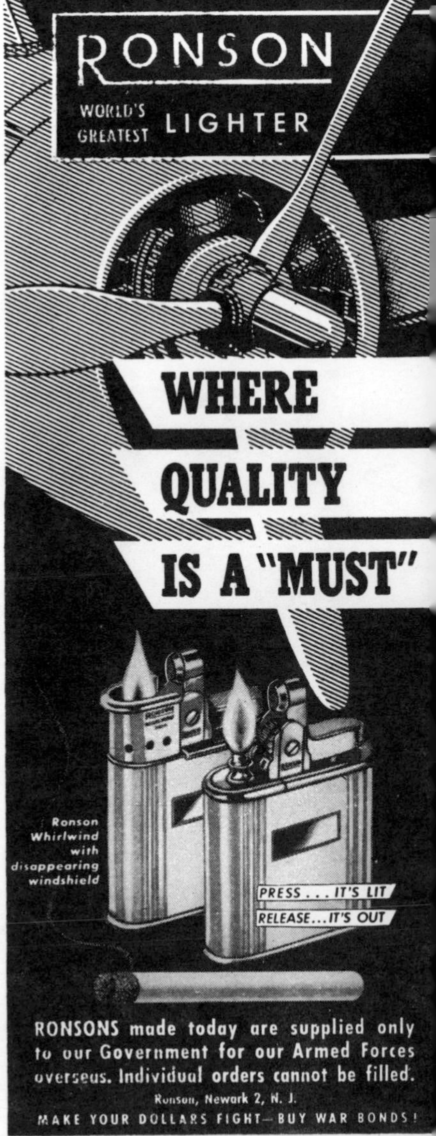

1944 Ronson WWII Magazine Ad

1930 CATALOG PAGE

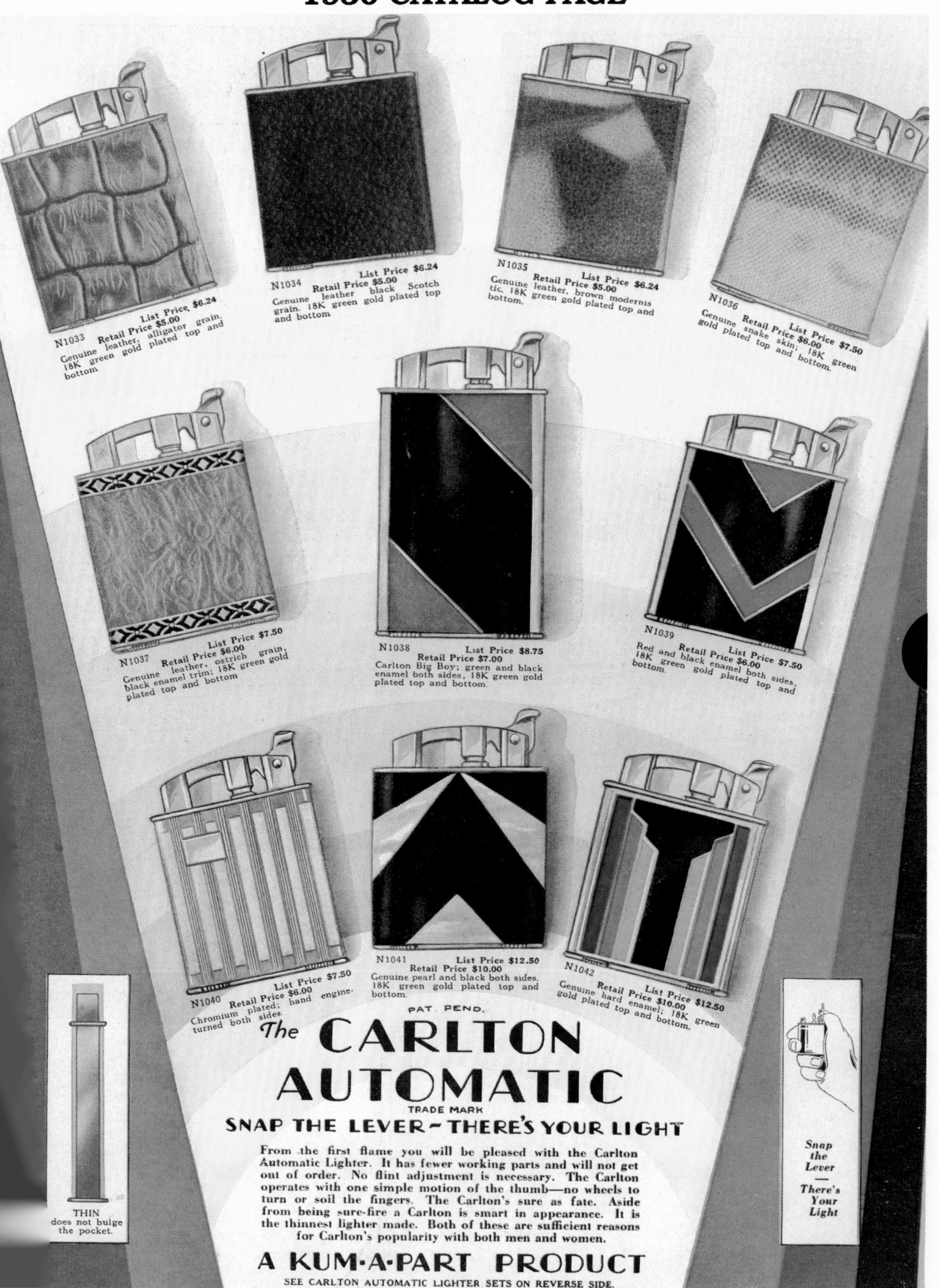

N1033 List Price $6.24 Retail Price $5.00
Genuine leather, alligator grain, 18K green gold plated top and bottom.
N1034 List Price $6.24 Retail Price $5.00
Genuine leather black Scotch grain. 18K green gold plated top and bottom.
N1035 List Price $6.24 Retail Price $5.00
Genuine leather, brown modernistic. 18K green gold plated top and bottom.
N1036 List Price $7.50 Retail Price $6.00
Genuine snake skin; 18K green gold plated top and bottom.
N1037 List Price $7.50 Retail Price $6.00
Genuine leather, ostrich grain, black enamel trim; 18K green gold plated top and bottom
N1038 List Price $8.75 Retail Price $7.00
Carlton Big Boy; green and black enamel both sides, 18K green gold plated top and bottom.
N1039 List Price $7.50 Retail Price $6.00
Red and black enamel both sides, 18K green gold plated top and bottom.
N1040 List Price $7.50 Retail Price $6.00
Chromium plated; hand engine-turned both sides.
N1041 List Price $12.50 Retail Price $10.00
Genuine pearl and black both sides, 18K green gold plated top and bottom.
N1042 List Price $12.50 Retail Price $10.00
Genuine hard enamel; 18K green gold plated top and bottom.
PAT. PEND.
The CARLTON AUTOMATIC
TRADE MARK
SNAP THE LEVER – THERE'S YOUR LIGHT
From the first flame you will be pleased with the Carlton Automatic Lighter. It has fewer working parts and will not get out of order. No flint adjustment is necessary. The Carlton operates with one simple motion of the thumb—no wheels to turn or soil the fingers. The Carlton's sure as fate. Aside from being sure-fire a Carlton is smart in appearance. It is the thinnest lighter made. Both of these are sufficient reasons for Carlton's popularity with both men and women.
THIN does not bulge the pocket.
Snap the Lever — There's Your Light
A KUM-A-PART PRODUCT
SEE CARLTON AUTOMATIC LIGHTER SETS ON REVERSE SIDE.

1930 CATALOG PAGE

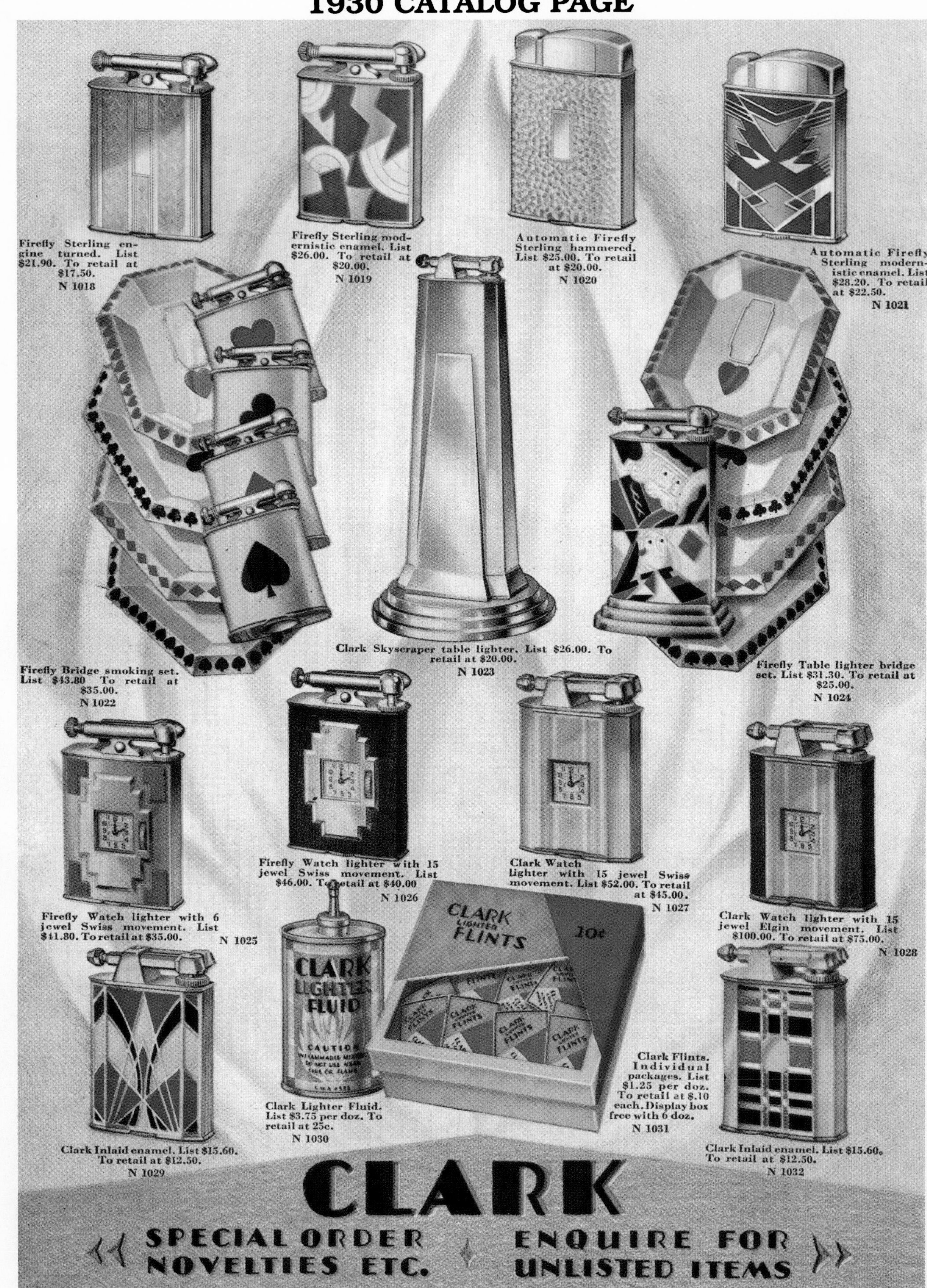

Firefly Sterling engine turned. List $21.90. To retail at $17.50.
N 1018
Firefly Sterling modernistic enamel. List $26.00. To retail at $20.00.
N 1019
Automatic Firefly Sterling hammered. List $25.00. To retail at $20.00.
N 1020
Automatic Firefly Sterling modernistic enamel. List $28.20. To retail at $22.50.
N 1021
Firefly Bridge smoking set. List $43.80 To retail at $35.00.
N 1022
Clark Skyscraper table lighter. List $26.00. To retail at $20.00.
N 1023
Firefly Table lighter bridge set. List $31.30. To retail at $25.00.
N 1024
Firefly Watch lighter with 6 jewel Swiss movement. List $41.80. To retail at $35.00.
N 1025
Firefly Watch lighter with 15 jewel Swiss movement. List $46.00. To retail at $40.00
N 1026
Clark Watch lighter with 15 jewel Swiss movement. List $52.00. To retail at $45.00.
N 1027
Clark Watch lighter with 15 jewel Elgin movement. List $100.00. To retail at $75.00.
N 1028
CLARK LIGHTER FLUID
CAUTION
CLARK LIGHTER FLINTS
10¢
Clark Inlaid enamel. List $15.60. To retail at $12.50.
N 1029
Clark Lighter Fluid. List $3.75 per doz. To retail at 25c.
N 1030
Clark Flints. Individual packages. List $1.25 per doz. To retail at $.10 each. Display box free with 6 doz.
N 1031
Clark Inlaid enamel. List $15.60. To retail at $12.50.
N 1032
CLARK
SPECIAL ORDER NOVELTIES ETC.
ENQUIRE FOR UNLISTED ITEMS

1930 CATALOG PAGE

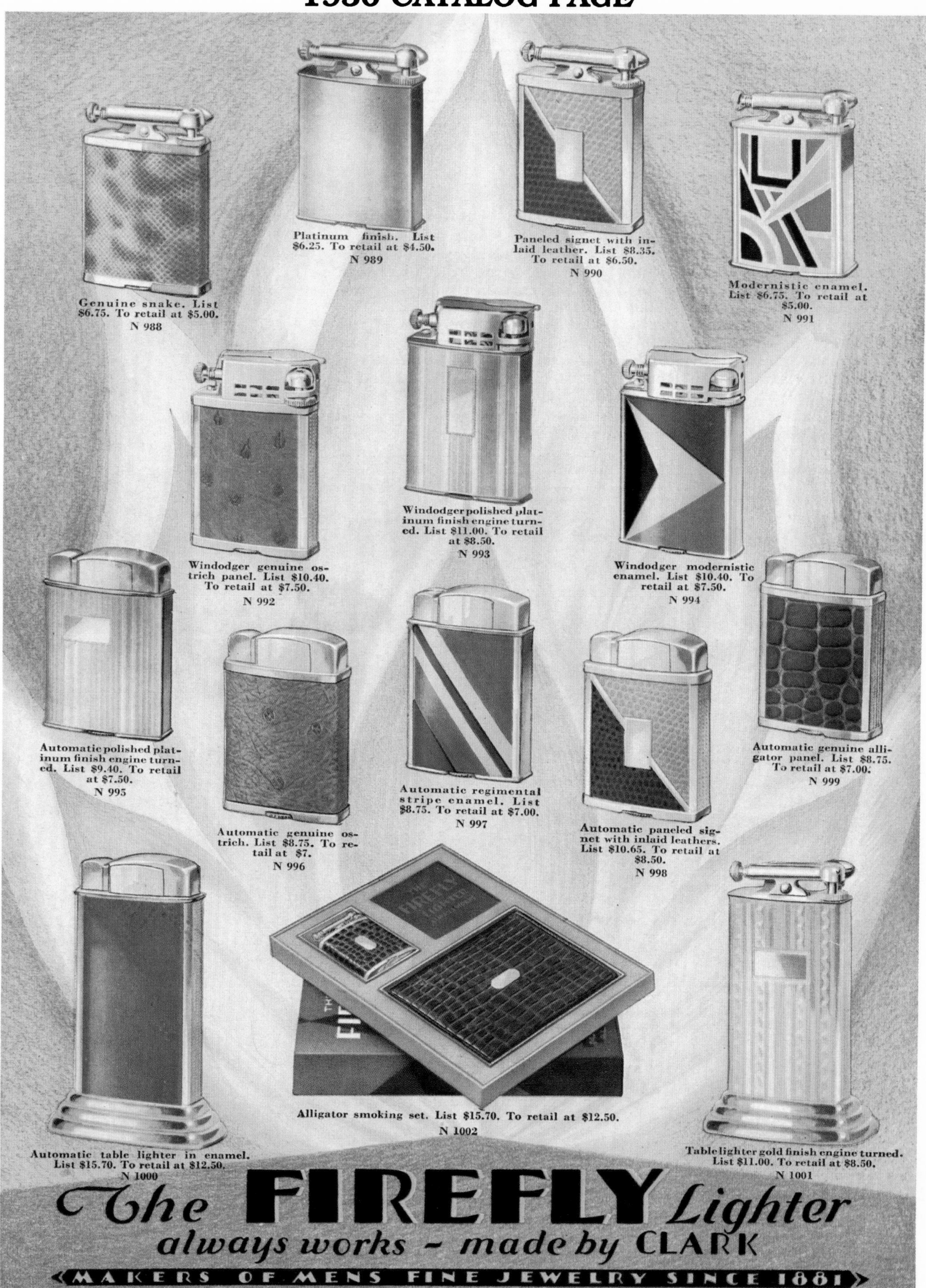

Genuine snake. List $6.75. To retail at $5.00. N 988
Platinum finish. List $6.25. To retail at $4.50. N 989
Paneled signet with inlaid leather. List $8.35. To retail at $6.50. N 990
Modernistic enamel. List $6.75. To retail at $5.00. N 991
Windodger genuine ostrich panel. List $10.40. To retail at $7.50. N 992
Windodger polished platinum finish engine turned. List $11.00. To retail at $8.50. N 993
Windodger modernistic enamel. List $10.40. To retail at $7.50. N 994
Automatic polished platinum finish engine turned. List $9.40. To retail at $7.50. N 995
Automatic genuine ostrich. List $8.75. To retail at $7. N 996
Automatic regimental stripe enamel. List $8.75. To retail at $7.00. N 997
Automatic paneled signet with inlaid leathers. List $10.65. To retail at $8.50. N 998
Automatic genuine alligator panel. List $8.75. To retail at $7.00. N 999
Automatic table lighter in enamel. List $15.70. To retail at $12.50. N 1000
Alligator smoking set. List $15.70. To retail at $12.50. N 1002
Table lighter gold finish engine turned. List $11.00. To retail at $8.50. N 1001
The FIREFLY Lighter
always works - made by CLARK
MAKERS OF MENS FINE JEWELRY SINCE 1881

1929 CATALOG PAGE

EVANS

EC300—White finish, hammered and engine turned design. ....$3.00 ea.

EC301—White finish, genuine leather cover, ostrich grain. ....$3.75 ea.

EC302—White finish, shark grain effect with modernistic design in contrasting French enamel colors. $4.50 ea.

EC303—White finish, French enamel front in contrasting colors..$6.00 ea.

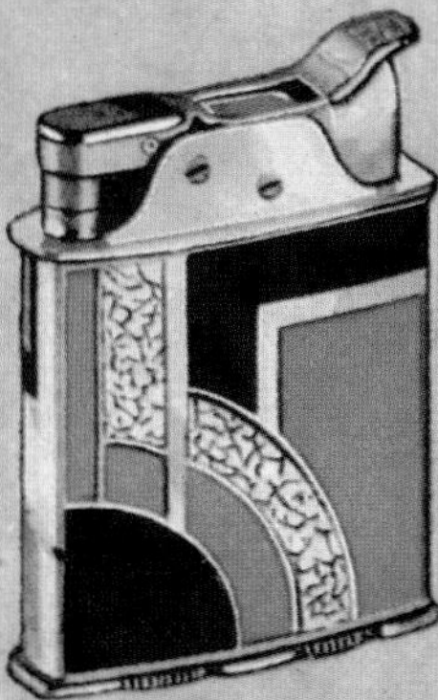

EC304—White finish, modernistic design with French enamel front with egg shell effect. $7.50 ea.

EC305—White finish, engine turned design with contrasting French enamel decoration....$6.00 ea.

EC306—White finish, modernistic design, French enamel front with egg shell effect. .....$7.50 ea.

EC307—Green gold finish with sterling silver top front in genuine hand painted Cloisonne enamel. $9.00 ea.

EC308—Green gold finish, sterling silver top front in genuine Cloisonne enamel. ....$9.00 ea.

EC309—White finish, French enamel front with genuine Cloisonne enamel decoration. ....$7.50 ea.

EC310—White finish, Automatic, Roller Bearing Desk or Table Lighter, French enamel front with genuine Cloisonne enamel decoration. ....$10.50 ea.

EC311—Big Boy model, Automatic Roller Bearing Pocket Lighter, white finish engine turned design with French enamel stripes, maximum fuel capacity for pocket lighter. ....$6.00 ea.

EC312—White finish, Sport model, Automatic Roller Bearing Pocket Lighter, modernistic design, French enamel front with egg shell effect. ....$9.00 ea.

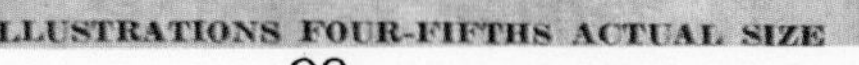

ILLUSTRATIONS FOUR-FIFTHS ACTUAL SIZE

1930 CATALOG PAGE

EVANS

N947—White finish basket weave design ....$6.00 ea.

— EVANS —
NEW ROLLER BEARING ACTION

Lighter Magic is achieved in the New Evans—the magic of modern mechanical perfection.

Cross Lever, Roller Bearing Action is a new principle in lighter building—exclusively Evans. It means smoother action, wider clearance between snuffer and wick, an almost complete revolution of the sparking wheel that spurts a veritable shower of sparks to insure ignition—not at one, but at several points in the revolution of the wheel, from just one pressure of the thumb. The removable wick holder is a unique convenience and all steel parts are specially hardened to assure long wear.

ITS STYLE NEVER FAILS TO REGISTER— ITS WICK NEVER FAILS TO LIGHT!

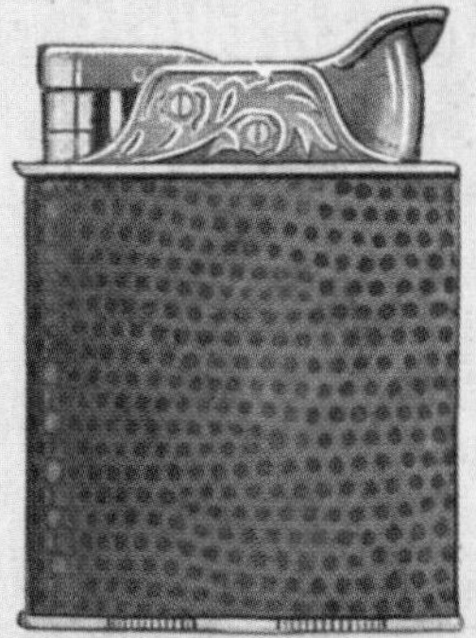

N948—White finish, genuine leather cover, lizard grain. $6.00 ea.

N949—White finish in contrasting French enamel front, neutral initial monogram design. $7.50 ea.

N950—White finish, engine turned design in modernistic pattern with hand painted French enamel decoration. $6.00 ea.

N951—White finish, modernistic design, of French enamel, shark grain background. $7.50 ea.

N952—White finish, modernistic design, French enamel front in contrasting colors. $7.50 ea.

N953—White finish, engine turned design with French enamel in contrasting color effects...............$7.50 ea.

N954—White finish, shark grain effect with French enamel stripes in contrasting colors. $7.50 ea.

N955—White finish, modernistic design, contrasting French enamel colors in shark grain effect background.....$7.50 ea.

N956—White finish, in all over French enamel effect in contrasting colors ....$7.50 ea.

N957—White finish, genuine Viennese egg shell enamel front with contrasting genuine hand engraved decoration...$12.00 ea.

N958—White finish, French enamel front in contrasting colors with egg shell design. $9.00 ea.

N959—Green gold finish, genuine ostrich cover with shield. $9.00 ea.

N960—White finish, genuine hand painted Dresden enamel front ....$12.00 ea.

Illustrations actual size.

The LINE with the STERLING TOUCH

1929 CATALOG PAGE

EVANS

E1600—Pony Pocket Lighter, hammered design...$3.00 ea.

E1604—Automatic Pocket Lighter, hammered design. $6.00 ea.

E1605—Automatic Pocket Lighter, hammered engine turned design......$6.75 ea.

E1601—Pony Pocket Lighter, genuine ostrich covered. $4.50 ea.

E1602—Standard Pocket Lighter, hammered design. $3.75 ea.

E1606—Automatic Pocket Lighter, genuine hand engine turned design..$7.50 ea.

E1607—Automatic Pocket Lighter, genuine hand engine turned design..$7.50 ea.

E1603—Standard Pocket Lighter, genuine leather covered............$4.50 ea.

E1608—Automatic Pocket Lighter, genuine leather covered, Hudson Seal. $7.50 ea.

E1609—Automatic Pocket Lighter, genuine Viennese enamel front in Lucky Elephant design......$12.00 ea.

E1610—Automatic Pocket Lighter, genuine Viennese enamel front......$12.00 ea.

E1611—Automatic Pocket Lighter, genuine ostrich covered...........$7.50 ea.

E1612—Combination Paper Weight and Automatic Desk Lighter..........$6.00 ea.

E1613—Automatic Desk Lighter or Table Lighter in contrasting lacquer and green gold finish......................$9.00 ea.

E1614—Combination Paper Weight and Automatic Desk Lighter, genuine leather covered, Hudson Seal............$7.50 ea.

Illustrations Four-fifths Size.

The LINE with the STERLING TOUCH

1929 CATALOG PAGE

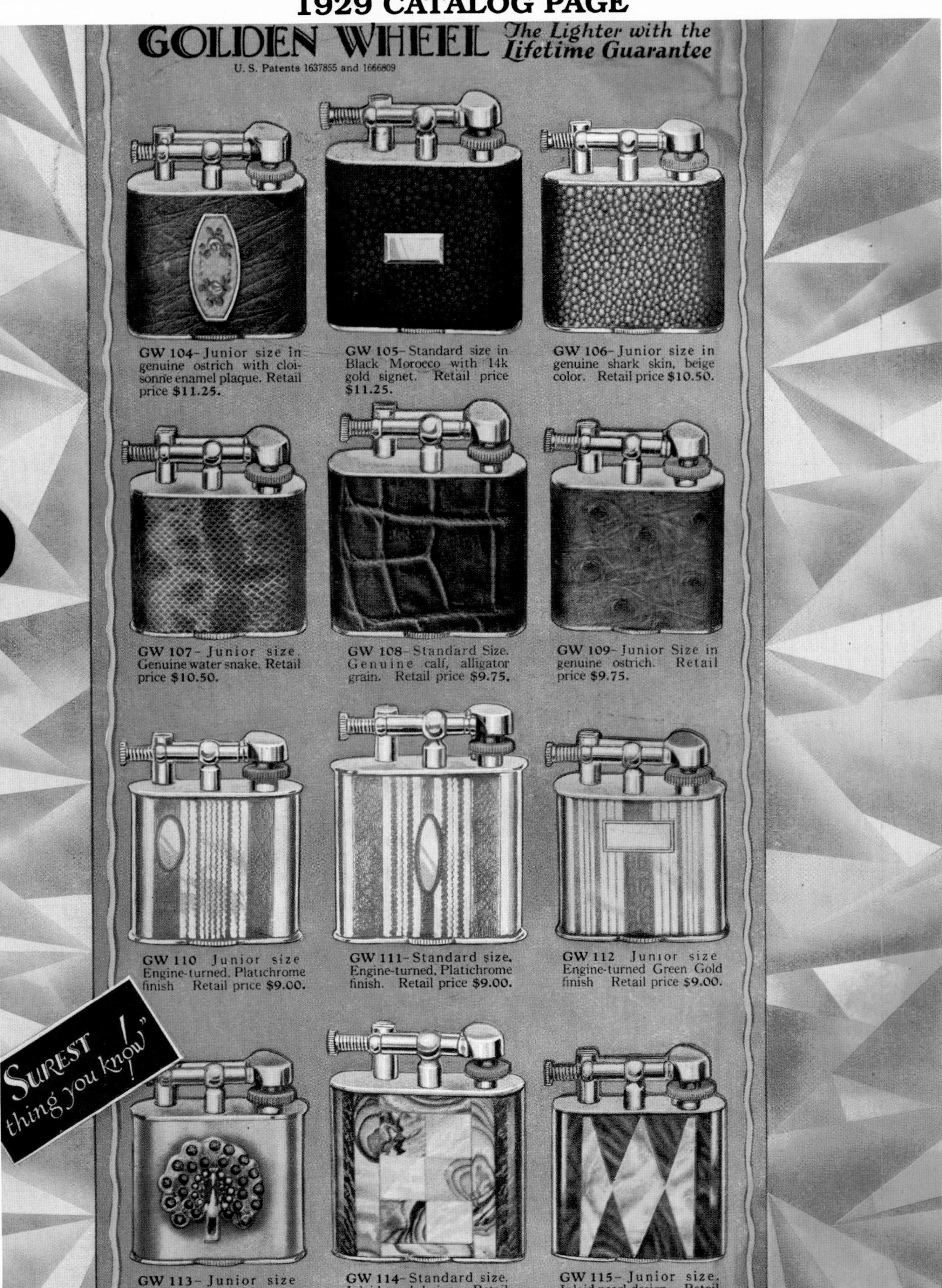

GOLDEN WHEEL The Lighter with the Lifetime Guarantee
U. S. Patents 1637855 and 1666809
GW 104–Junior size in genuine ostrich with cloisonne enamel plaque. Retail price $11.25.
GW 105–Standard size in Black Morocco with 14k gold signet. Retail price $11.25.
GW 106–Junior size in genuine shark skin, beige color. Retail price $10.50.
GW 107– Junior size. Genuine water snake. Retail price $10.50.
GW 108–Standard Size. Genuine calf, alligator grain. Retail price $9.75.
GW 109–Junior Size in genuine ostrich. Retail price $9.75.
GW 110 Junior size Engine-turned. Platichrome finish Retail price $9.00.
GW 111–Standard size. Engine-turned, Platichrome finish. Retail price $9.00.
GW 112 Junior size Engine-turned Green Gold finish Retail price $9.00.
"SUREST thing you know!"
GW 113– Junior size Antique gold finish-stone-set peacock design. Retail price $10.50.
GW 114–Standard size. Inlaid pearl design. Retail price $13.50.
GW 115– Junior size. Inlaid pearl design. Retail price $13.50.

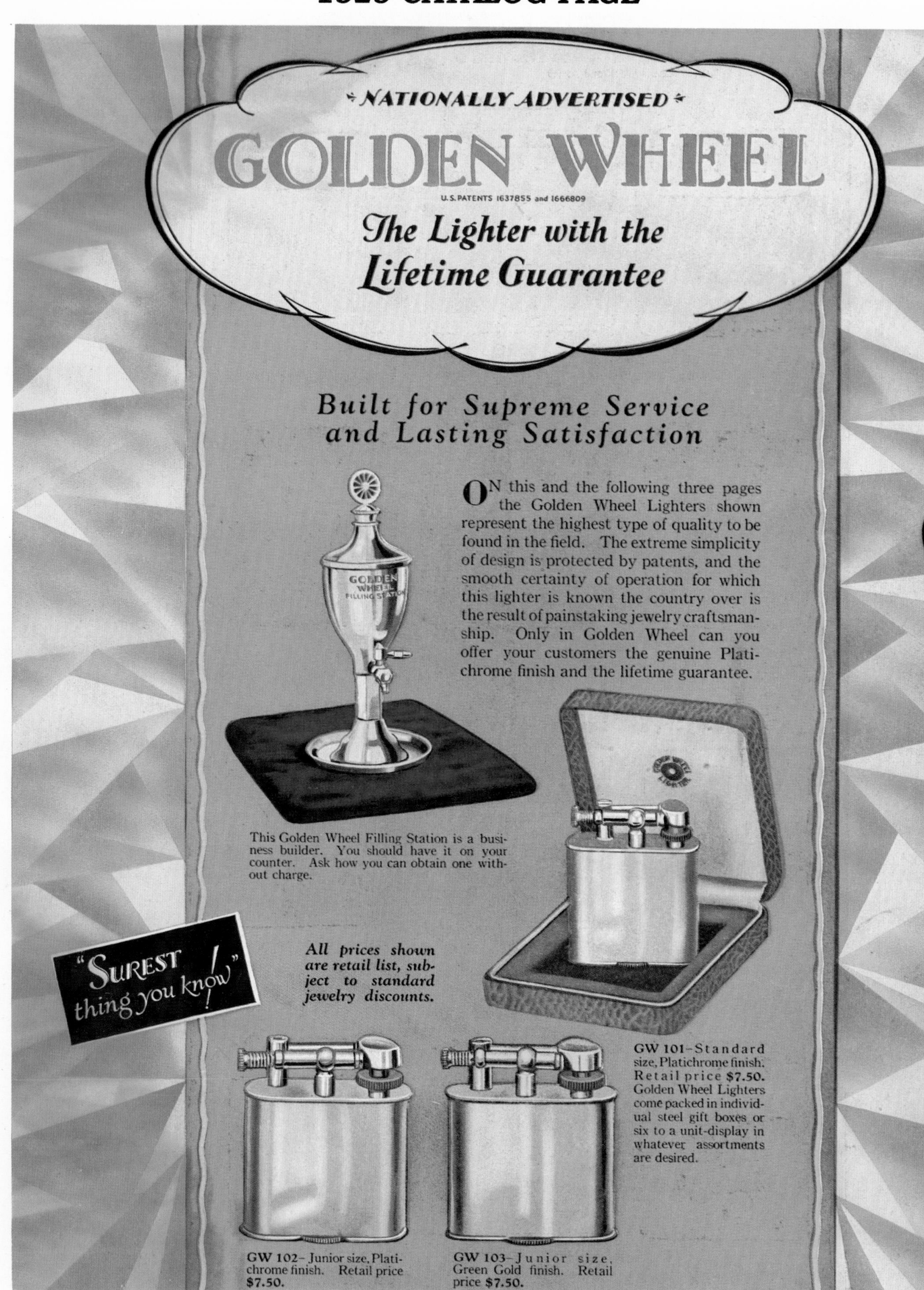
NATIONALLY ADVERTISED
GOLDEN WHEEL
U.S. PATENTS 1637855 and 1666809
The Lighter with the Lifetime Guarantee
Built for Supreme Service and Lasting Satisfaction
ON this and the following three pages the Golden Wheel Lighters shown represent the highest type of quality to be found in the field. The extreme simplicity of design is protected by patents, and the smooth certainty of operation for which this lighter is known the country over is the result of painstaking jewelry craftsmanship. Only in Golden Wheel can you offer your customers the genuine Platichrome finish and the lifetime guarantee.
GOLDEN WHEEL FILLING STATION
This Golden Wheel Filling Station is a business builder. You should have it on your counter. Ask how you can obtain one without charge.
"SUREST thing you know!"
All prices shown are retail list, subject to standard jewelry discounts.
GW 101–Standard size, Platichrome finish. Retail price $7.50. Golden Wheel Lighters come packed in individual steel gift boxes or six to a unit-display in whatever assortments are desired.
GW 102– Junior size, Platichrome finish. Retail price $7.50.
GW 103– Junior size, Green Gold finish. Retail price $7.50.

1929 CATALOG PAGE

GOLDEN WHEEL

SPIN·TYPE AUTOMATIC

Lighters

N 1069

~~GW222~~-Automatic with Cigarette Case of genuine leather, snake grain, to match. Platichrome signets. **$9.00.**

N 1070

~~GW223~~-Spin-type, junior size, in Longchamps enamel. **$9.00.** ***Lifetime Guarantee.***

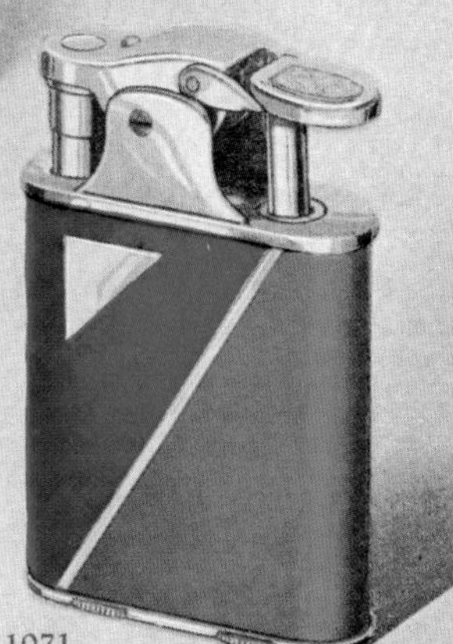

N 1071

~~GW224~~-Automatic. Polished enamel with Platichrome signet and trim—**$9.00.**

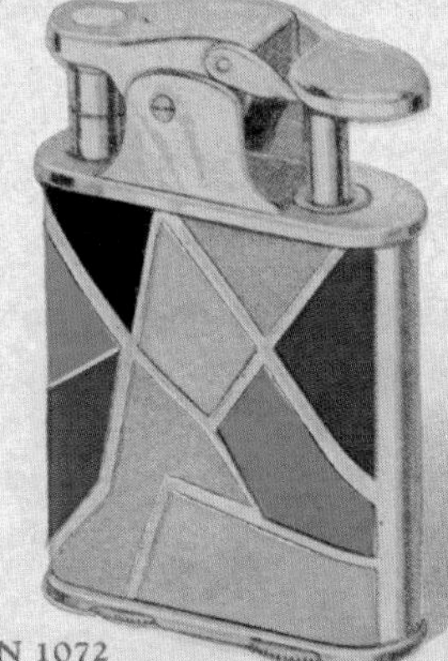

N 1072

~~GW225~~-Automatic. Longchamps enamel, modernistic design. **$7.50.**

N 1073

~~GW226~~-Spin-type, junior size, in polished enamel. Platichrome signet and trim. **$10.50.** ***Lifetime Guarantee.***

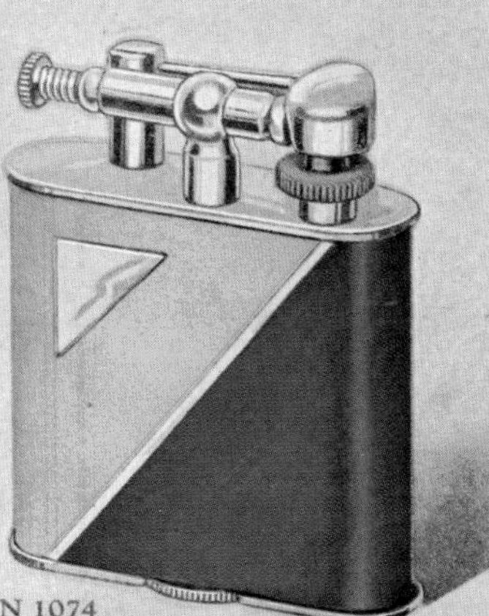

N 1074

~~GW227~~-Spin-type, standard size, in polished enamel. Platichrome signet and trim. **$10.50.** ***Lifetime Guarantee.***

"SUREST
hing you know!"

N 1075

~~GW228~~-Automatic Table Lighter. 4 inches high—several months' fuel capacity. In polished enamel—**$12.00.**

All Prices Are Retail List

1930 CATALOG PAGE

THE WORLD'S GREATEST LIGHTER

"A Flip -and it's lit!"

RONSON *De-light*

"Release -and it's out!"

PATENTED. OTHER PATS. PDG. TRADE MARKS REGISTERED

Illustrations of individual Lighters about four-fifths actual size.

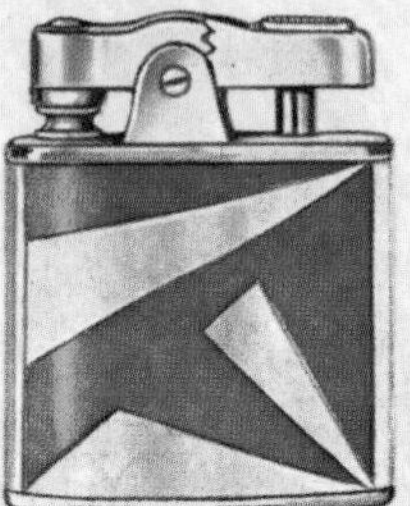

PRINCESS "MODERNISTIC"
Enamel

No.		List each	Retail each
01101	Red Enamel	$9.05	$6.50
01101	Black Enamel	9.05	6.50

PRINCESS "SOPHOMORE"
Enamel

No.	Color Combinations	List each	Retail each
01304	Black, Blue, Green	$9.05	$6.50
01303	Brown, Tan, Red	9.05	6.50

STANDARD "MODERNISTIC"
Enamel

No.		List each	Retail each
1101	Black Enamel	$9.05	$6.50
1101	Brown Enamel	9.05	6.50

STANDARD "SOPHOMORE"
Enamel

No.	Color Combinations	List each	Retail each
1303	Brown, Tan, Red	$9.05	$6.50
1301	Black, Blue, Orange	9.05	6.50

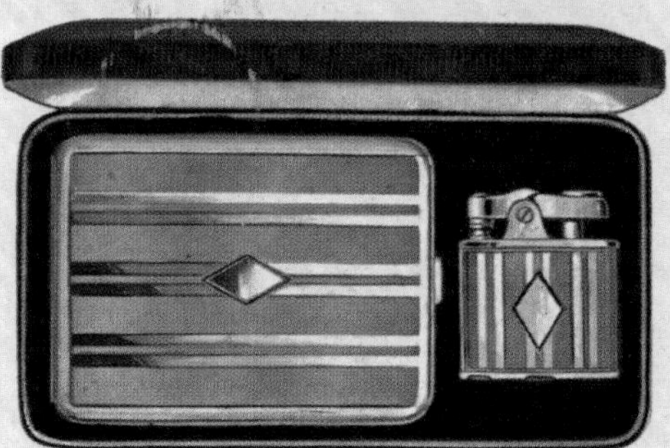

RONSON SETS
Chromium Plate, Engine Turned

No.		List set	Retail set
13042	with Standard Model No. 17	$18.80	$13.50
13043	with Princess Model No. 12351	18.80	13.50

RONSON SETS
Chromium Plate, Enameled

No.		List set	Retail set
13040	with Standard "Twin Bar" Black Enamel	$21.00	$15.00
13041	with Princess "Twin Bar" Blue Enamel	21.00	15.00

RONSON SETS
Ladies' Size
Chromium Plate, Enameled

No.		List set	Retail set
13064	with Princess Two-Tone Blue Enamel	$17.40	$12.50

RONSON SETS
Chromium Plate, Enameled

No.		List set	Retail set
13038	with Standard "Modernistic" Red	$21.00	$15.00
13039	with Princess "Modernistic" Black	21.00	15.00

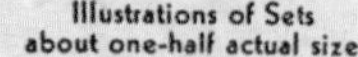

Illustrations of Sets about one-half actual size.

PRINCESS "CAMPUS"
Enamel

No.	Color Combinations	List each	Retail each
01203	Red and Black	$9.05	$6.50
01201	Black and Orange	9.05	6.50

PRINCESS "TWIN BAR"
Enamel

No.		List each	Retail each
01102	Green Enamel	$9.05	$6.50
01102	Blue Enamel	9.05	6.50

STANDARD "CAMPUS"
Enamel

No.	Color Combinations	List each	Retail each
1202	Red and Blue	$9.05	$6.50
1201	Orange and Black	9.05	6.50

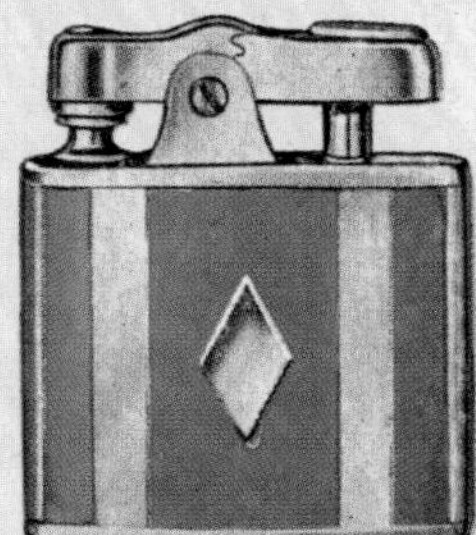

STANDARD "TWIN BAR"
Enamel

No.		List each	Retail each
1102	Blue Enamel	$9.05	$6.50
1102	Black Enamel	9.05	6.50

1930 CATALOG PAGE

THE WORLD'S GREATEST LIGHTER

"A Flip -and it's lit!"

RONSON De-light

"Release -and it's out!"

PATENTED. OTHER PATS. P'D'G. TRADE MARKS REGISTERED

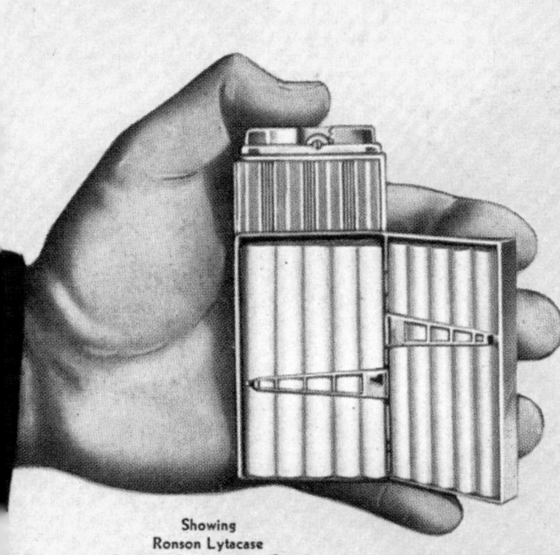

Showing Ronson Lytacase Cigarette Compartment, Open

Showing Ronson Lytacase De-Light Lighter in Action

RONSON LYTACASE No. 12939 Combination Ronson De-Light and Cigarette Case

LYTACASE No. 12939 Chromium Plate Engine Turned
List each - $14.00
Retail each - 10.00

Illustrations on this page are actual sizes

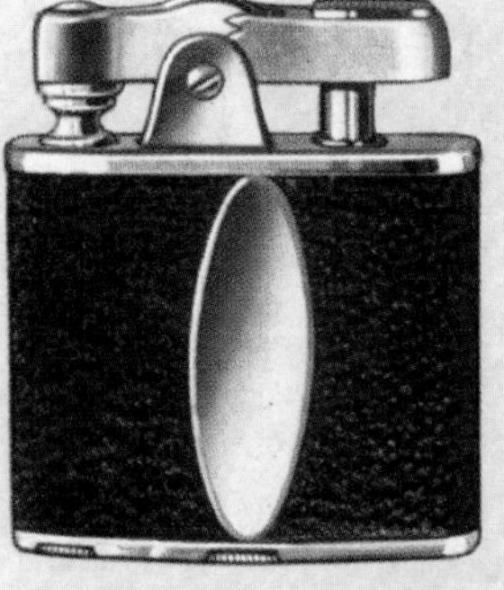

STANDARD MODEL

No.		List each	Retail each
1	Black Leather	$7.00	$5.00
4	Green Leather	7.00	5.00

PRINCESS MODEL

No.		List each	Retail each
02	Red Leather	$7.00	$5.00
016	Brown Leather	7.00	5.00

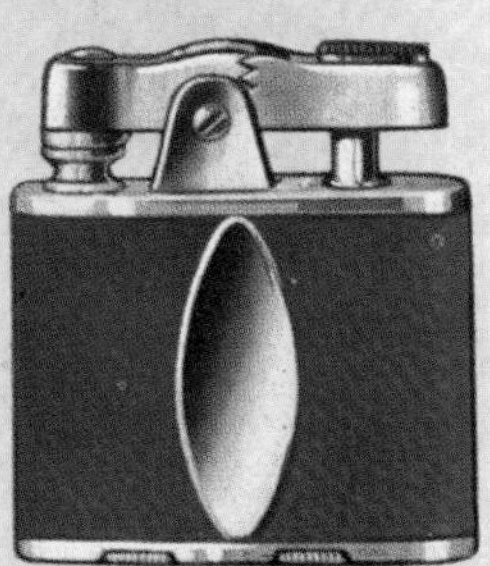

JUNIOR MODEL

No.		List each	Retail each
64	Blue Leather	$7.00	$5.00
49	Tan Leather	7.00	5.00

STANDARD "WINDBREAK"

No.		List each	Retail each
1007	Alligator Skin	$13.25	$9.50
01001	Princess "Windbreak" Black Leather	10.50	7.50

STANDARD MODEL
Chromium Plate

No.		List each	Retail each
17	Engine Turned	$9.05	$6.50
21	Butler Finish	7.00	5.00

JUNIOR MODEL
Chromium Plate

No.		List each	Retail each
151	Engine Turned	$9.05	$6.50
153	Butler Finish	7.00	5.00

PRINCESS MODEL
Chromium Plate

No.		List each	Retail each
12351	Engine Turned	$9.05	$6.50
021	Butler Finish	7.00	5.00

JUNIOR SPORT MODEL
Chromium Plate

No.		List each	Retail each
100	Engine Turned	$11.85	$8.50
90	Black Leather	10.50	7.50

Various World War I Lighters

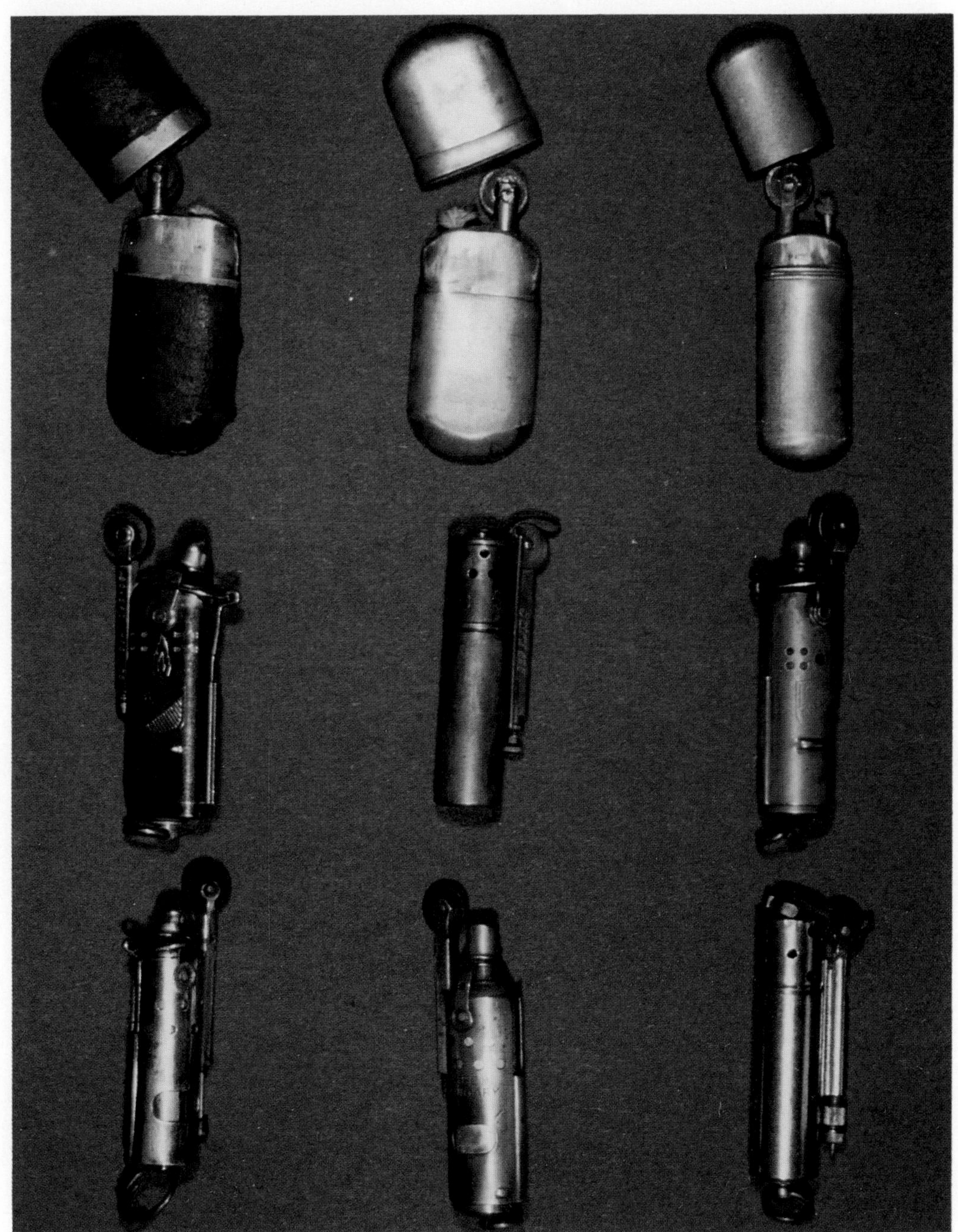

1. Unknown	2. Unknown	3. Unknown
4. Bowers	5. Austria	6. Bowers
7. Occupied Japan	8. Hungary	9. Hungary

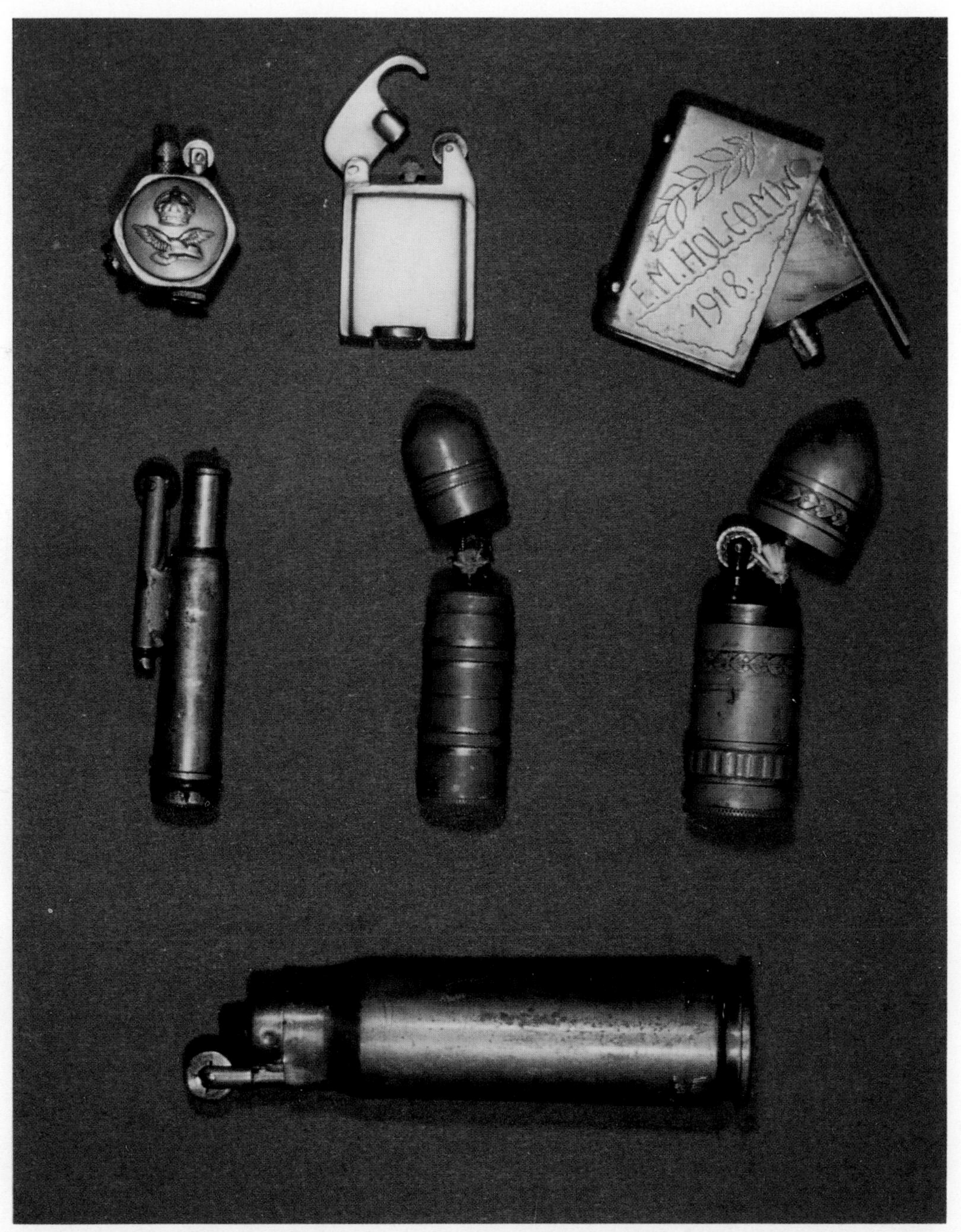

1. German
2. Unknown
3. English
4. Unknown
5. French
6. French
7. USA

Unknown

Gold on Silver – Mexico

Zippo Rip-Off

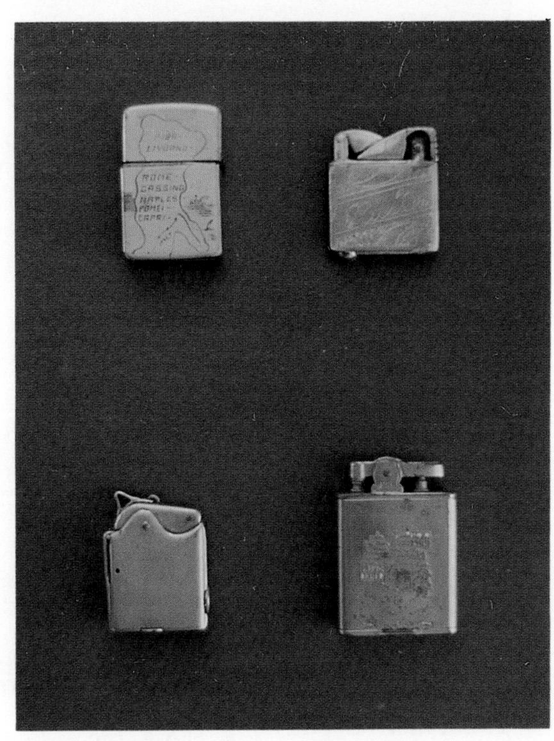

1. Zippo
2. Unknown
3. Unknown
4. Japan

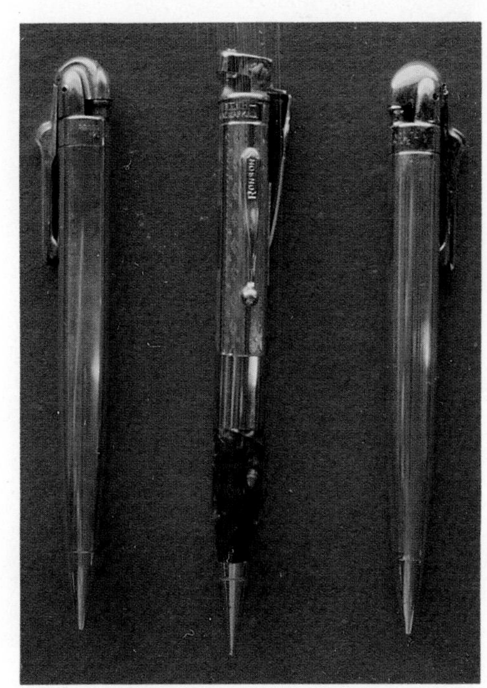

All Ronson Pencil Lighters

1. Royalite – Japan
2. Bowers
3. Continental – Japan
4. Ronson Whirlwind – Mack
5. Ritepoint
6. Pack Lite – Korea
7. Made in USA
8. Windette – Japan
9. Pack Lite – Korea

1. Maru Man Halley
2. - 9. (all) Ronson

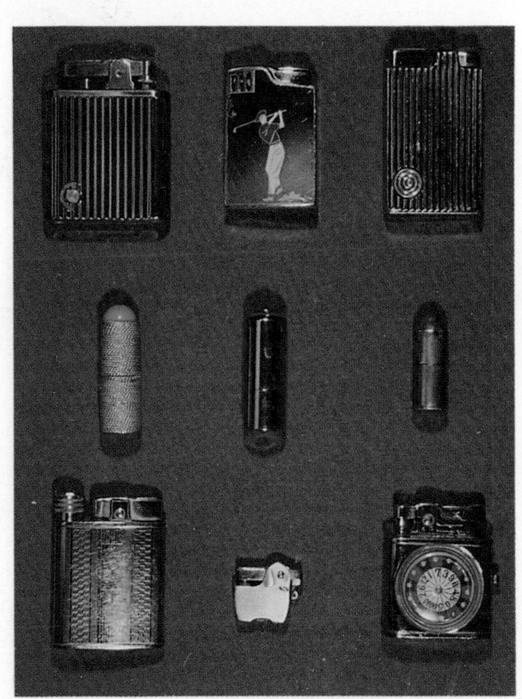

1. Musical
2. Hadson – Musical
3. Pac Musical
4. Florenza
5. Strike-a-lite
6. Japan
7. Duralux
8. Crown
9. Monte Carlo – Roulette Wheel

1. Coronet – Japan
2. Dundee – Japan
3. Japan
4. Rosen – Japan
5. Rolex – Japan
6. E.A.A. Inc. – Japan
7. Brother-Lite – Japan
8. Little Billboard
9. Playboy – Japan
10. Howard – Japan

1. Hesti
2. Continental
3. Wellington Balboa
4. Continental
5. Gal Par
6. Rolex
7. Elgin American
8. Ryan
9. Warco

1. Bentley
2. Bentley
3. Marxman
4. Modern Gas
5. Deluxe
6. Rogers
7. Globe - Musical
8. Elgin American
9. Penguin

1. Automatic Surelite
2. Firefly
3. Dura Light
4. Shalco
5. Japan
6. Colvair
7. Bowers – Stolen from Olsen & Johnson
8. Korea
9. Arrow Hologram

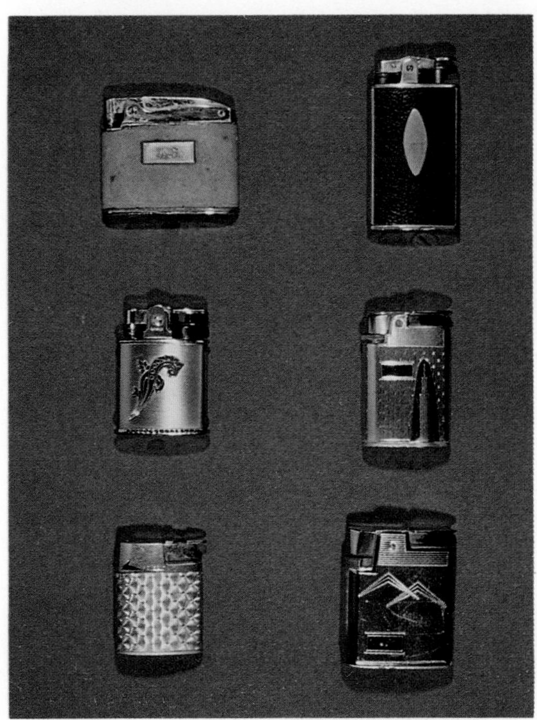

1. Ronson Adonis
2. Ronson Delight
3. Ronson Princess
4. Ronson Starfire Gas
5. Ronson Butane
6. Ronson Varaflame Standard

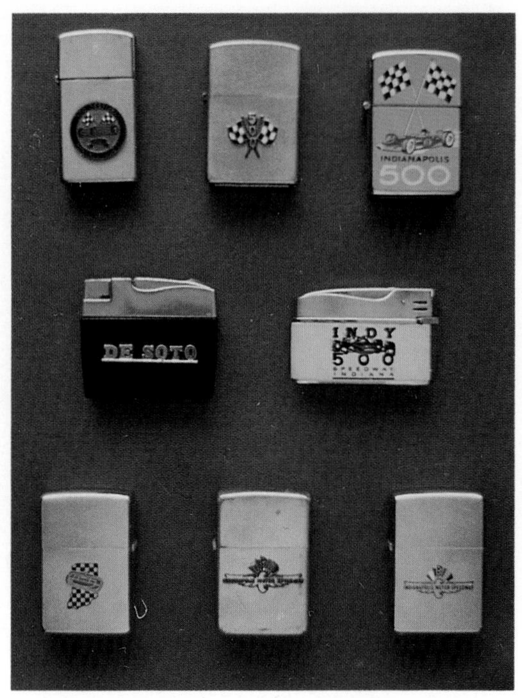

All Lighters Are Advertising The Indy 500

1. Idealine
2. Windsor
3. Japan
4. 1956 Pace Car
5. Noble Gas
6. Zippo, 1964
7. Zippo, 1946
8. Zippo, 1964

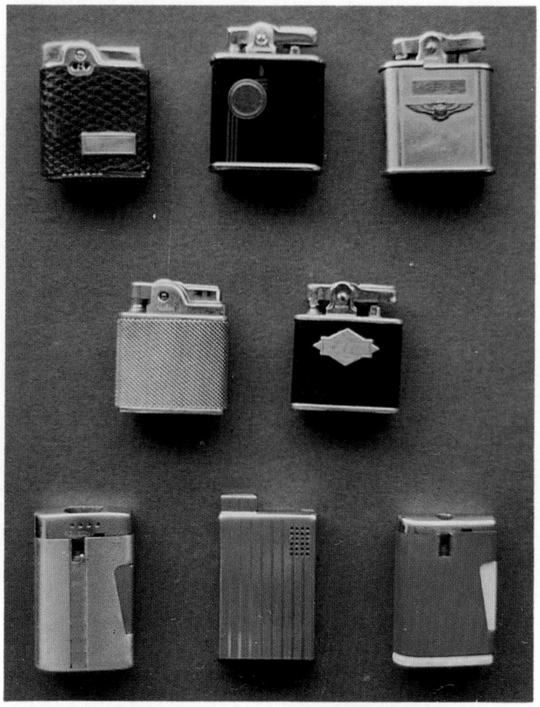

1. Ronson
2. Ronson Gas
3. Ronson
4. Ronson
5. Ronson
6. Ronson Gas
7. Ronson Gas
8. Ronson Gas

Top: Rouen
Bottom: Unknown

Top: Unknown
Bottom: Japan

Match King

The Match King

The Match King

Match King

Permanent Match –
Japan

U.S. Match Co.

1. Warner
2. Japan
3. Storm Master
4. Japan
5. Weso
6. Barlow
7. Rite Point
8. Hong Kong
9. Unknown

1. Hurricane F.O.E.
2. Golden Arrow
3. Franklin
4. Thorens

1. Royal Star
2. Brother-Lite
3. Seabury
4. Balboa
5. Little Billboard
6. Olympia Lite
7. Ryan
8. Sarome
9. Rolex

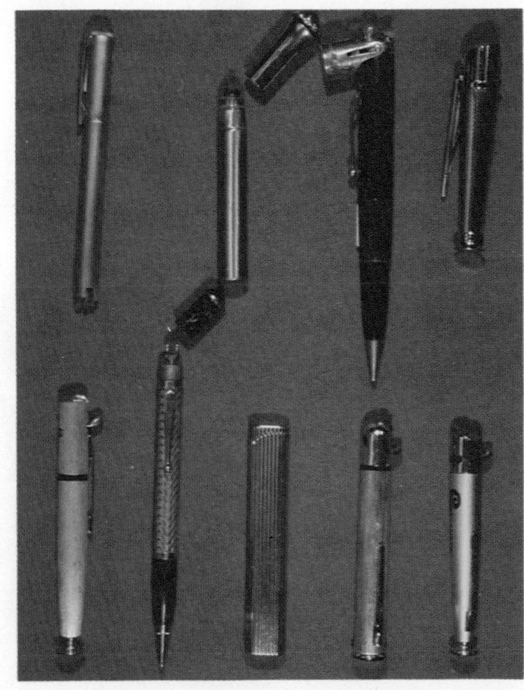

1. Colibri
2. Japan
3. Havalite
4. Super Clip
5. Crown Sangyo
6. Unknown
7. Capri
8. Flamex
9. Japan

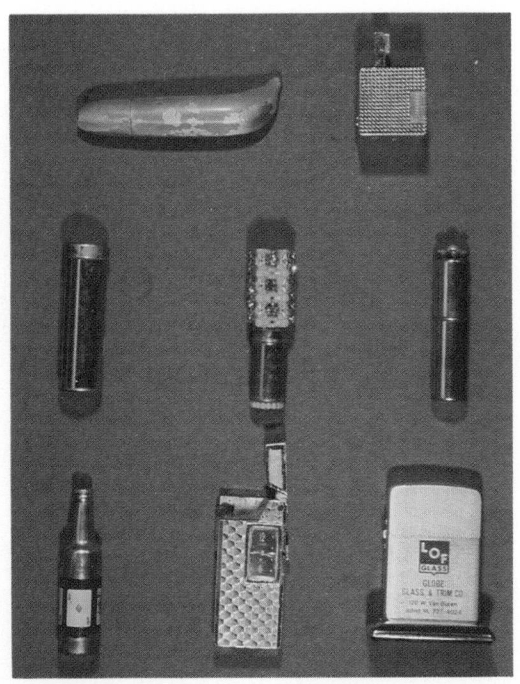

1. Banana
2. Ippag Dice
3. Japan
4. Japan
5. Hi-Glo
6. Kem
7. Swank with watch
8. Ad Table Lighter

1. Warren - Japan
2. 1982 Worlds Fair
3. Everready – Map of W. Germany
4. A.T.C. – Japan
5. Elgin American
6. Unknown
7. Nesor
8. Crown – Japan
9. Sunex – Korea

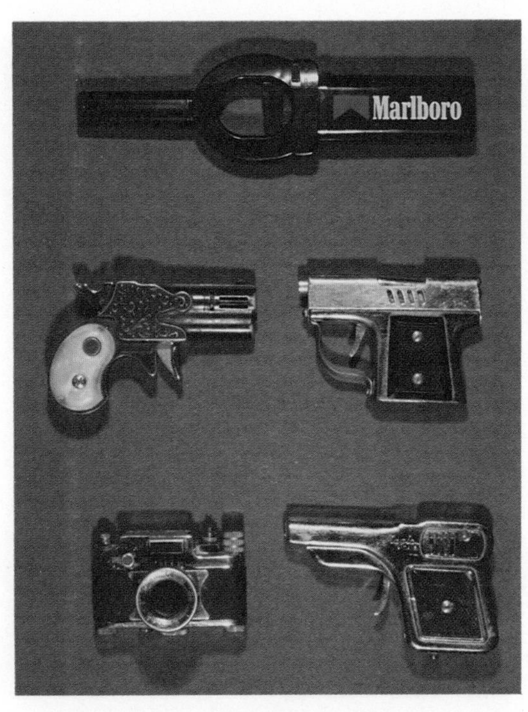

1. Japan
2. Mascot – Japan
3. Japan
4. Lucky Lite – Occ. Japan
5. Magic

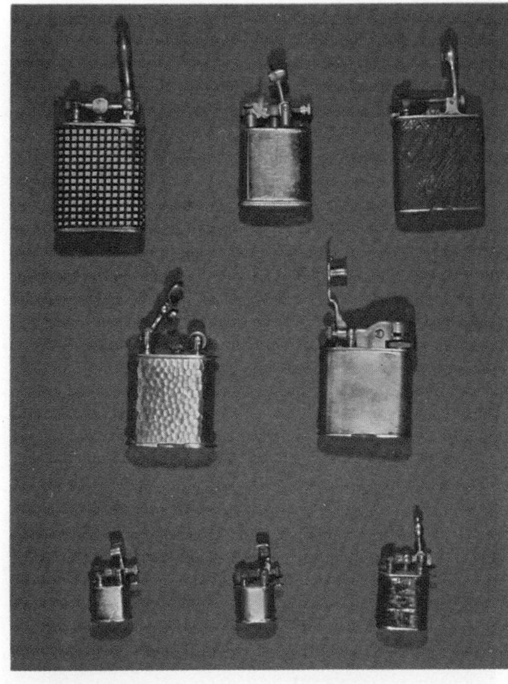

1. Unknown
2. Japan
3. Clark Firefly
4. Evans
5. Sterling Silver
6. Empress – Japan
7. Empress – Japan
8. Occupied Japan

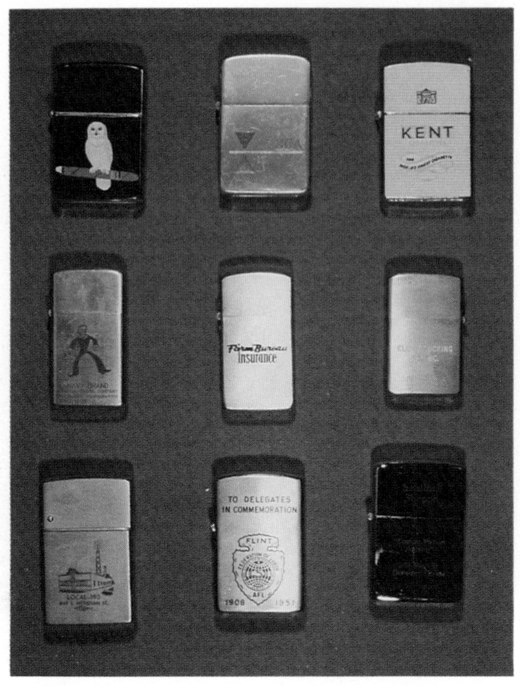

1. White Owl
2. Park-Alcoa
3. Hudson
4. Vulcan-Navybrand
5. Park
6. Windette Ellis Trucking
7. Windmaster
8. Barlow
9. Hi-Lite Sentinel Shoppe

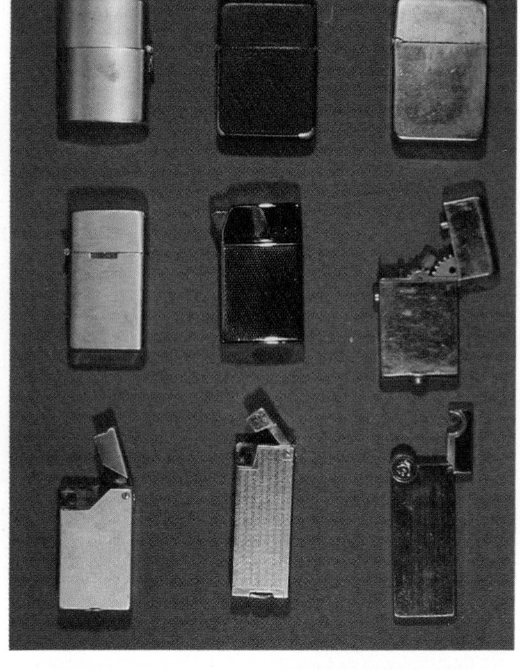

1. Elegant Occupied Japan
2. Matawan
3. Neff
4. Sovereign Nasco – Japa
5. Bentley
6. Hahway
7. Swing
8. Cygnus Japan
9. Japan

1. Custom Gas
2. Sterling Silver – Japan
3. PAC
4. Silver Inlay
5. Silver Inlay
6. Japan
7. American
8. Unknown
9. Unknown

1. Modern
2. Thames
3. Continental
4. Japan
5. Realite
6. Master Craft
7. Trickette
8. Japan
9. Playboy
10. Buxton

1. Japan
2. Sterling – Zippo inside
3. SHS – Silver
4. Unknown
5. Unknown
6. Unknown
7. Unknown – Sterling 950
8. Windsor – Japan
9. Japan
10. Japan
11. Japan

1. President – Japan
2. Ronson
3. The Windy
4. Royalite – Japan
5. Firebird – Korea
6. Supreme – Korea
7. Korea
8. ATC – Japan
9. Minex – Japan

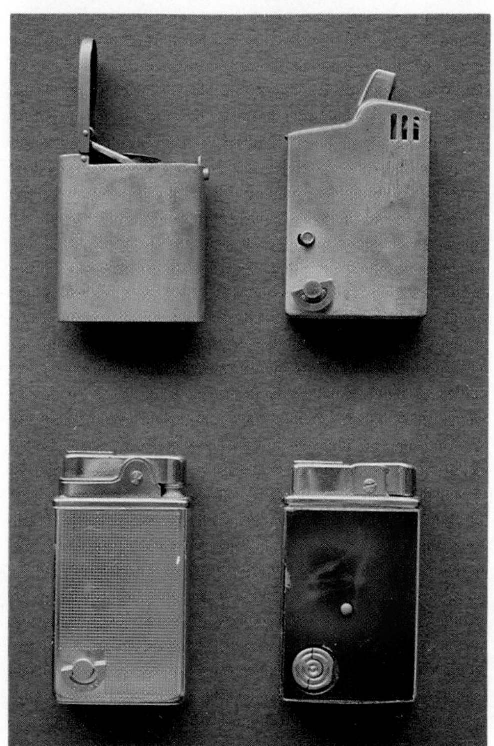

1. Lektrolite
2. Blue Bird – Japan Perry Como's Kraft Music Hall
3. Pacton – Japan Music Hall
4. Continental Music Lighter – Japan

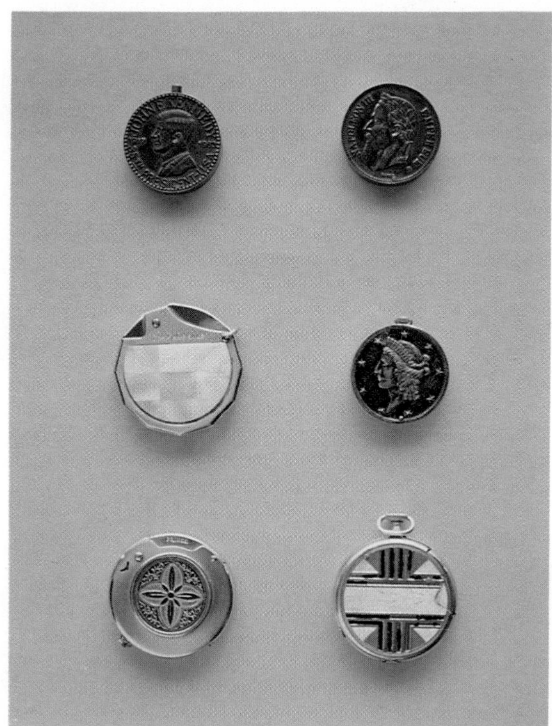

1. JFK – Japan
2. Napolean – Japan
3. Penguin Smile – Japan
4. Windsor – Japan
5. Prince (Rotary) – Japan
6. Unknown

COCA-COLA ADVERTISING LIGHTERS

Musical Lighter
White 1970's
Red 1950's

1. 1960's Scripto lighter
2. 1960's Lighter
3. 1950's Zippo lighter in box
4. 1950's Rosen lighter
5. 1960's Chatanooga Btgl. Co. Lighter
6. 1950's Bottle lighter, pull-apart
7. 1950 Dispoz.-A-Lite
8. 1950's Balboa lighter
9. 1950's Lighter
10. 1960's Lighter Par
11. 1960's Lighter Zippo applied bottle
12. 1960's Lighter Scripto
13. 1950's Lighter Rosen
14. 1960's Lighter Supreme

Courtesy of Collectors Guide to Coca-Cola, Al Wilson

1. Occupied Japan (mini)
3. Silver (Mexico)
5. Unknown
7. Golden Wheel (mini)

2. Marathon Co.
4. Unique – Dunhill (Swiss)
6. Empress – Japan (mini)

1. Crest-Craft – Japan
3. Vulcan – Japan
5. Vulcan – Japan
7. Beta One Hundred – Japan

2. Zippo 1987
4. Ronson (Cadet)
6. Jbelo Monopol
8. Zippo

The Giant
Bentley – Austria
Continental - CMC
ATC Super Deluxe – Japan
Brother Lite – Japan
1. Coronet – Japan

2. Unknown
4. Tarlton
6. Prince Gardner – Japan
8. Ronson
10. Ronson

1. Ronson
3. Hahway – German
5. Nimrod Pipe
7. Ronson
9. National Chemsearch
11. Champ – Austrian

2. Bowers
4. Bentley – Austrian
6. PAC – Japan
8. Swank – Japan
10. Ziama Cord – Japan
12. Deville – Japan

1. Supreme Sculptured
2. Supreme Sculptured
3. Supreme Sculptured
4. USS Alamo
5. Sarome
6. Morlite
7. Japan
8. Japan
9. Korea

1. Wind Master
2. Scripto-Butane
3. L.D.L.
4. Idealine
5. Idealine
6. Wellington Junior
7. Park
8. USA
9. Hava Liter

1. Barlow
2. Berkeley
3. Continental – Japan
4. Flamex Slimlite – Japan
5. Rogers – Japan
6. Storm King
7. Reliance Pipe – Japan
8. Champ – Austria
9. Rogers – Japan

1. Park
2. Japan
3. P.M. USA
4. Park
5. Wellington
6. Penguin
7. Park
8. USA
9. Japan

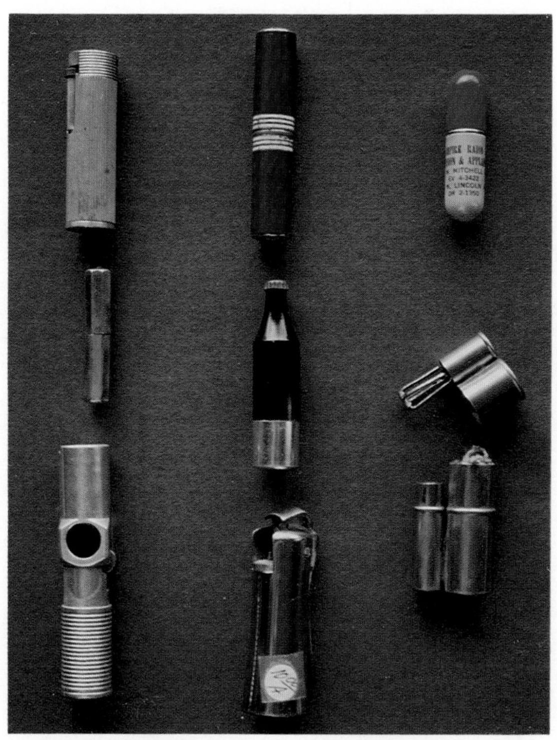

1. Automet
2. Weston
3. Allbright
4. Japan
5. Unknown
6. Unknown
7. Nimrod Pipeliter
8. Ronson

1. Park Lighter
2. Unknown (Winston)
3. Korea (Camel)
4. Park Lighter (Autolite)
5. Continental – Japan (L&M)
6. Park Lighter (AAA)
7. Shaw-Barton – Japan
8. Park Lighter (RCA)
9. Austria (Heineken)

1. Evans Trig-a-Lite
2. Kwik - Fil by Continental
3. Globe – Japan
4. Evans
5. Ruby
6. Longins – Tokyo Japan
7. Continental CMC
8. Kreisler
9. Lansing - Japan
10. Rogers
11. Japan
12. Berkeley

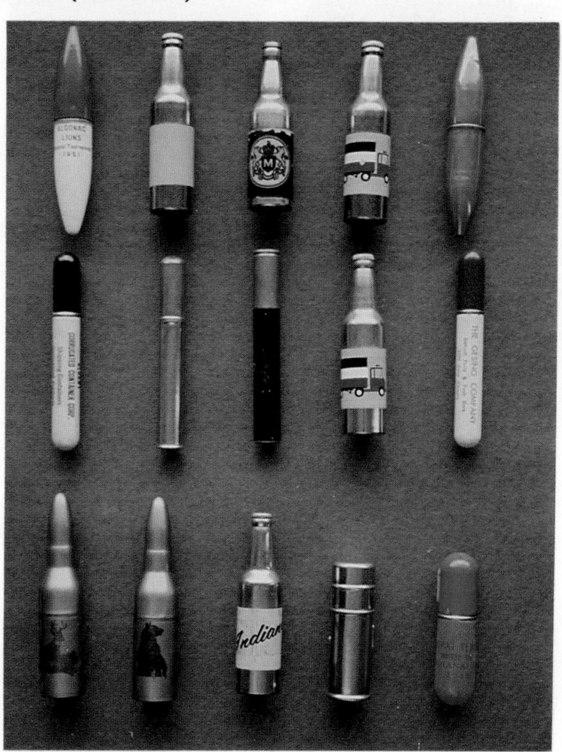

1. Unknown (Algonac Lions)
2. Kem Co.
3. Unknown (Royal Amber)
4. Kem Co.
5. Unknown
6. Redilite
7. Unknown
8. Redilite – City Service
9. Kem Co.
10. Redilite
11. Kem
12. Kem
13. Kem co.
14. Bowers – Rope
15. Strikalite

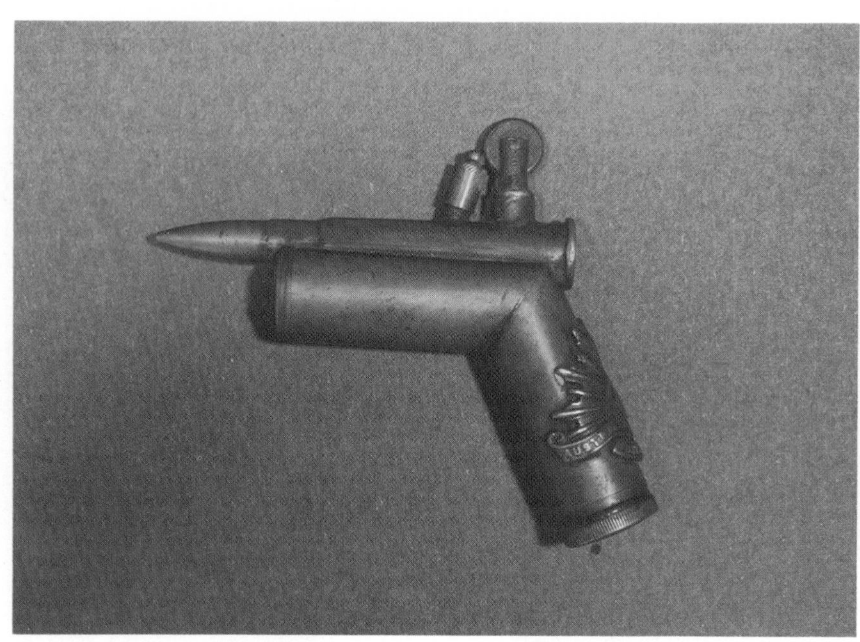

Australia Commonwealth Military Force
4 inches long

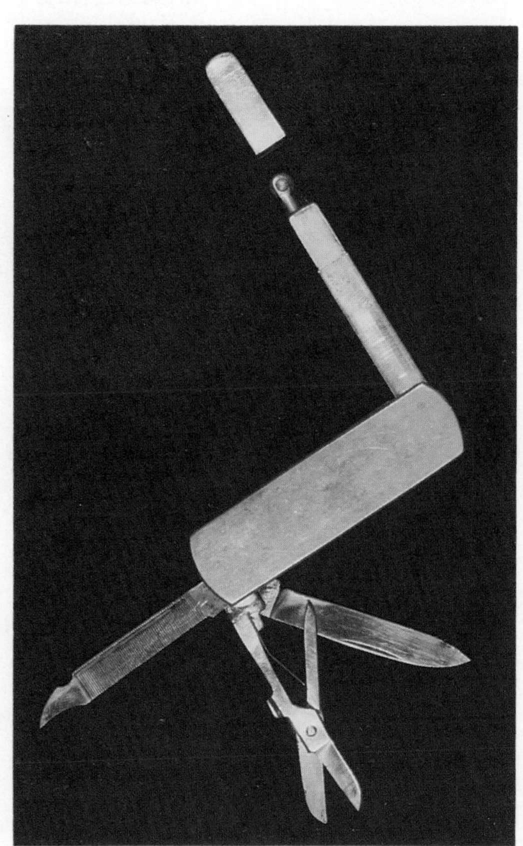

Unknown

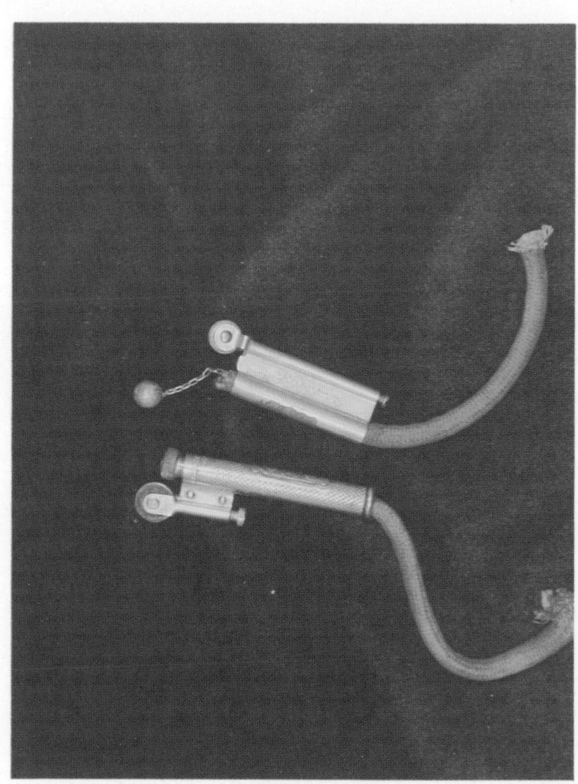

Top: Dunhill Sterling
Bottom: Briquet Tempete Depose

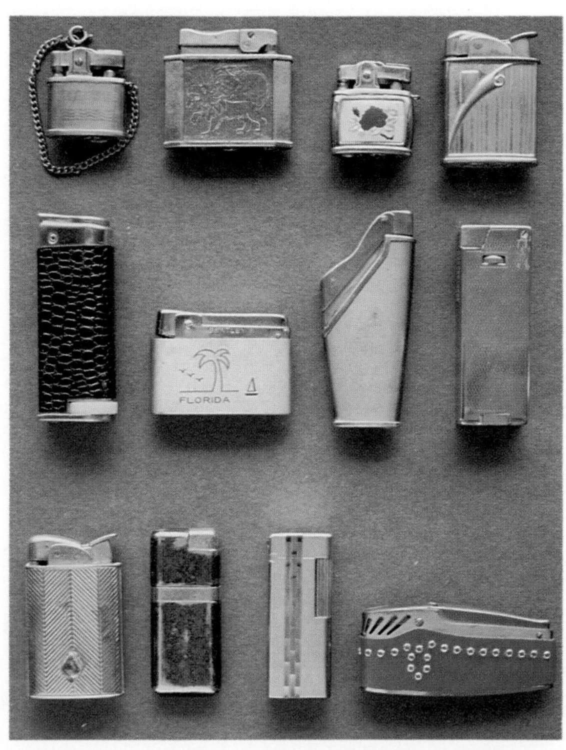

1. Royal Star - Japan
2. Rogers – Japan
3. Penguin
4. Evans
5. Champ Ariel – Austria
6. Bentley – Austria
7. Crown Harp – Japan
8. Hamilton (Deville) – Japan
9. Evans
10. Colibri – Japan
11. Nesor – Japan
12. Prince Gardner – Japan

1. Kreisler
2. Beattie Jet Lighter
3. Colibri by Kreisler
4. Evans
5. Ronson
6. Kreisler
7. SMC – Japan
8. Omega – Japan
9. Modern (Modernlite) – Japan
10. Prince – Japan
11. Brother – Japan
12. Gas Lite – M'Boro

1. Little Billboard – Japan
2. Japan
3. Storm Master
4. Vu-Lighter by Scripto – Canada
5. Barlow
6. Korea
7. Adver. Barnes – Detroit
8. Scripto

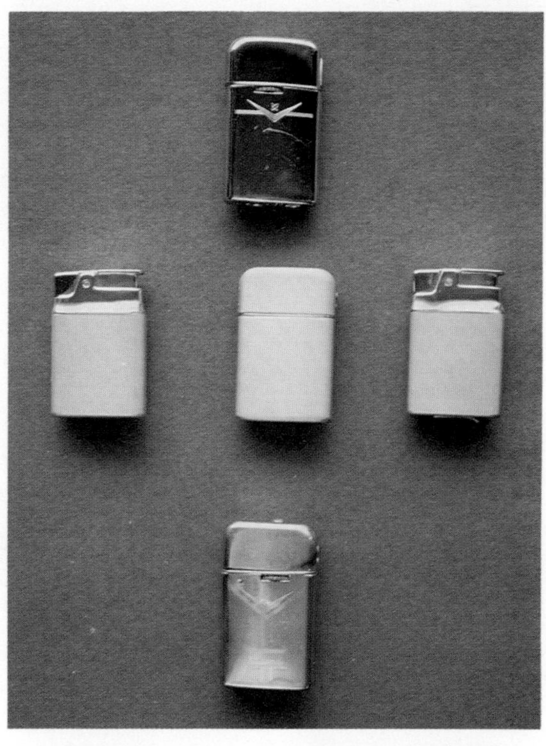

1. Ronson
2. Ronson Pioneer
3. Ronson Typhoon
4. Ronson Pioneer
5. Ronson

Windsor

Storm Master

1. Evans
2. Evans International Date Line
3. Ronson - Capri
4. Pigeon
5. Ronson Princess
6. Pereline - Japan

Unknown (very early)

1. Conty
2. Zippo
3. Windmaster
4. Unknown
5. Japan "W"
6. Penguin Mate

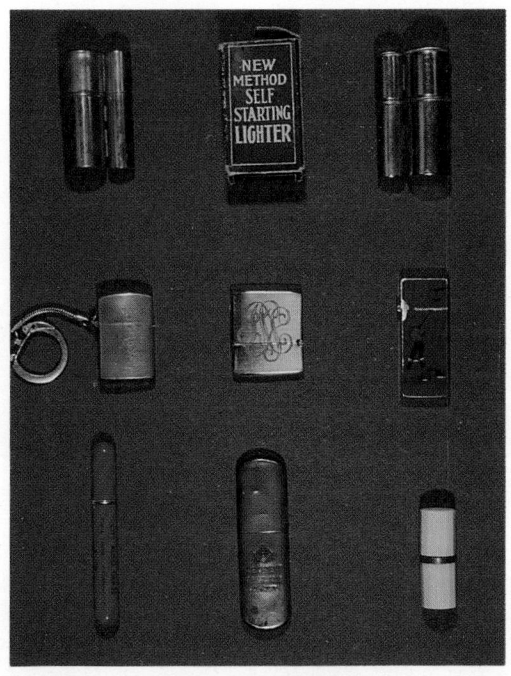

1-3. New Method
4. Japan
5. Japan
6. Penguin
7. USA City Auto Glass
8. MB 1912
9. Glo-Lite

1. Match King – Edwin Cigar
2. Denturaids
3. Permanent Match
4. Match King – 1933 Century of Progress
5. Nude
6. Vogue
7. Japan
8. Permanent Match
9. Fire Chief

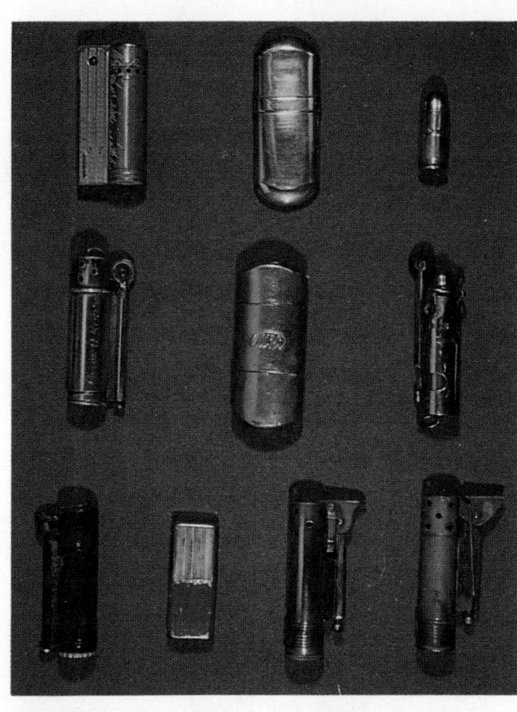

1. IMCO
2. USA
3. Bullet U.S.C.C.D.
4. Dunhill Sterling Silver
5. K-W
6. Occupied Japan
7. Dunhill
8. Strike-A-Lite
9. Austria
10. Austria

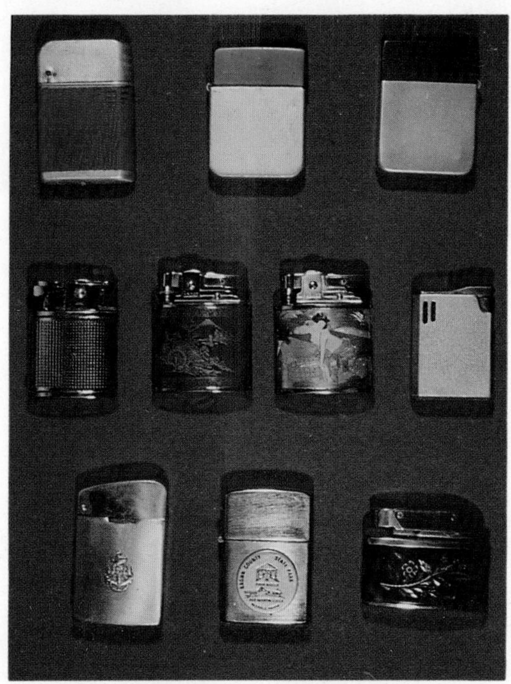

1. Bowers
2. Berkeley
3. Berkeley
4. Kalman
5. Prince
6. Prince
7. Firebird
8. Zaima
9. Aro
10. Consul

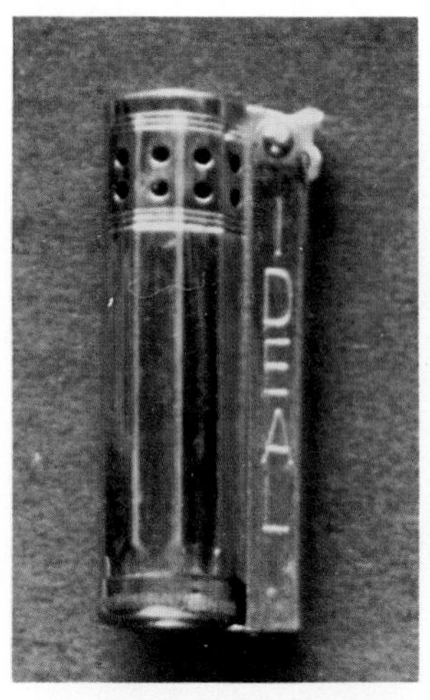

Ideal – W. Germany

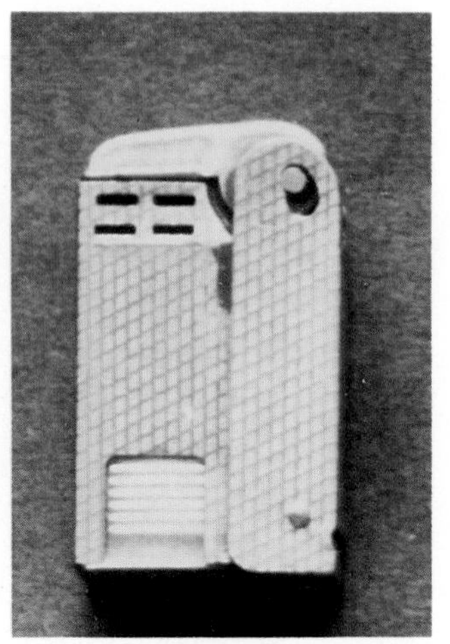

Regens

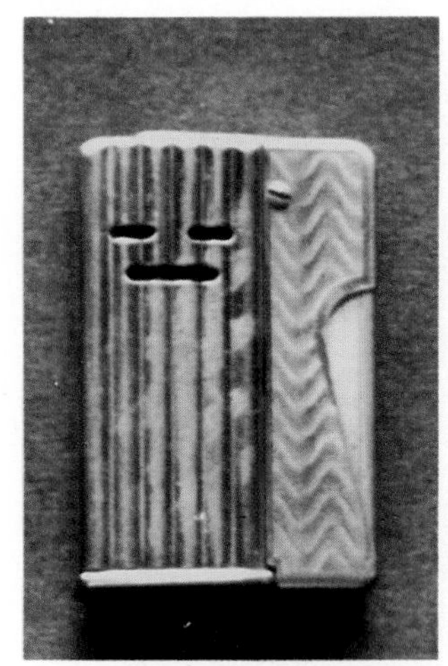

Karat – Austria

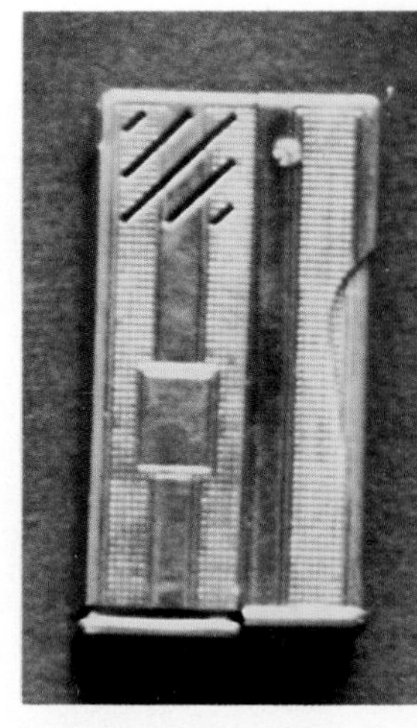

Karat 99 – Austria

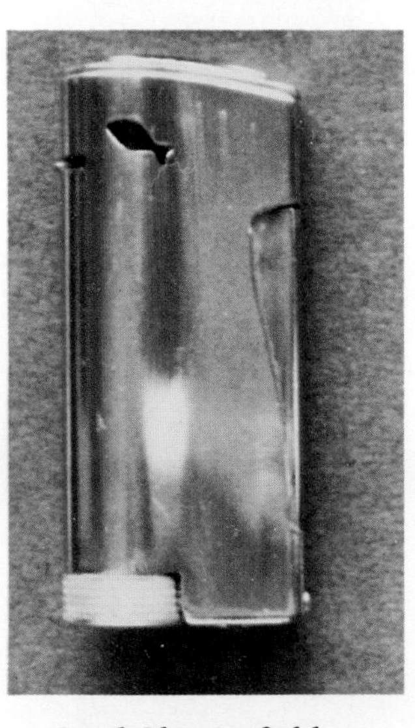

Lord Chesterfield – Japan

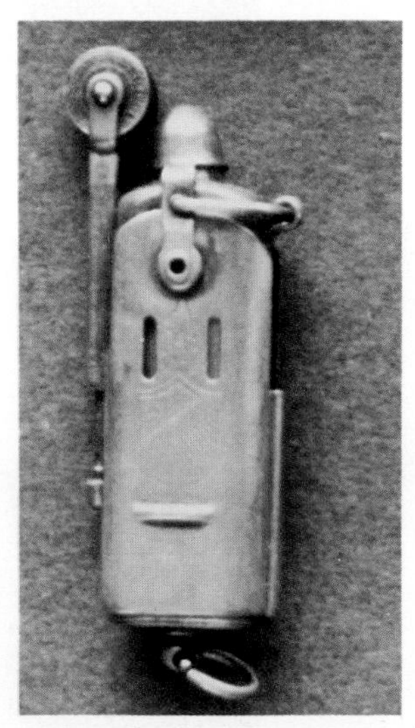

Bowers

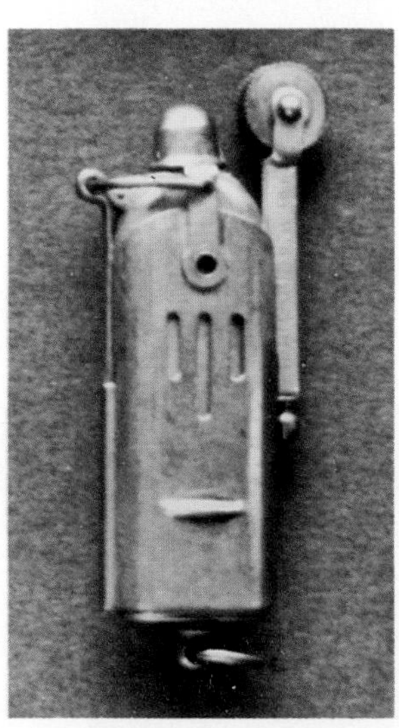

Bowers

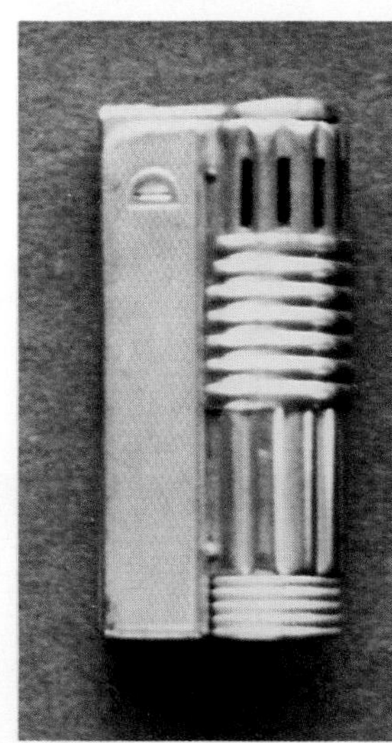

Imco Triple X – Austri

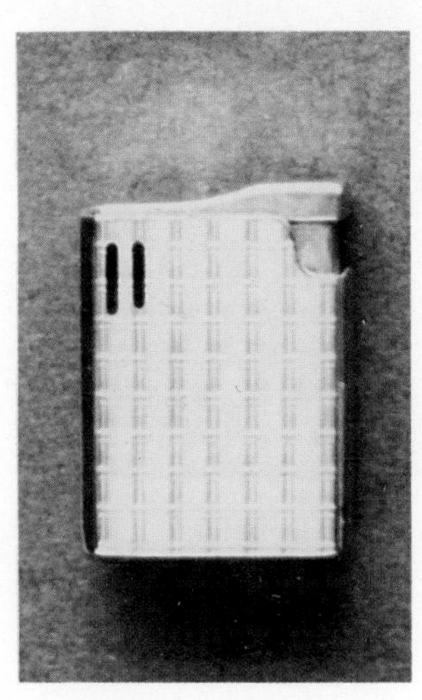

Colibri – Japan

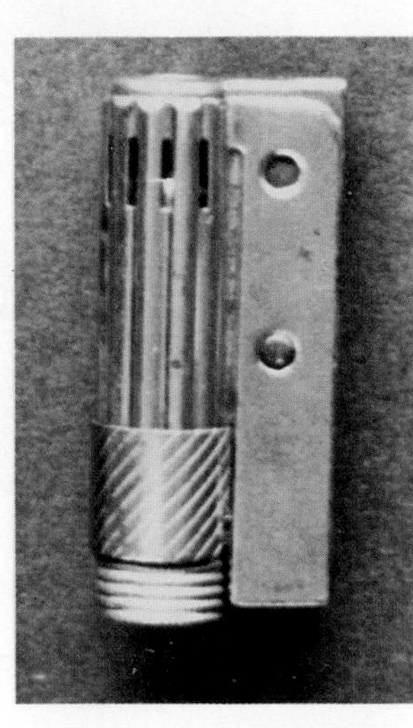

Triple X – French Zone – Austria

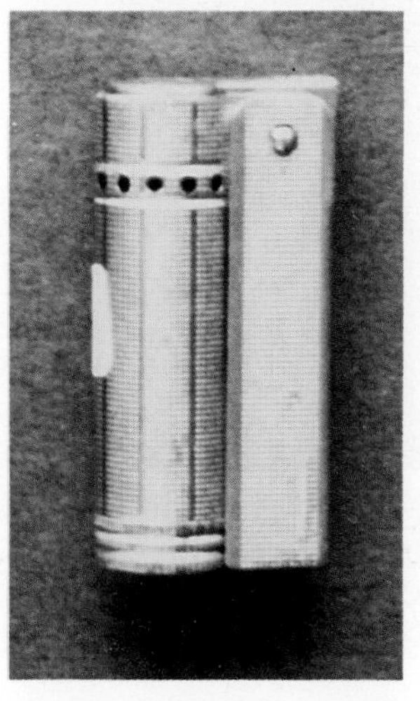

Imco – Triple X Junior – Austria

Clinton – Austria

1973 Zippo

1977 Zippo

1975 Zippo

1935 Zippo

1968 Zippo

1976 Zippo

1952 Zippo

1991 Zippo

1965 Zippo

1948 Zippo

1952 Zippo

1977 Zippo

1958 Zippo

1968 Zippo

1962 Zippo

1963 Zippo

1967 Zippo

1. Zippo 1977
2. Zippo 1979
3. Zippo 1953
4. Zippo 1992
5. Zippo 1991
6. Zippo 1972
7. Zippo 1966 – Air Force
8. Zippo 1954 – Marines
9. Zippo 1955

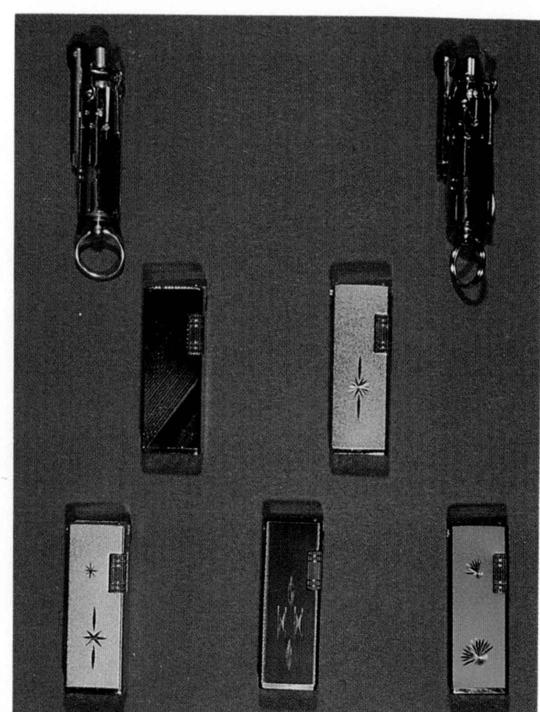

All New 1992

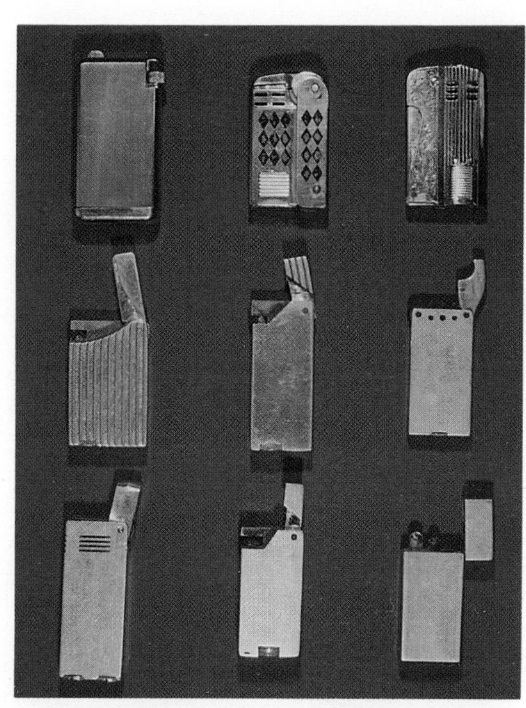

1. Parker Pen
2. Regens
3. Corona – Made in Occupied Japan
4. Aluminum
5. Aluminum
6. Ampg Alum.
7. General Research
8. Aluminum
9. Knapp Aluminum

1. Gas Can
2. B & R
3. Schick
4. Evans
5. Korea
6. Evans
7. Japan
8. Japan
9. Japan

All Lighters Above Are 1993 Zippos

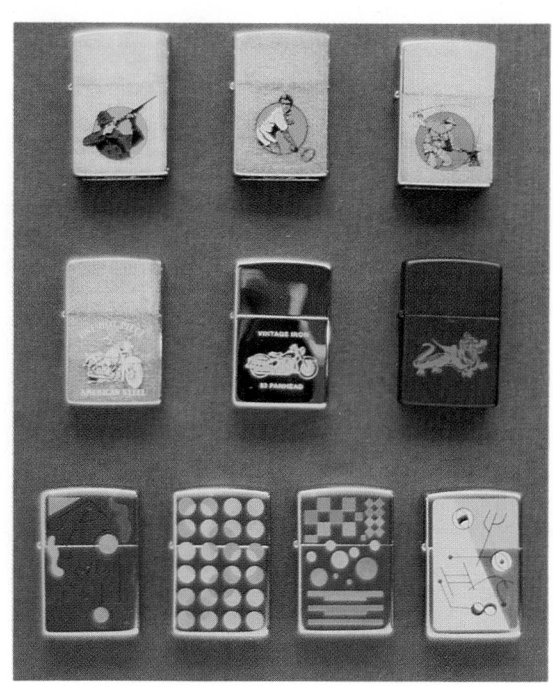

All Lighters Above Are 1993 Zippos

All Lighters Above Are 1993 Zippos

1. Zippo, 1957
2. Zippo, 1978
3. Zippo, 1962
4. Zippo, 1960
5. Zippo, 1990
6. Zippo, 1962
7. Zippo, 1989
8. Zippo, 1990

1. Zippo 1985 – Masonic
2. Zippo 1960 – Maccabees
3. Zippo 1962 – U.S.S. Liddle
4. Zippo 1960
5. Zippo 1946
6. Zippo 1958
7. Zippo 1992
8. Zippo 1992
9. Zippo 1989

1. Toral
2. Bic Pipe Reamer
3. Feudor
4. Scripto – China
5. Popeye
6. Korea
7. Jehvani

All lighters in this picture are gas

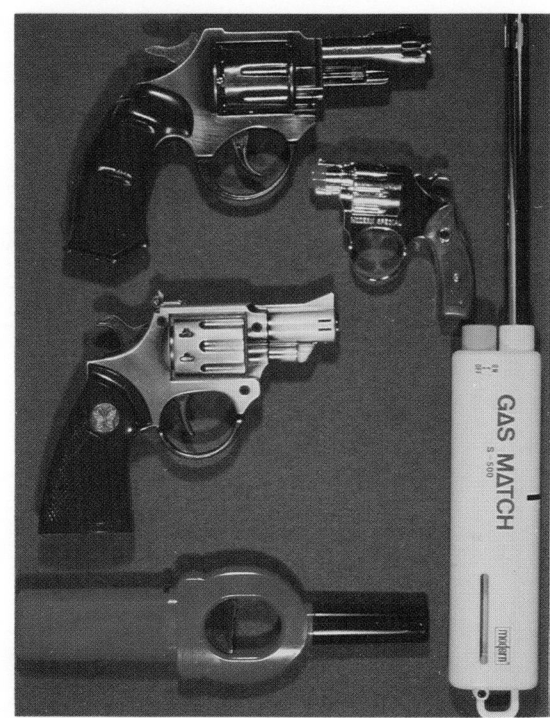

1. Super Magnum Gun
2. Modern Special Gun
3. JS 38 Gun
4. Gas Match
5. T.C. – Japan

All lighters in this picture are gas

1. Modern
2. Japan
3. Lip-Lite
4. Japan
5. Cowboy – Korea
6. Japan

All lighters in this picture are gas

Top: Evans
Bottom: Evans

Top: Occupied Japan
Bottom: Idealine Award Lighter
for WPTA-TV, Fort Wayne, IN

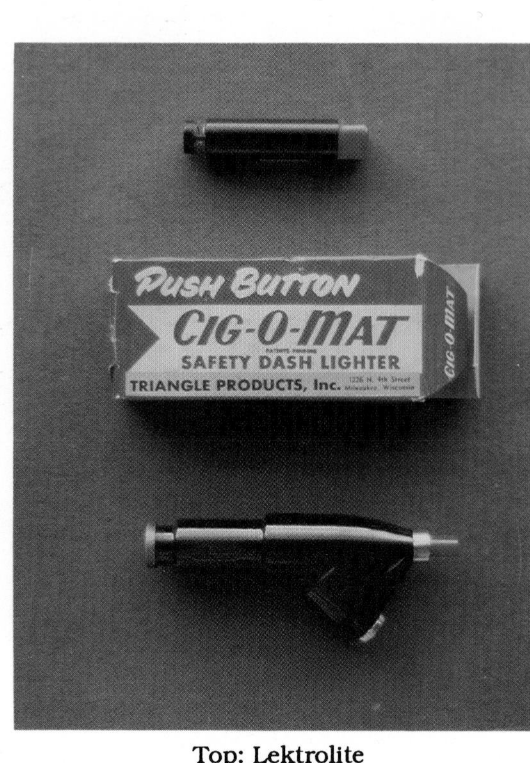

Top: Lektrolite
Bottom: Cig-O-Mat

1. Red Devil's Lighter Fluid Can
2. Spotlight Lighter Fluid Can
3. Texaco Lighter Fluid Can

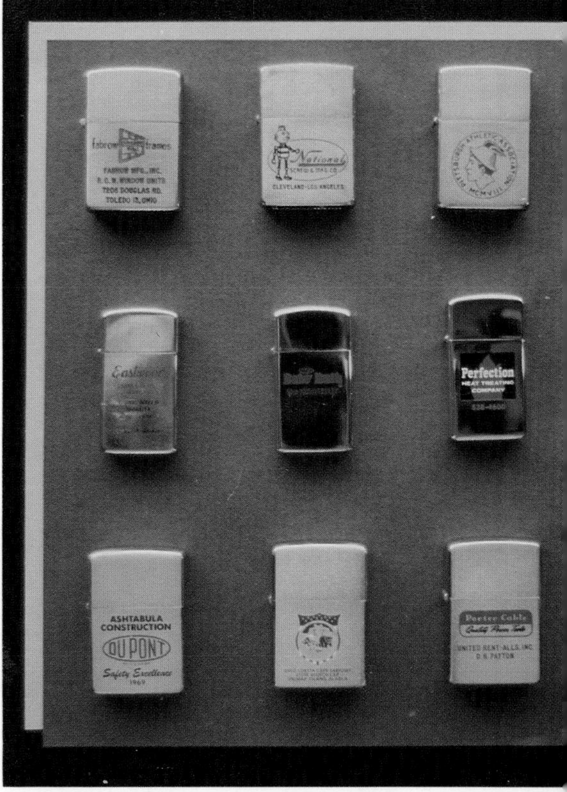

1. Zippo, 1948
2. Zippo, 1963
3. Zippo,
4. Zippo, 1980
5. Zippo, 1971
6. Zippo,
7. Zippo, 1968
8. Zippo, 1970
9. Zippo,

Top: Strikalite Bottom: Strikalite

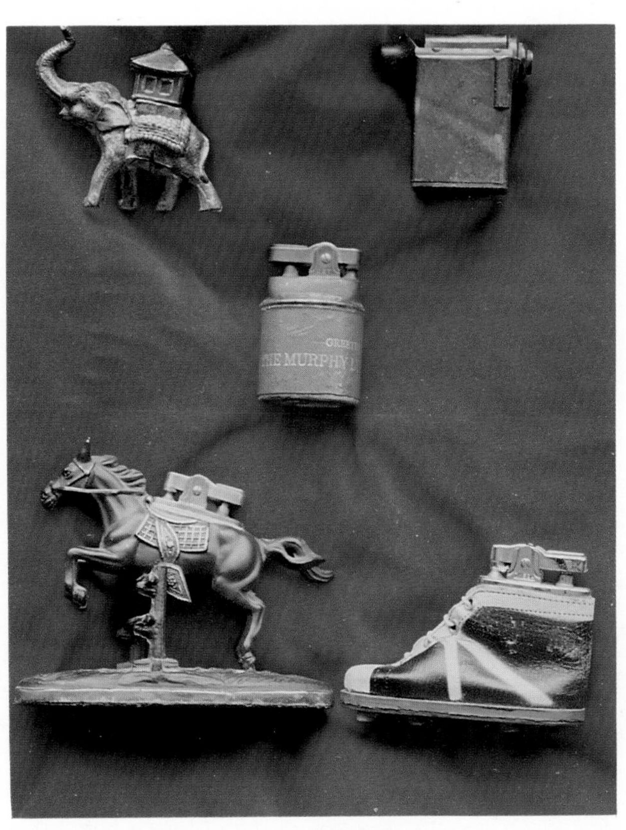

1. Japan 2. USA
3. Jet - Japan
4. Japan 5. Omega

. Cont-Lite – Occupied Japan
. Royal Cart
. Marbo-Lite – Japan
. GE (General Electric)
5. Magna W-Lite (German)
6. Ramba w/watch
7. Auer w/tape

Japan (both)

Thorens

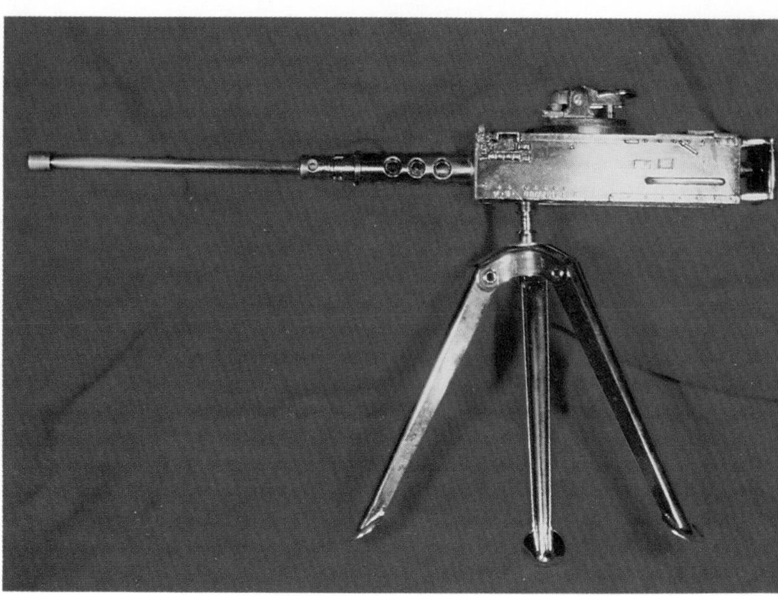

Browning Automatic Rifle - Japan

Japan Sports Series

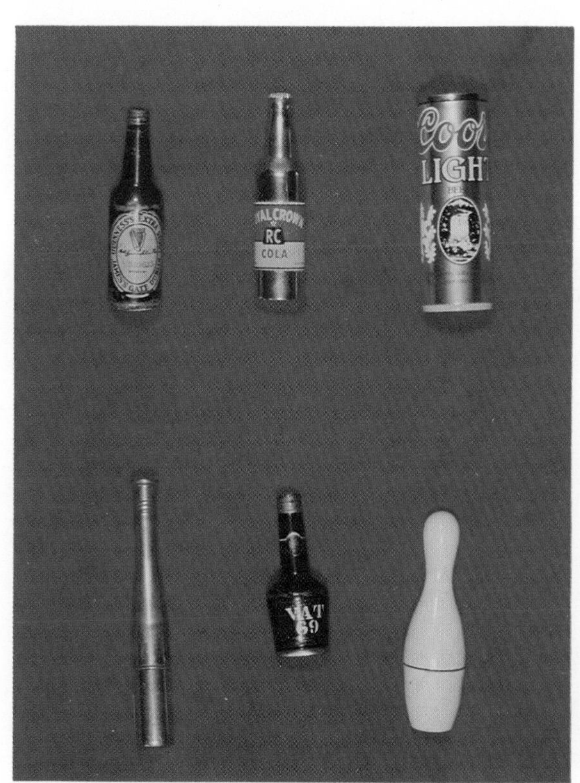

1. Germany
2. Kem Co.
3. Beer Light - Japan
4. The Big Leaguer
5. Prince
6. Kem Inc.

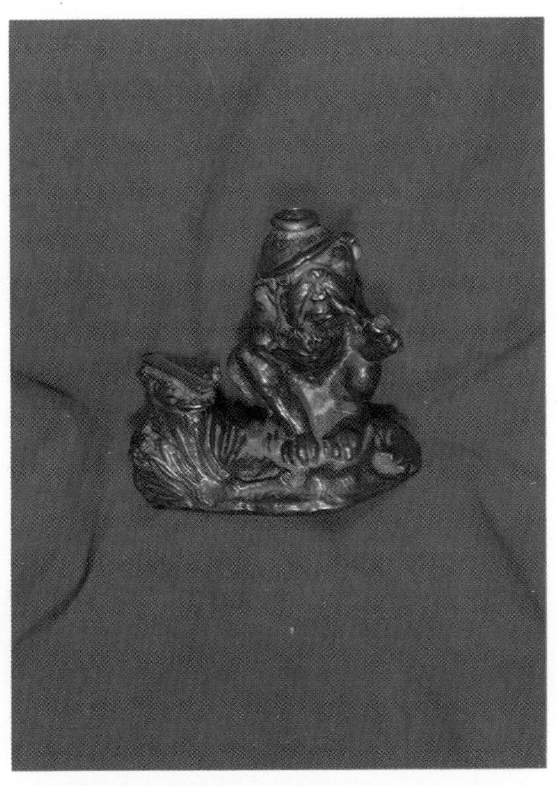

Bulldog Striker – (Sherlock Holmes?)

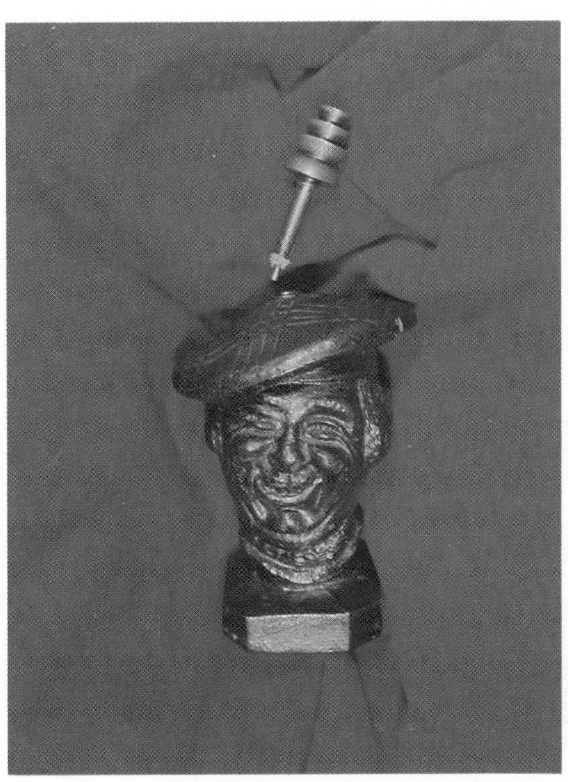

Golfer Striker

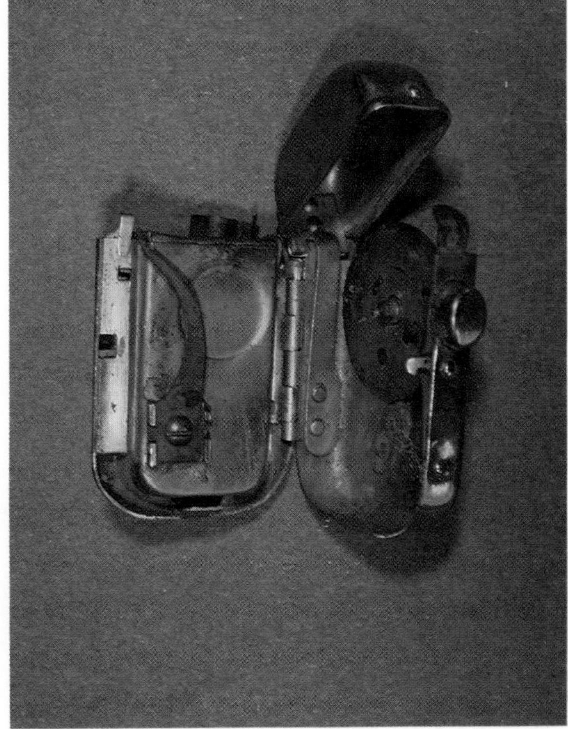

Magic Pocket Lamp – Koomans Patent 1889

All Lighters Above Are Korean

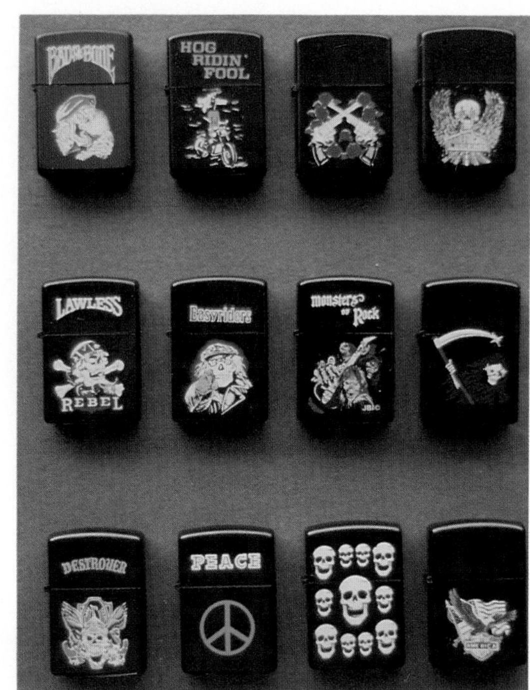

All Above Lighters Are Korean

1. Japan
2. Japan
3. Japan
4. Japan

"Kwik-Lite" Lighter Fluid Can, 1929

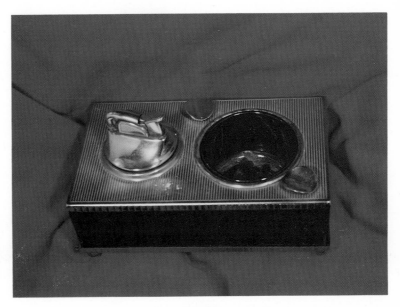

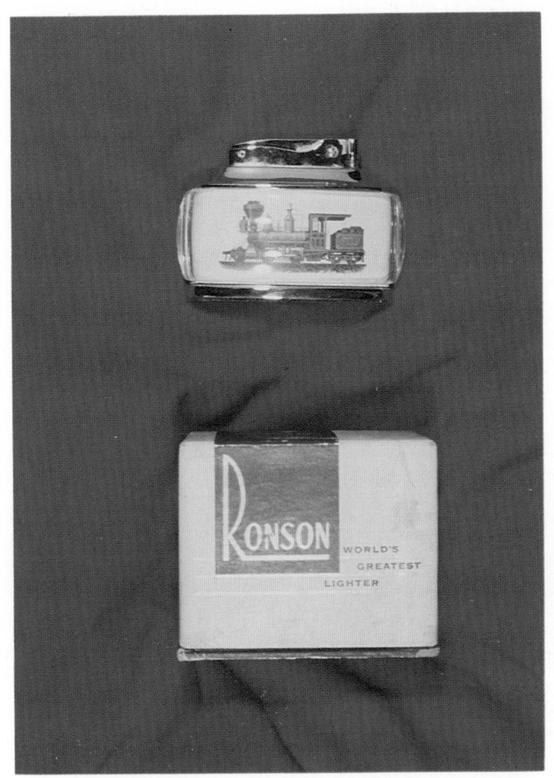

Ronson Trophy with box

Evans

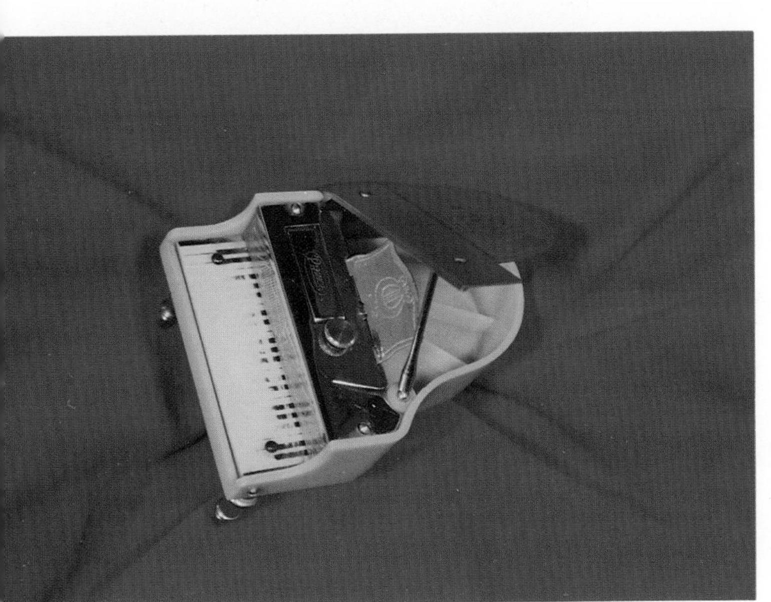

Made in Occupied Japan (Prince)

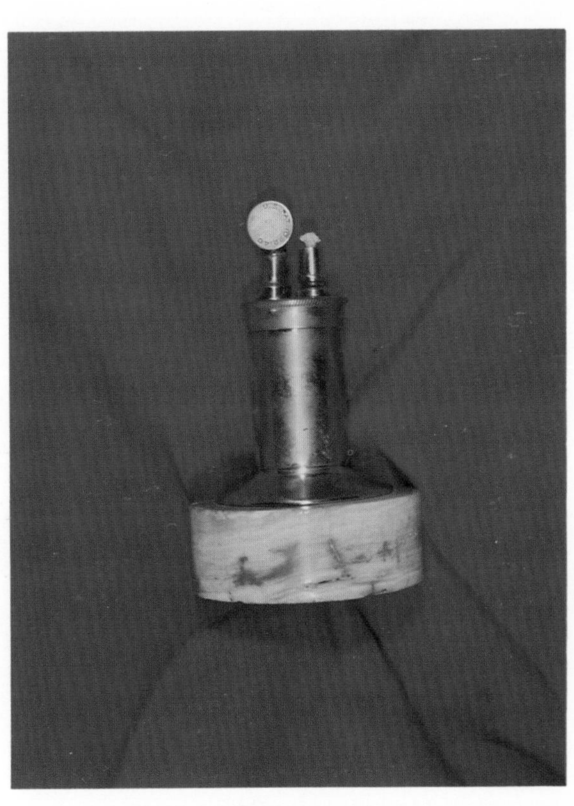

Unknown

1. Japan 2. Evans
3. Evans 4. MTC – Japan

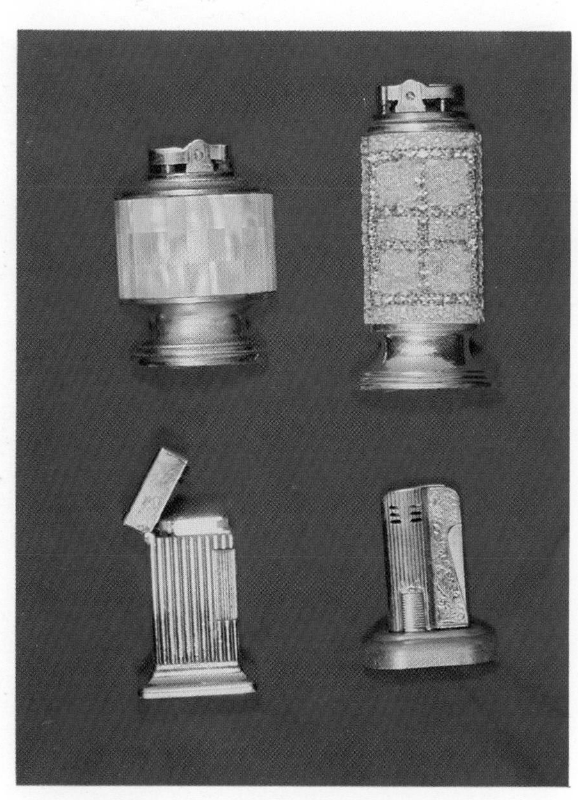

1. Marhill 2. Trickette
3. Parker 4. Made in Occupied Japan

1. Japan 2. Japan
3. Japan (Wood) 4. Made in Occupied Japan

1. Penguin – Japan
2. Occupied Japan
3. Continental – Occupied Japan

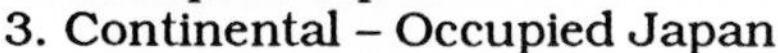

Japan

Japan

1. Unknown WWI
2. Unknown WWI
3. Unknown WWI
4. USA WWII

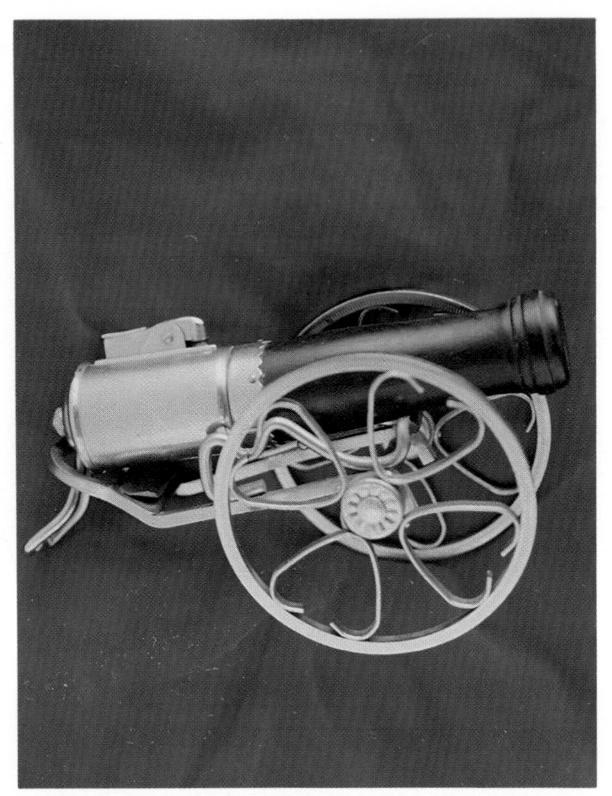

Japan

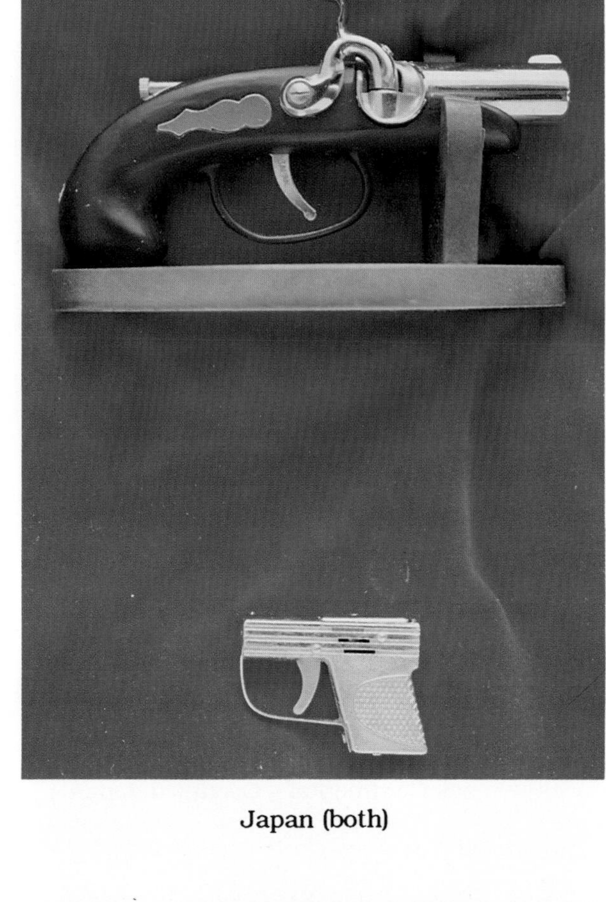

Japan (both)

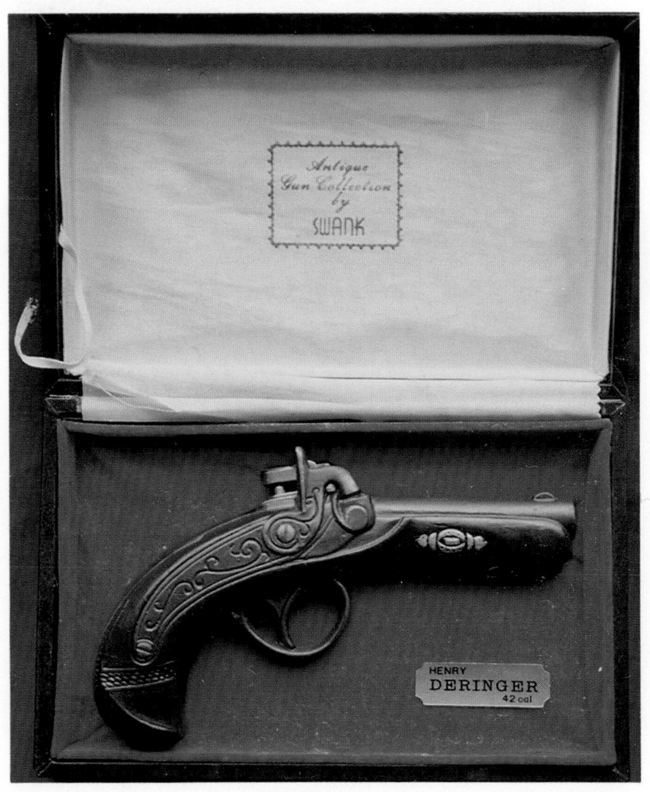

Swank

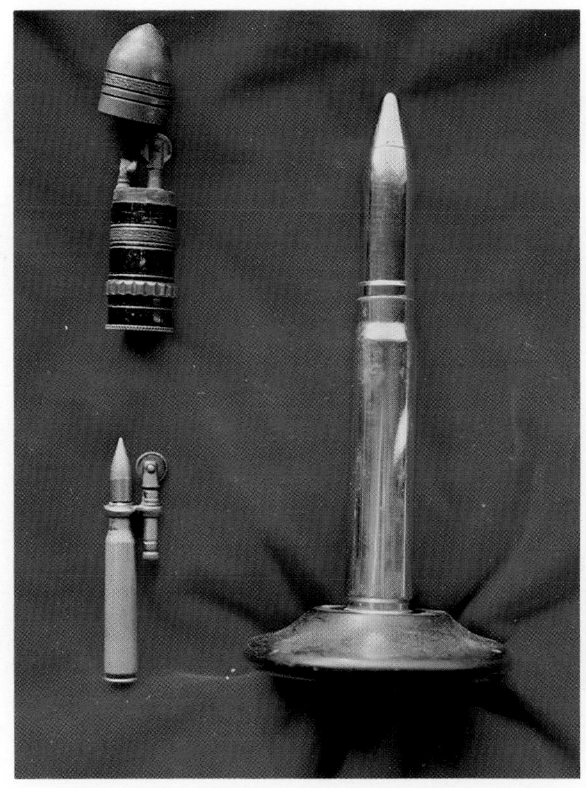

Top left: French Shell – France
Bottom left: P.C. Co., Pat. Dec. 23, 1919
Bottom right: Edas

Top: Japan (both)
Middle: USA (both)
Bottom left: Occupied Japan Bottom right: USA

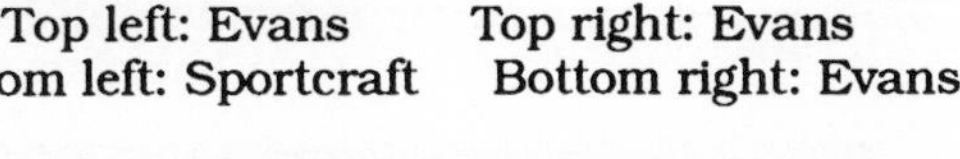

Top left: Evans Top right: Evans
Bottom left: Sportcraft Bottom right: Evans

Top set: Ronson
Bottom set: West German

Top set: Wedgewood Bone China – England – Florentine
Bottom left: Penguin – Japan
Bottom right: Orlik – France

Top left: Evans Top right: Japan
Bottom left: Unified Bottom right: Ronson Varaflame Saturn

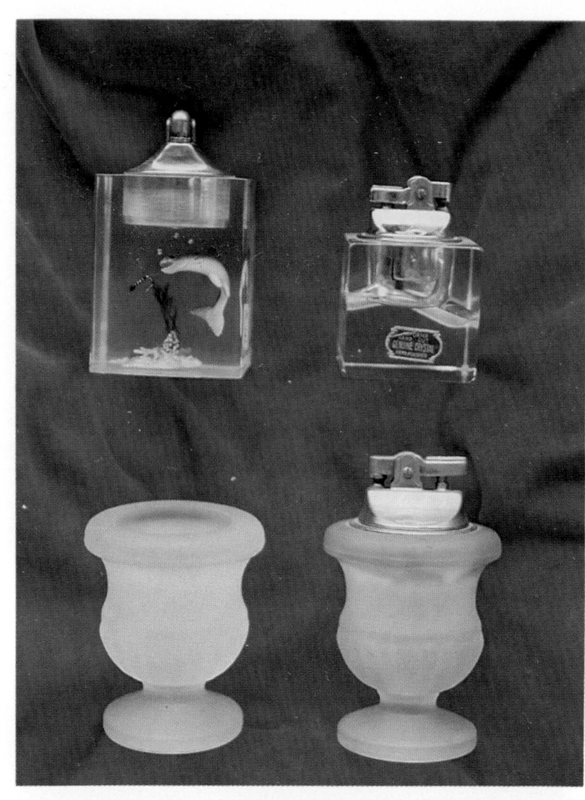

Top left: Evans Top right: Japan
Bottom: Japan

Top: Evans Bottom: Japan

Scripto

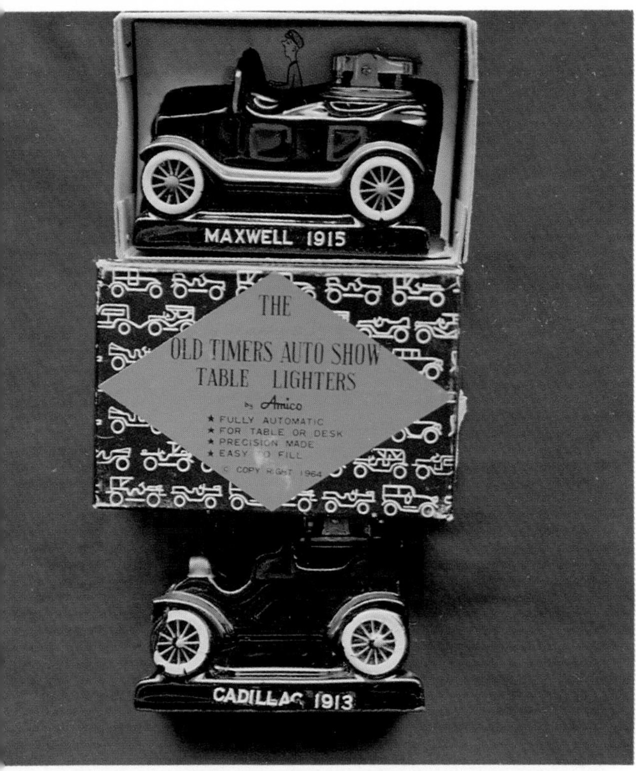

Top: Amico – Japan
Bottom: Amico – Japan
o made in a 1908 Ford, 1913 Cadillac, 1909 Stanley
amer, 1905 Packard, 1915 Maxwell. Also made in mis-
laneous trains.

Nesor

Top: Art Mark – Japan
Bottom: Japan

Top left: Am Leatherline – Japan
Top right: Dabs – Japan
Bottom left: Ronson – Leona
Bottom right: Japan

Top left: Penguin Top right: Vu Lighter by Scripto
Bottom: Japan (Ross) – Gas Lucite

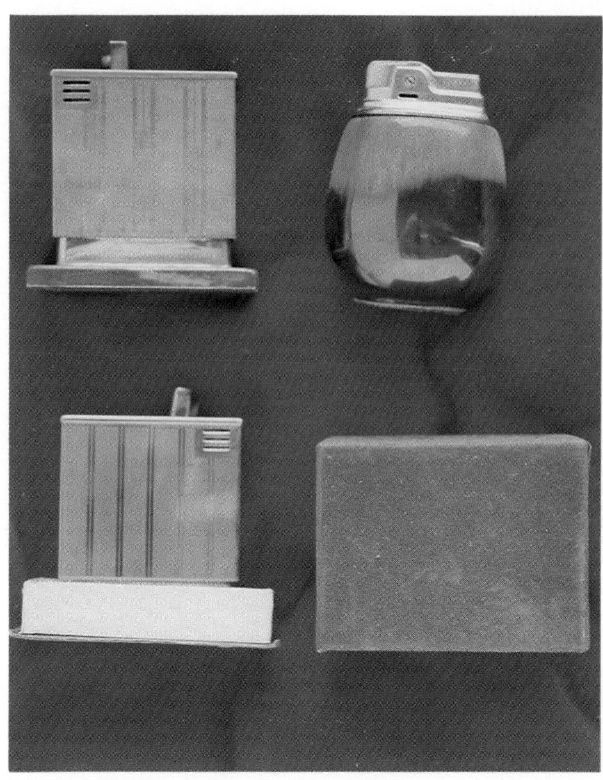

Top left: Lifto-Lite Top right: Ronson
Bottom: Lifto-Lite

Top left: Fortune – Japan Top right: Unknown
Bottom left: Bic Bottom right: Japan

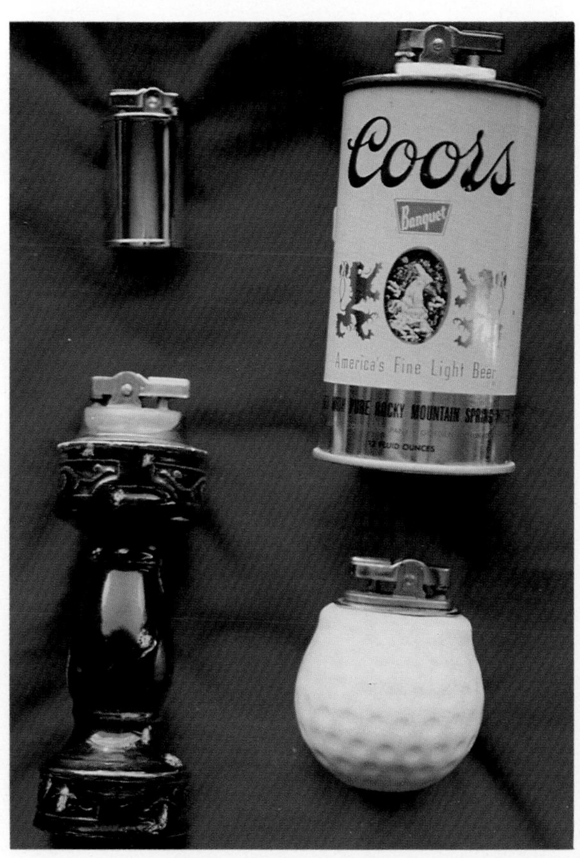

Top (both): Japan
Bottom (both): Japan

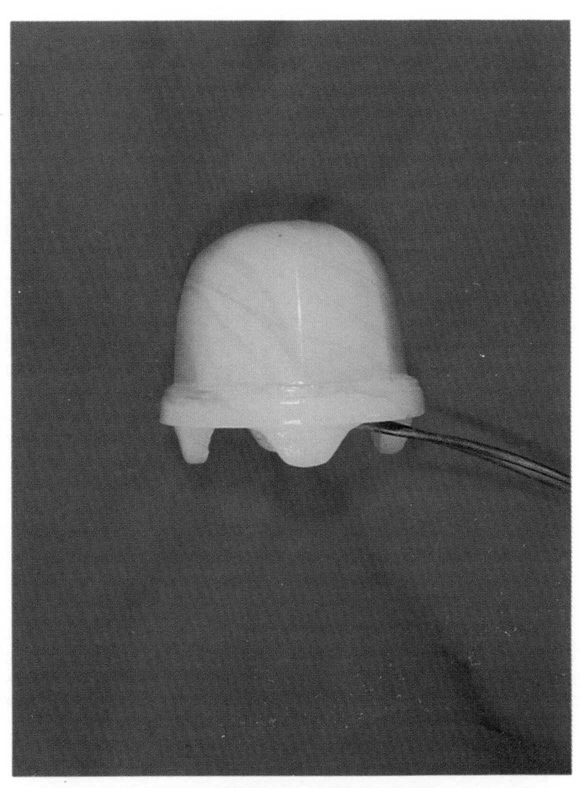

Unknown - Akro Agate

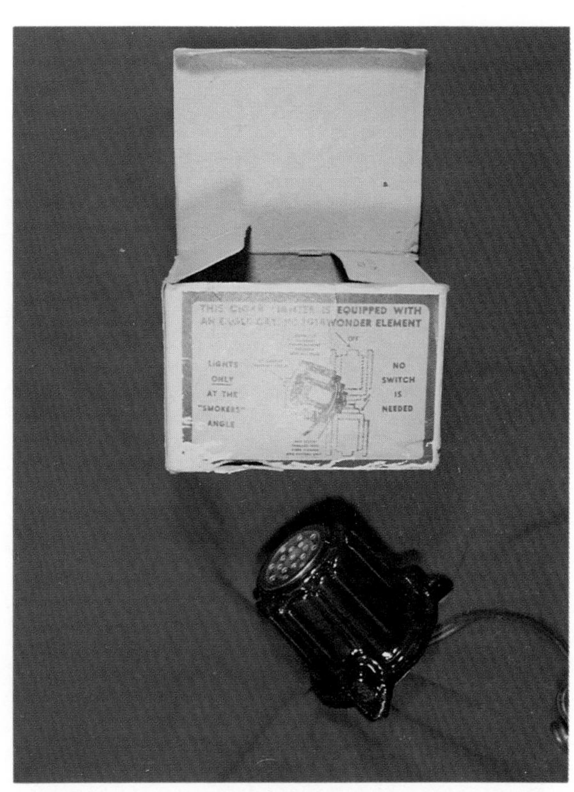

Eagle with box

Unknown-Top of smoking stand with electric lighter

Tassel Lighter Co. - Electric

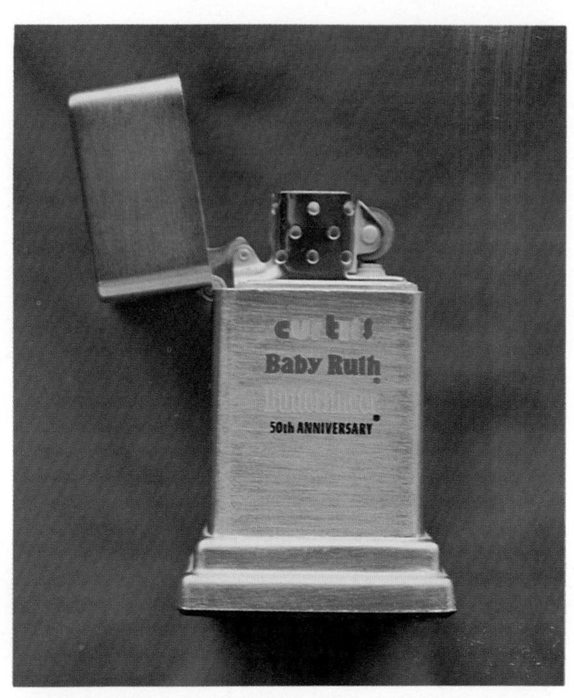

Zippo

1. Japan
2. Arrow

Stratoflame

Crown

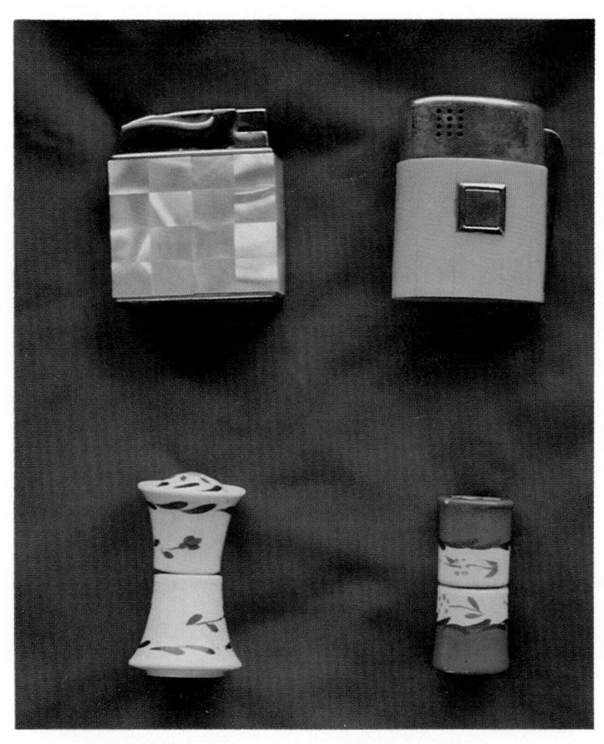

1. Unknown 2. Unknown
3. Japan 4. Japan

1. Torchcraft – Japan 2. Japan
3. Dal-Tis 4. Unknown

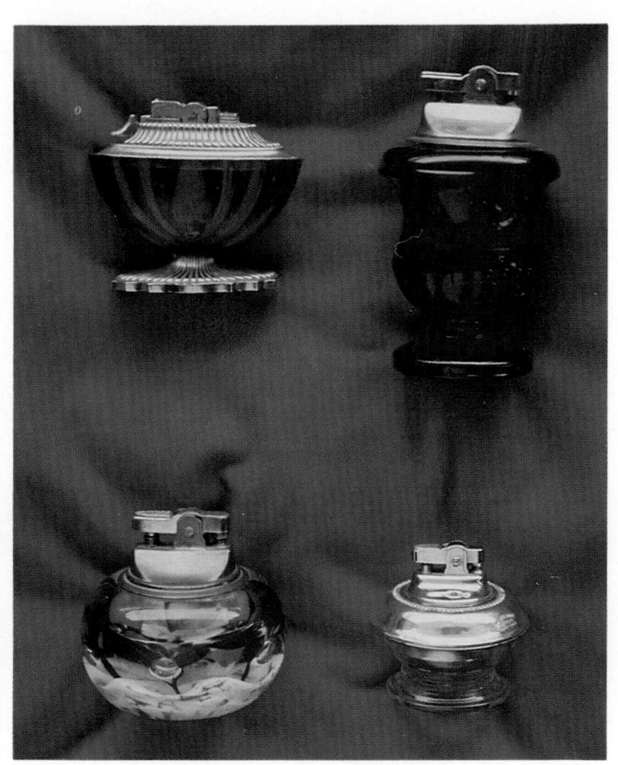

1. A.S.R. 2. Japan
3. Japan 4. Sterling Silver

1. Evans – Italian Porcelain 2. Japan
3. Italian 4. Evans

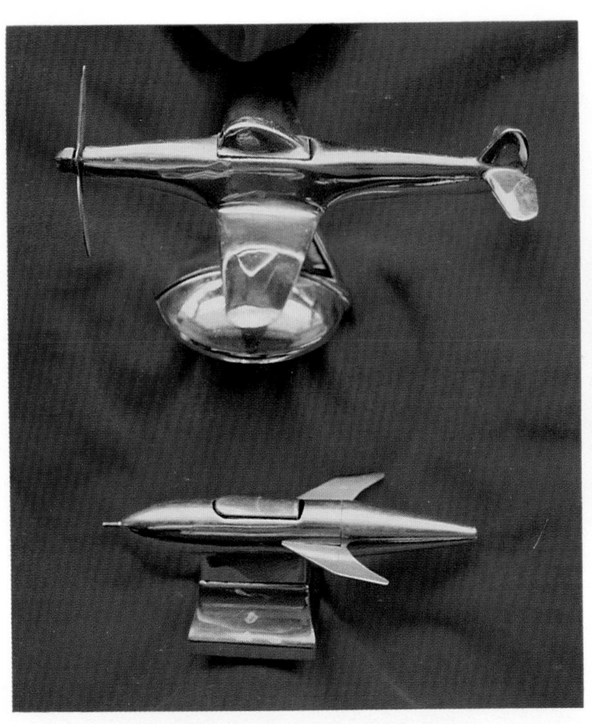

Top: Negbaur – Made in USA
Bottom: Continental - Japan
(nose cone is missing)

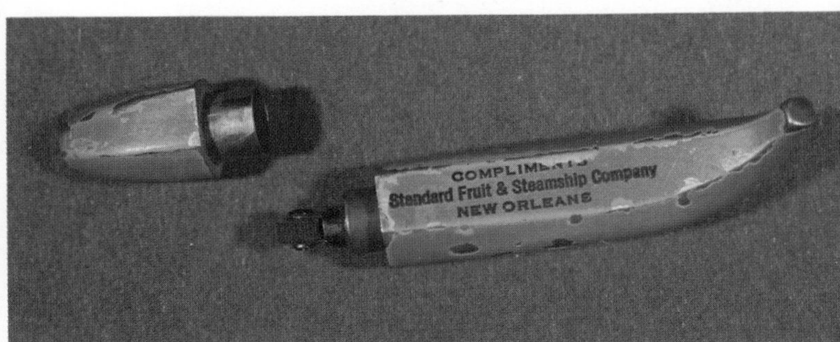

A very early Advertising Lighter

1. Modern 45 – Japan 2. Occupied Japan
3. Japan
4. Japan

Top: USA Electric (Mico)
Bottom: Aluminum – Africa (Pipe Lighter)

Ronson Striker

Ronson Striker

Ronson – Touch Tip

Real Bottle Lighter

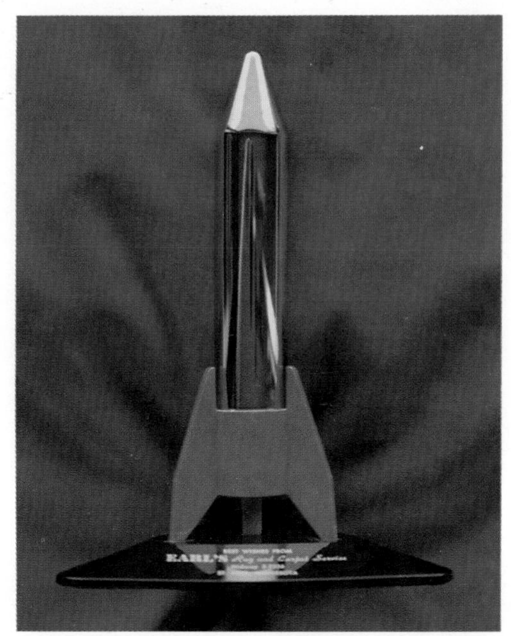

Made in USA

Made from actual beer can

Miscellaneous Advertising Lighters

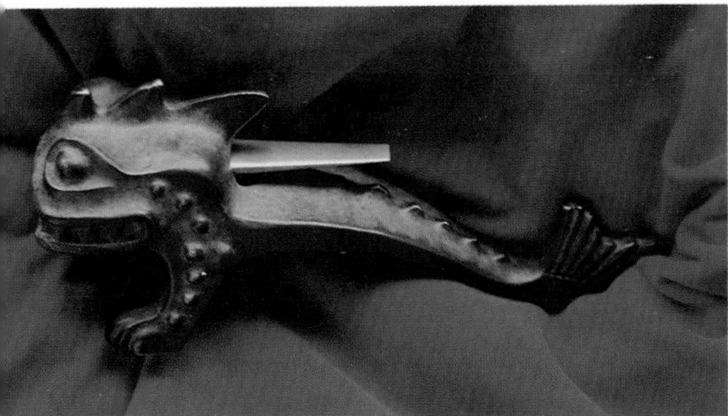

Germany

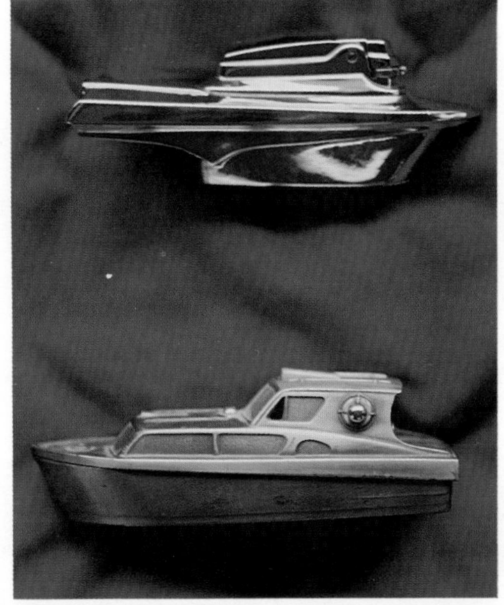

Top: Futura Bottom: Shields – Japan

1. Japan 2. Japan
3. Unknown 4. Unknown

Top: Japan
Bottom: Windsor – Japan

1. Negbaur 2. Negbaur
3. Made in Occupied Japan

Top Set - USA
Bottom: USA

1. Omsco lite – Japan
2. Varaflame Dane
3. Unknown
4. Excello – Japan

1. Sterling Silver
2. Ronson – Rondo
3. Ford City Advertising

1. Ronson – LaRonde
2. Unknown
3. Eight Ball
4. Evans – Egg

1. Ronson 2. Evans
3. Japan 4. Ronson

1. Japan 2. Japan
3. Japan 4. Japan

1. Japan 2. Japan
3. Ronson 4. Evans

1. Japan 2. Japan
3. Evans 4. Evans

Prince

Japan

Rony – Japan

Japan

Patja

Japan

1. Ronson
2. Japan
3. Erhard
4. Evans

1. Pine Hill – Japan (H & C)
2. Germany
3. Japan
4. ATC

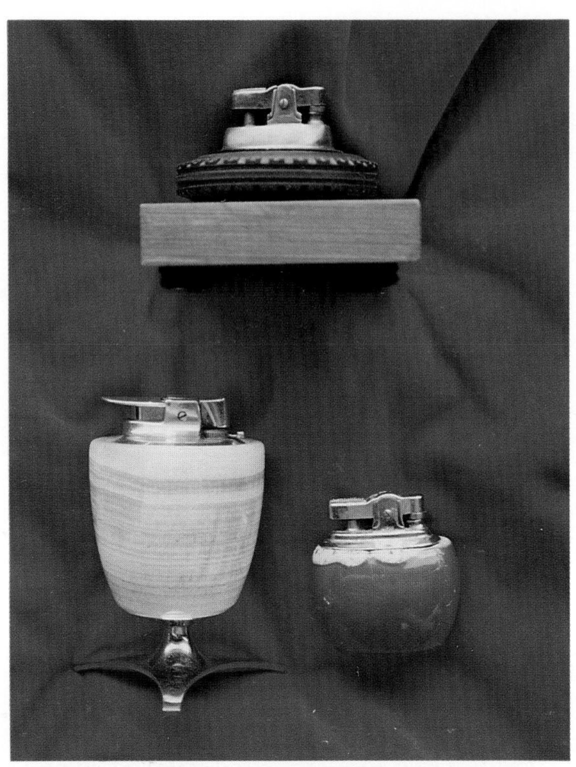

Top: USA
Bottom left: Ronson – England
Bottom right: – Japan

Top left: Blenko Handcraft – Japan
Top right: Japan
Bottom left: Japan   Bottom right: Swank – Gas

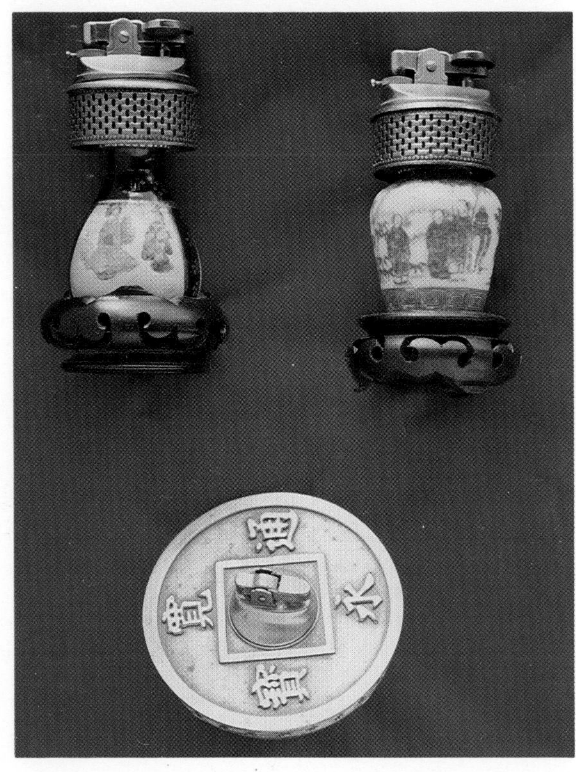

Top left: Japan – Gas   Top right: Japan – Gas
Bottom: Japan

Both Evans

Japan

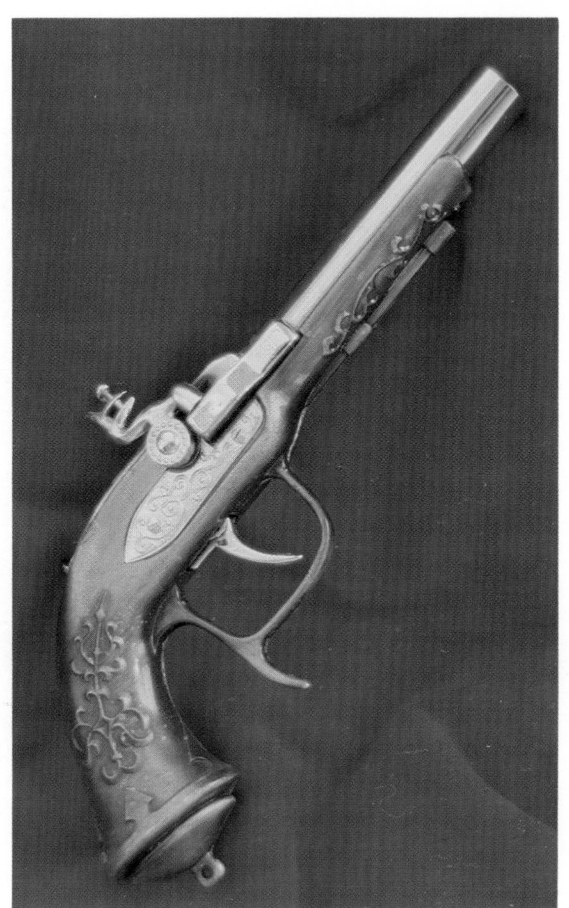
Japan

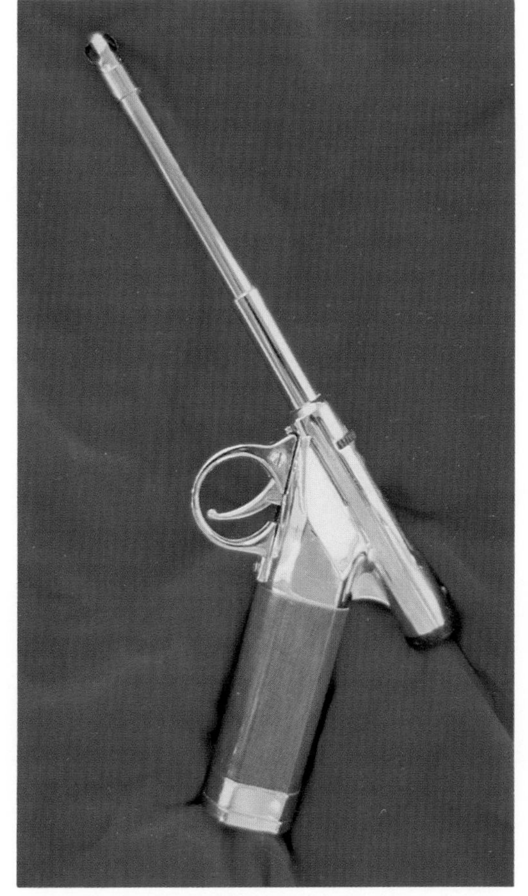
Japan

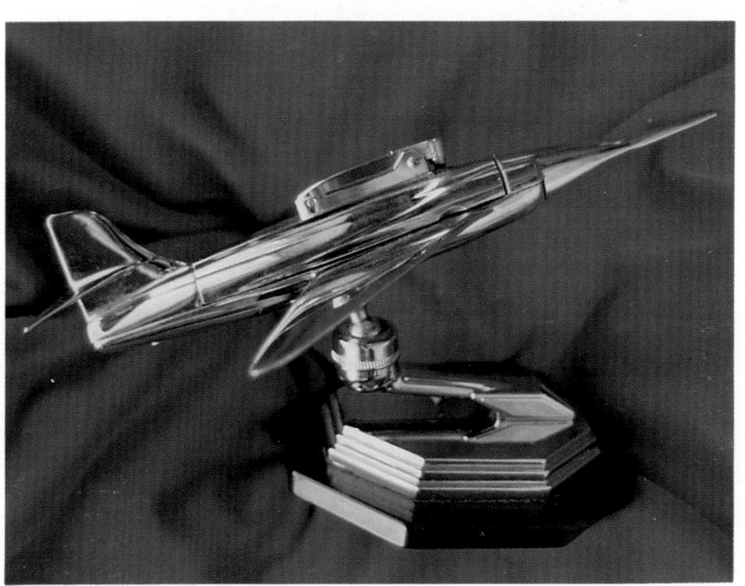
Japan

Japan

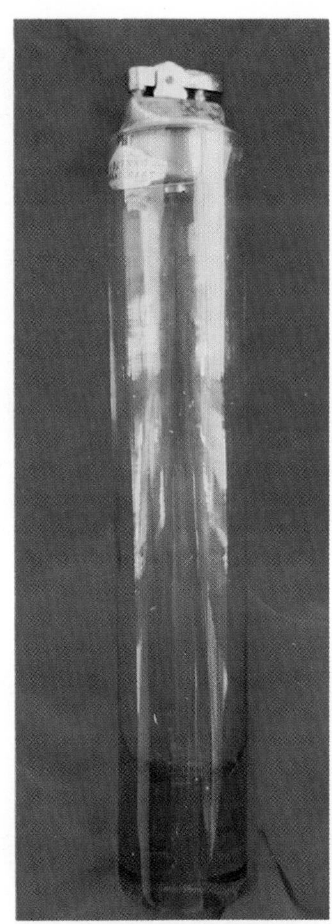

Blenko Glass

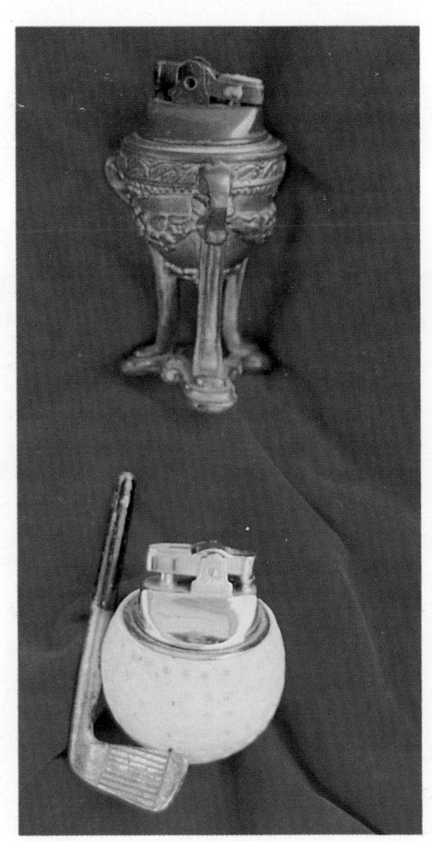

Both Japan

Japan

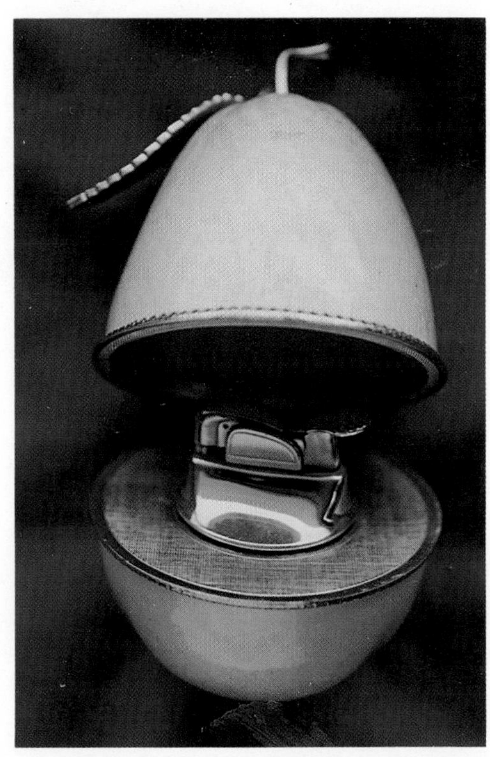

Evans Pear

Unknown

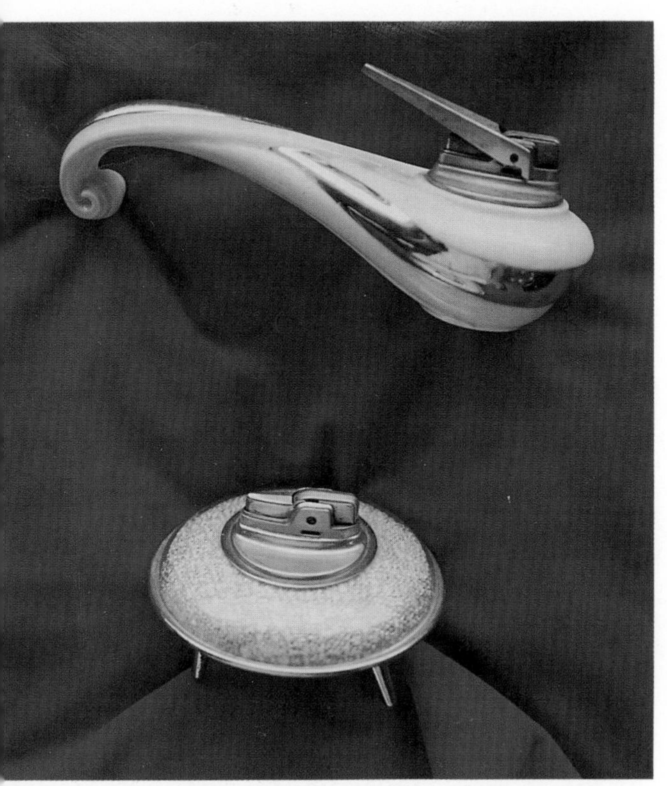

1. Ronson – Fantasy
2. Ronson – Decor

Electro-Match (Hong Kong)

Top: Arrow
Bottom: Parker – Silent Flame Table Lighter

USA

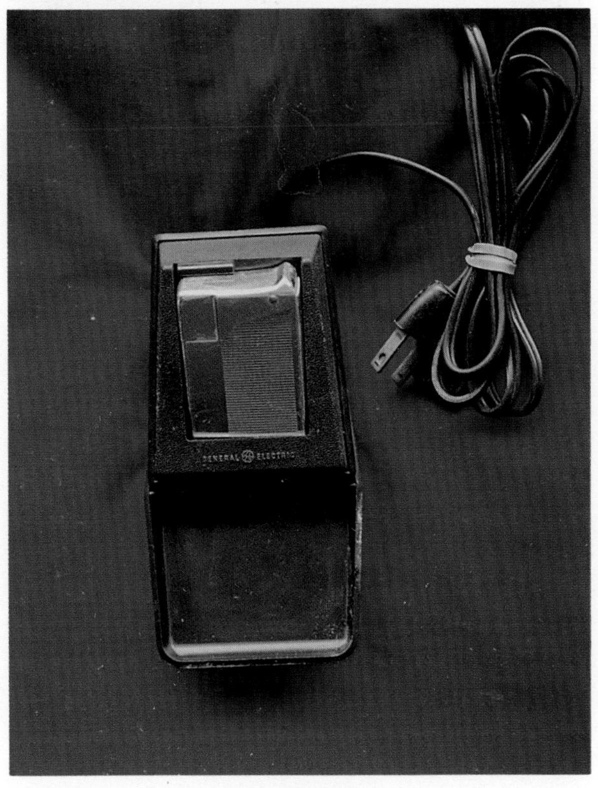

General Electric

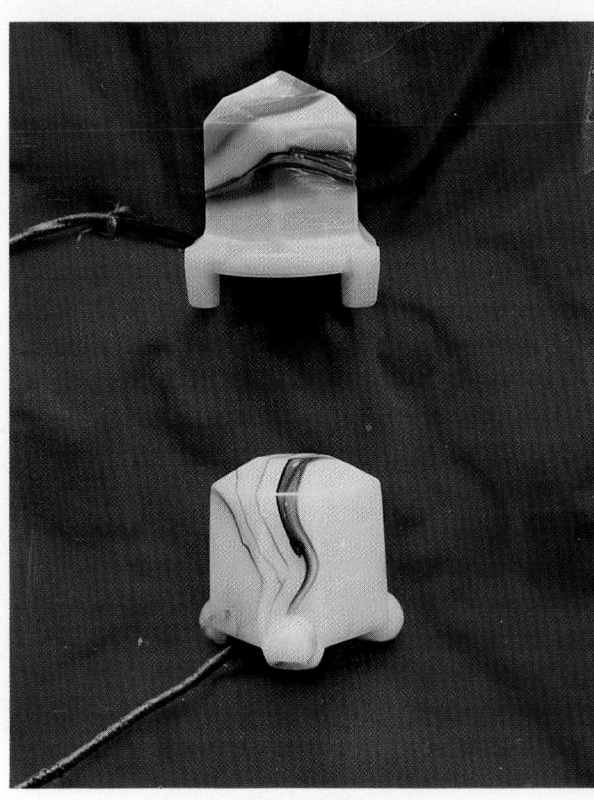

Akro Agate Electric Lighters

Top left: Strike-A-Lite Top right: Everflow
Bottom left: Japan Bottom right: Ronson

Top left: Kreisler Top right: Ronson
Bottom left: Supreme – Japan Bottom right: Japan

Top left: Castleton - Japan
Top right: Wales – Japan
Bottom: Both are Japan

Top left: Ronson Top right: Ronson – Trophy
Bottom left: Ascot – USA Bottom right: Evans

Top left: West Germany Top right: Ronson
Middle: Ronson – Senator
Bottom left: A.S.R. Bottom right: Japan

Top left: Amico Top right: Japan
Bottom: Both are Occupied Japan

Top: Both are Ronson
Bottom left: Dragon Bottom right: Ronson

Top left: Unified Top right: Japan
Bottom left: Kreisler Bottom right: Japan

Rechargeable Plug-in Lighter

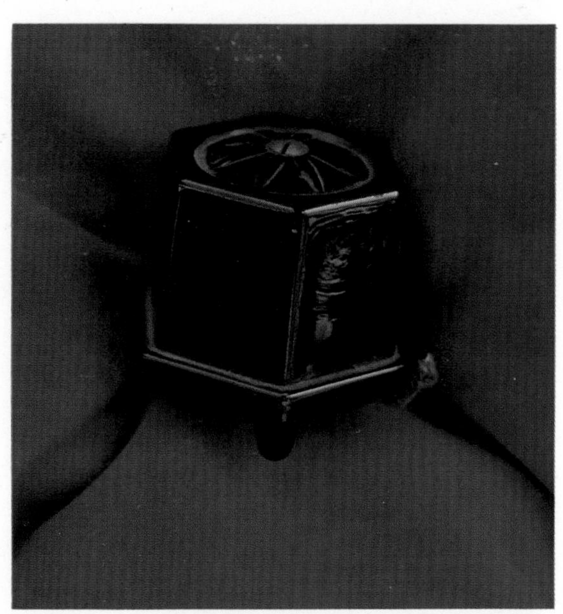
Black glass - electric

Gubelin - Germany

Aluminum

Japan

Ronson Striker

Unknown

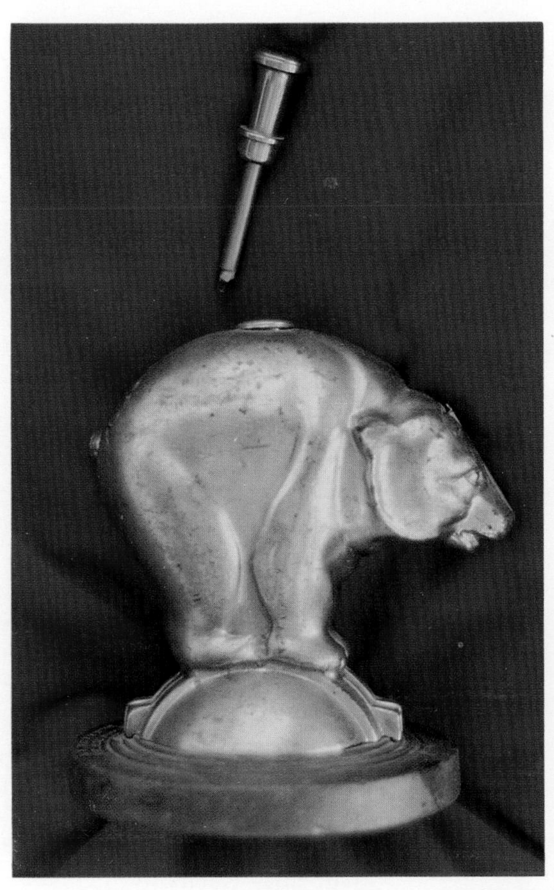

Ronson Striker

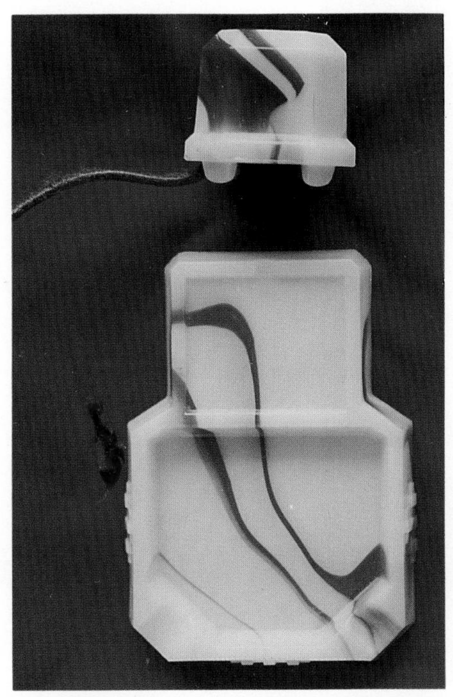

Unknown – Akro Agate (USA)

Swank

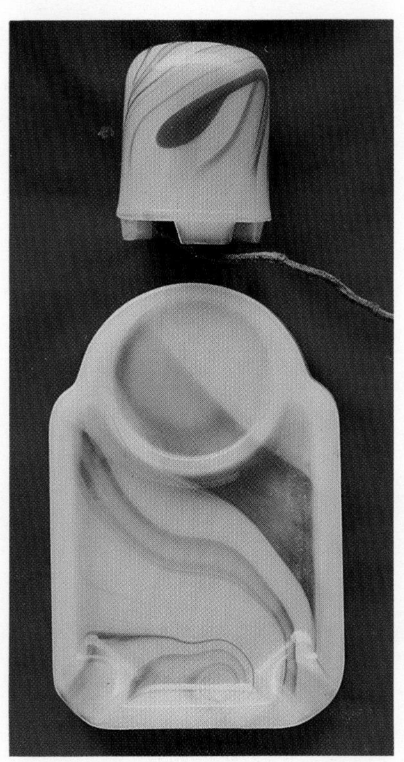

Unknown – Akro Agate (USA)

Japan

Ronson Touch Tip
Enamel and Gold Plated

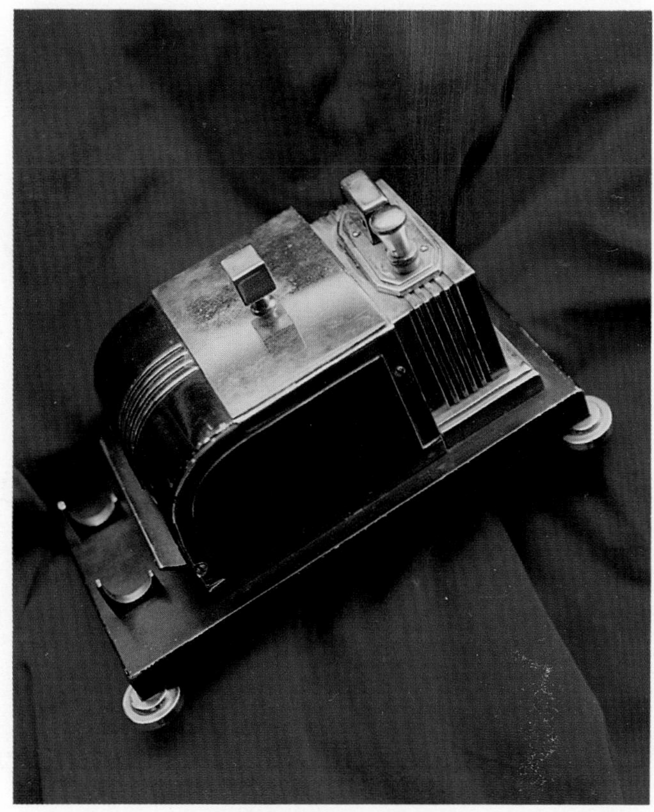

Ronson Touch-Tip
Cigarette Dispenser

Ronson Touch-Tip Octette

Top left: Evans Top right: Japan
Bottom left: Japan Bottom right: Supreme

Left: Rosenthal Netter
Top right: Evans Bottom right: Evans Boot

MaruMan Cut Glass

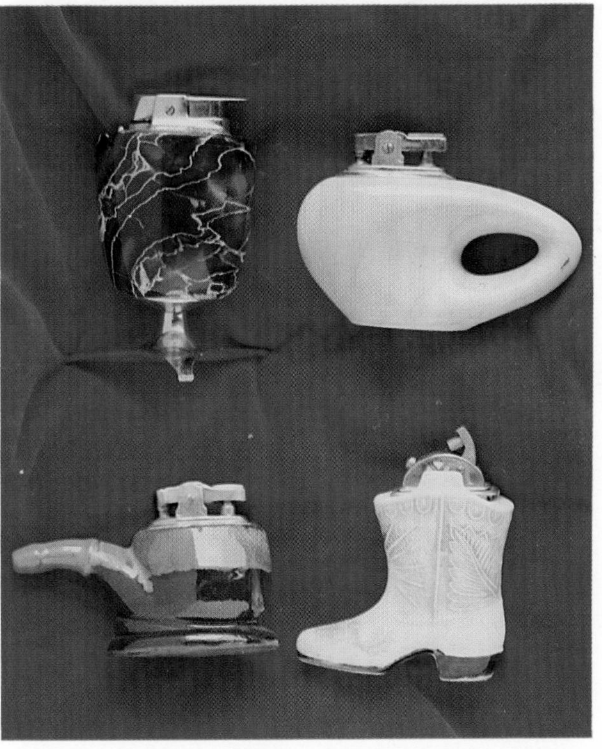

Top left: Ronson Top right: Japan
Bottom left: USA Bottom right: Reliance – Japan

Japan

Demley

AGM

Eric Wedemeyer, Inc. – USA

Japan

1. Japan
2. Zippo – Standard Model

Corona

1. Unknown
2. Blenko Glass – Japan
3. Evans
4. Japan

All Japan

1. Fortune – Japan
2. Penguin - Japan
3. Japan
4. Japan

1. Japan
2. Evans
3. Evans
4. Evans

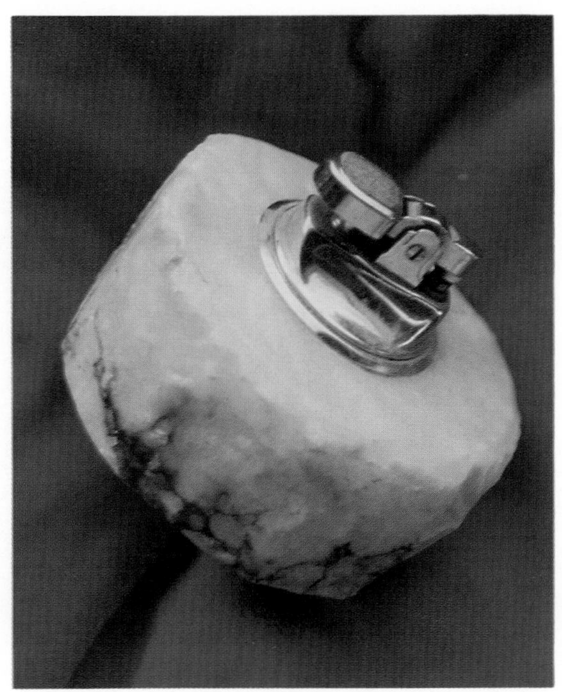
Japan

Unknown

Japan

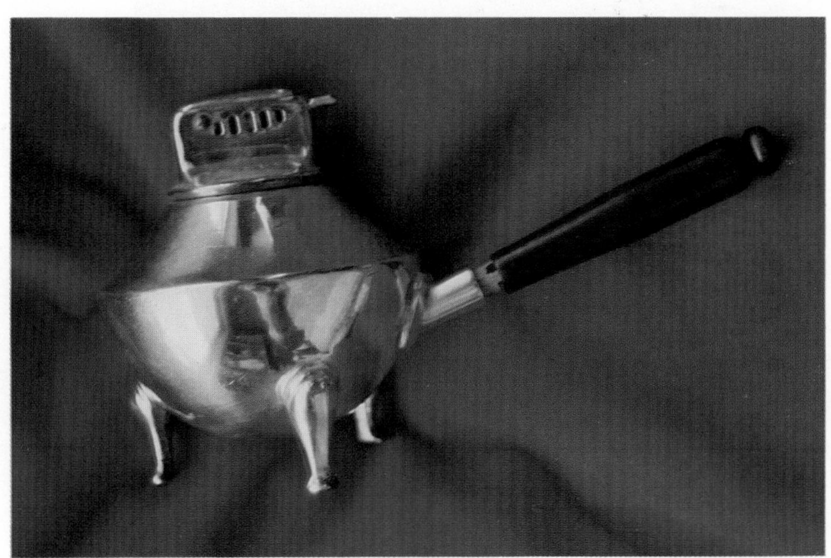
Japan

Left: Unknown
Right: Advertisement on Bottom

Grinding Stone - Japan

Bowling Ball & Pins - Japan

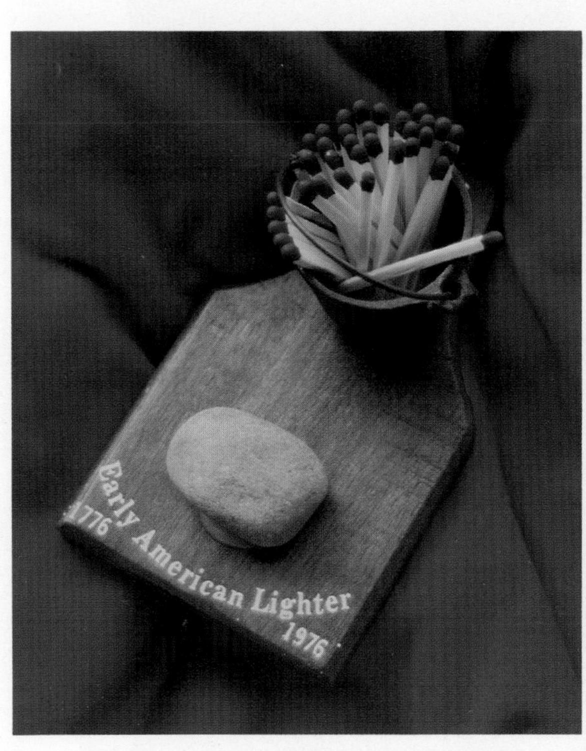

Early American Lighter - Home Made

Top: Hamilton Bottom: Hamilton

Top left: Japan Top right: Japan
Bottom: Japan

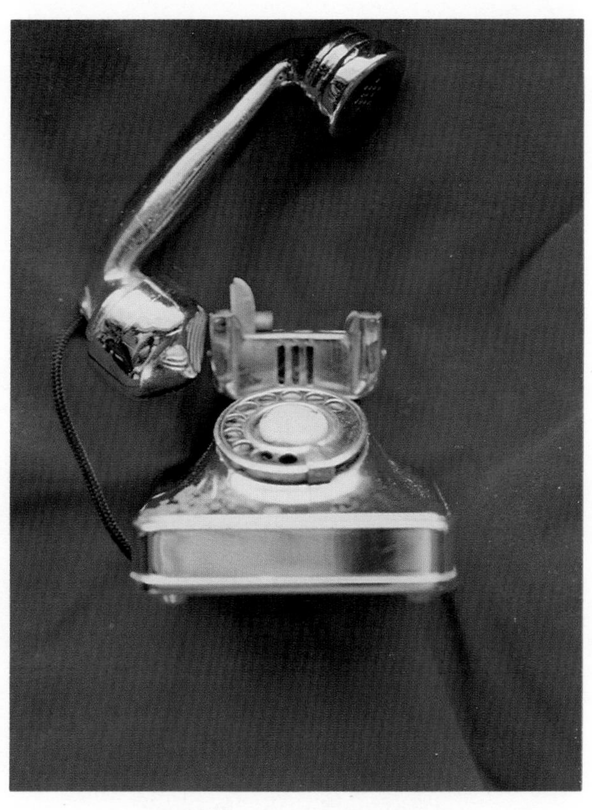

Peacock – Occupied Japan

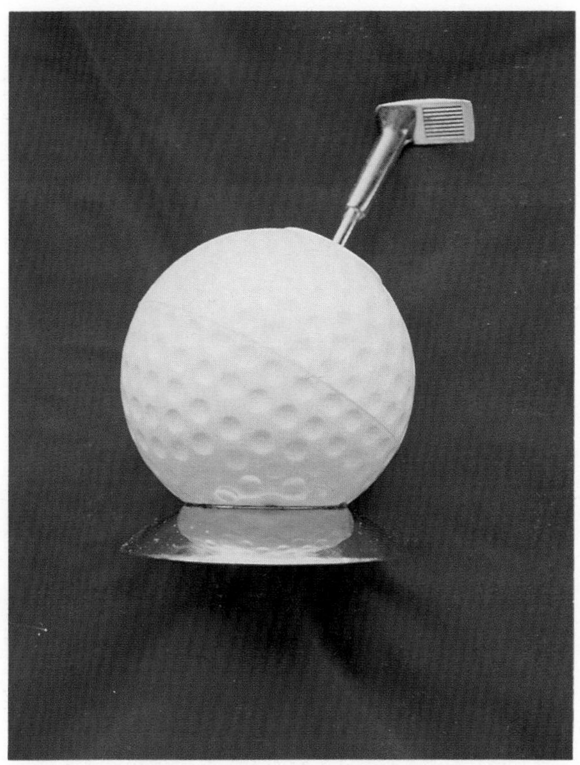

Supermatch

Ronson Striker
(looks like a Pelican)

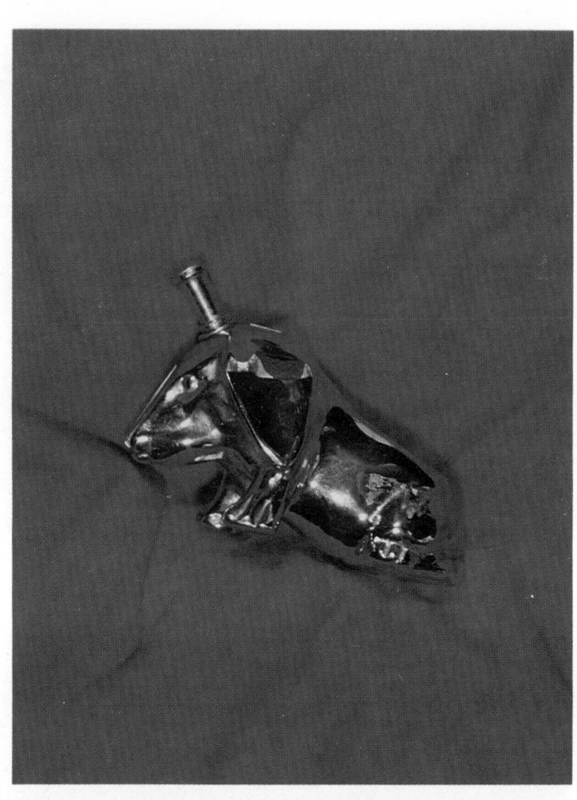

Pup with pipe holder striker

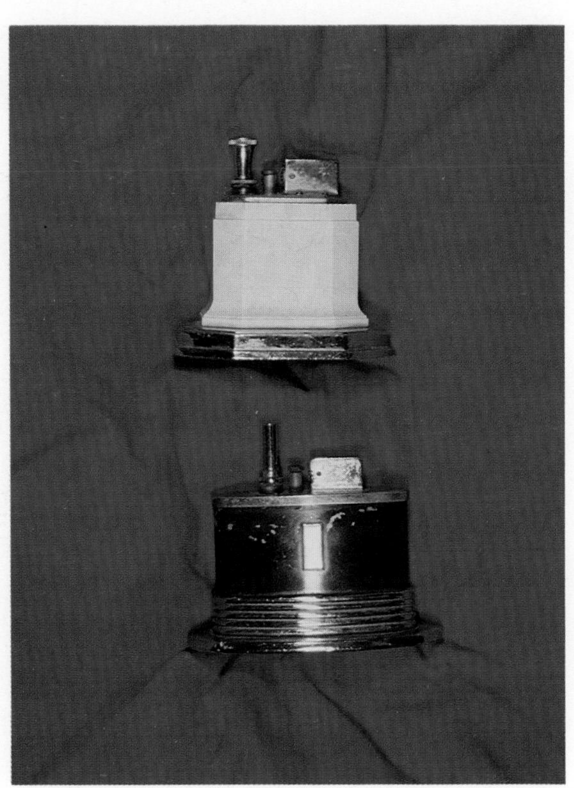

Top: Octette – Ronson Touch-Tip
Bottom: Ronson Touch-Tip Oval

Ronson Touch-Tip Clock

Electromatch

Classic Jumbo – England

1. Japan
2. Holland Wooden Shoe 3. Japan

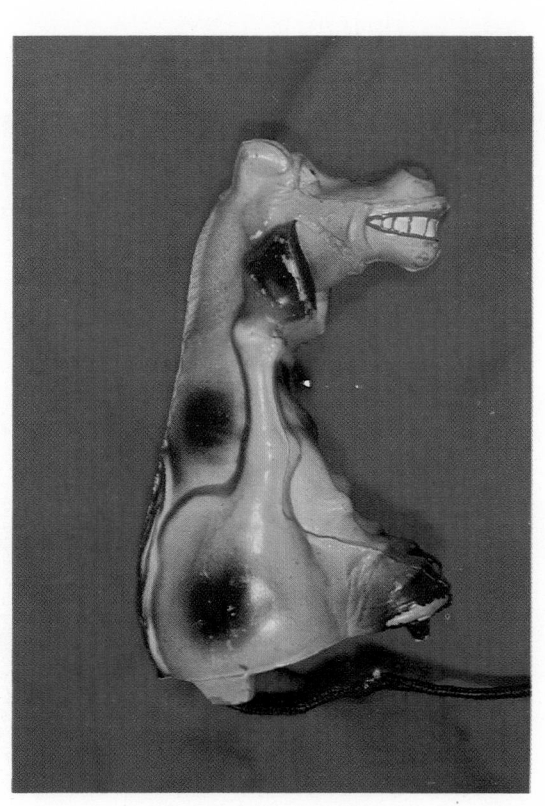

Unknown – Electric

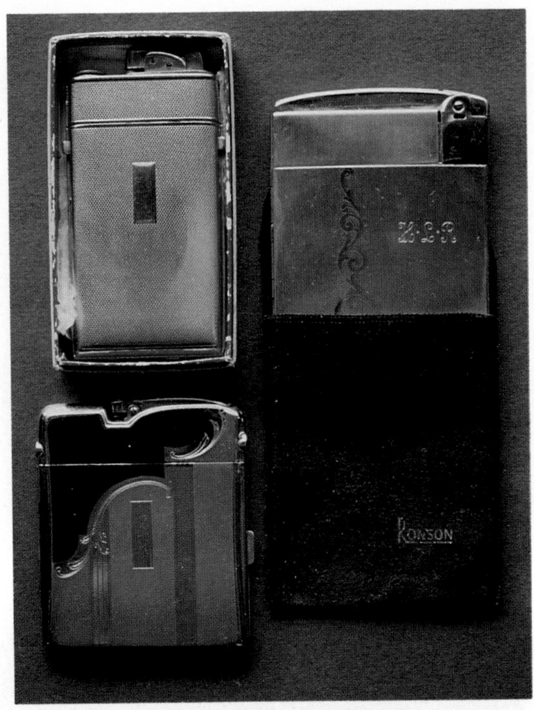

Top left: Evans
Right: Ronson Escort
Bottom left: Ronson

1. Ronson (Sport case)
2. Ronson (Master case)
3. Ronson (Ten a case)
4. Ronson (Master case)

Top left: Ronson Top right: Evans
Bottom: Both are Evans

Left side: Partlow Kase Liter
Top right: Royal Case Light
Bottom right: Magic Case

1. Ronson w/Removable Adonis Lighter
2. Fuzi Art Deco Case
3. Ronson
4. Japan

Top: Elgin American Lite-O-Matic
Bottom: Ronson Magnacase

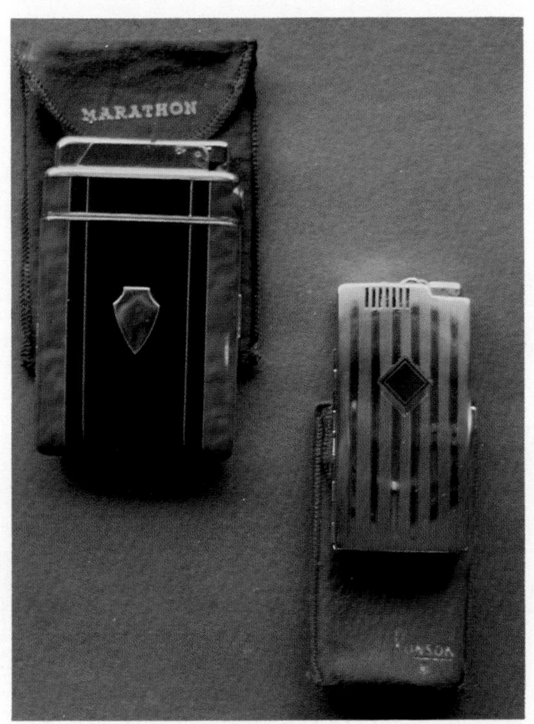

Top: Marathon
Bottom: Ronson

Cigarette Case w/Lighter - Japan

Bentley display card with lighters

Display pen shield – full card

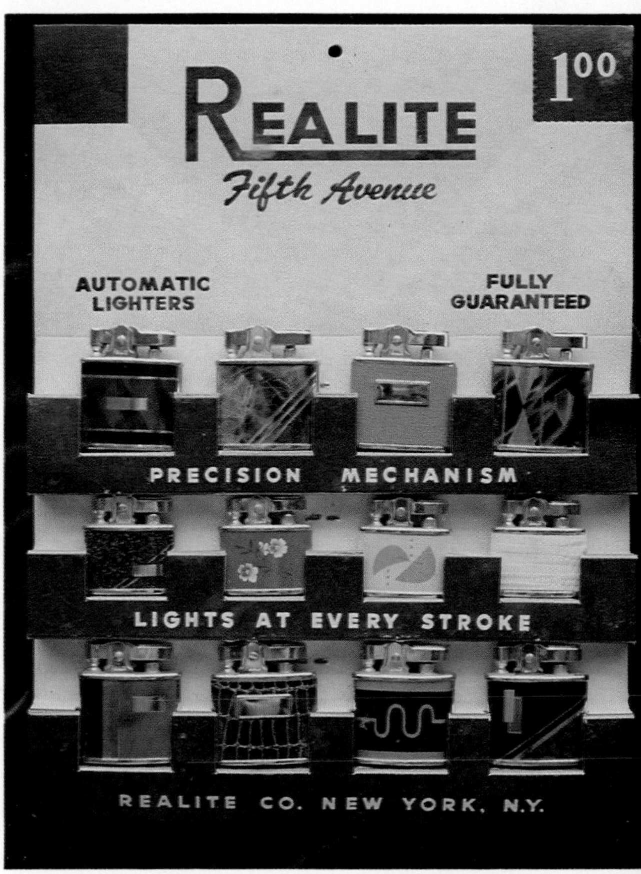

Display card with 12 lighters

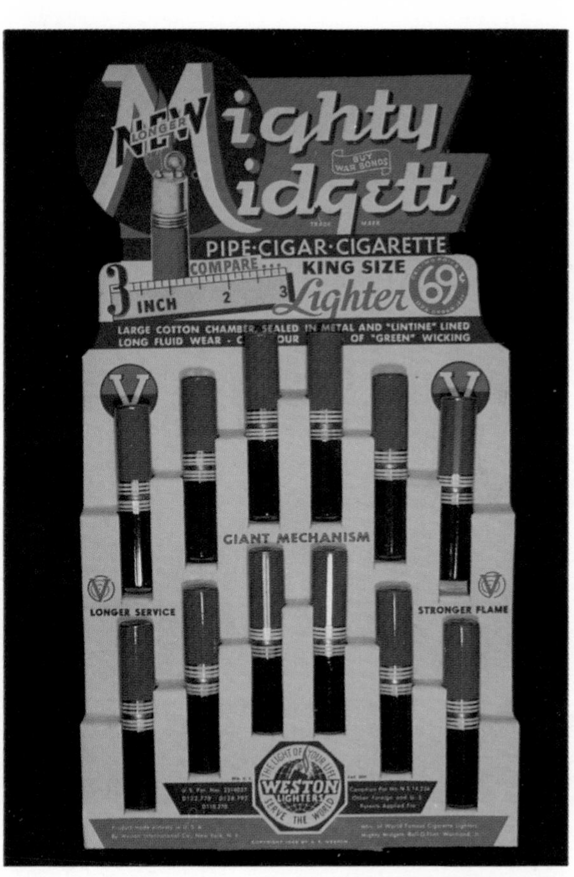

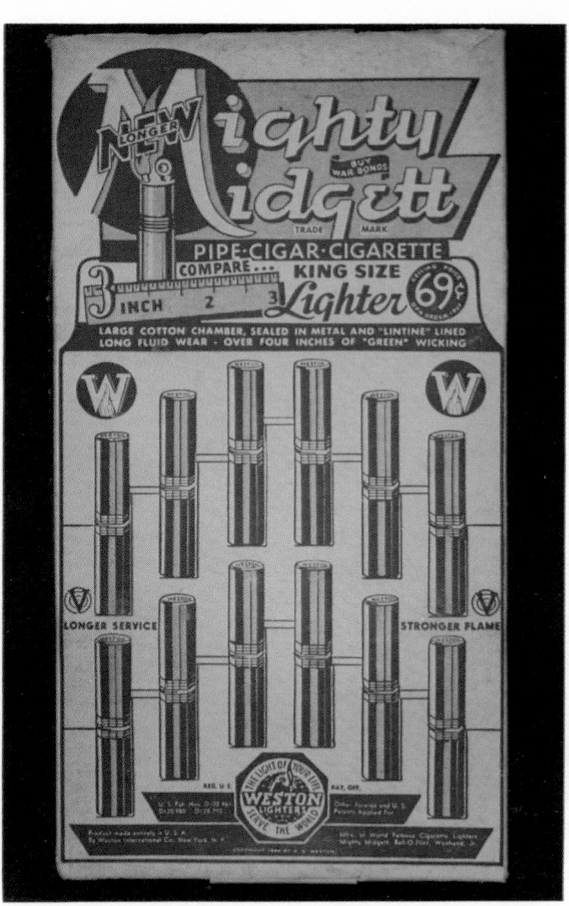

Weston's Mighty Midgett – full card with box

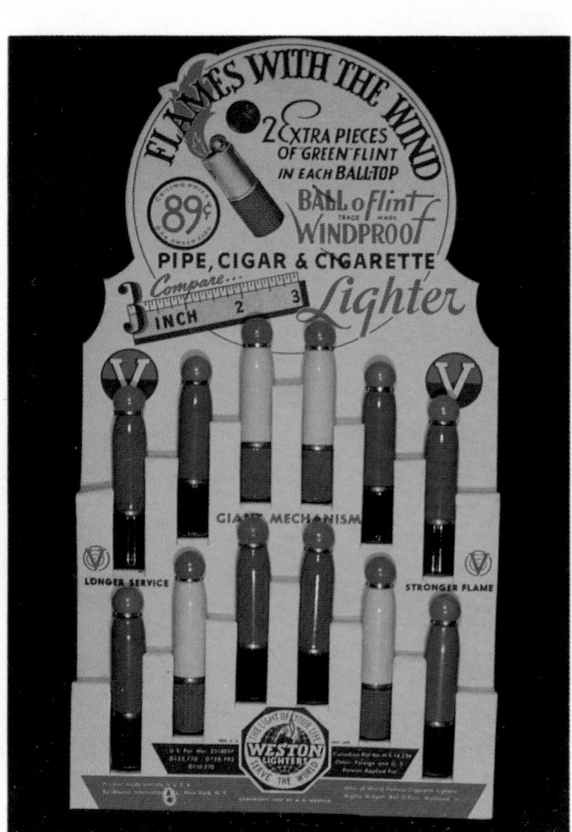

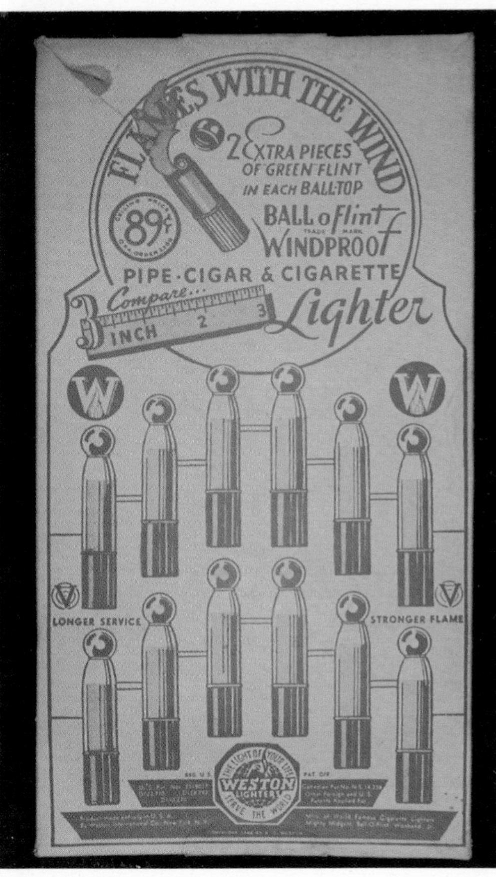

Weston Lighters – full card with box

Display Card w/6 Lighters
(Spesco C-Thru)

Zippo Display w/lighters

Companion EzLite
Display card with 11 lighters

1975 Zippo Display card with 4 lighters

INDEX FOR BRANDS & MANUFACTURERS

INDEX FOR BRANDS & MANUFACTURERS

INDEX FOR BRANDS & MANUFACTURERS

INDEX FOR BRANDS & MANUFACTURERS

INDEX FOR TYPES OF LIGHTERS

PRICE GUIDE

Page 8
55452 - $650+
S523 - $40+
S974 - $40+
S972 - $60+
N718 - $50+
566209 - $40+
S1657 - $40+
S957 - $40+
Page 9
400 - $75+
4574 - $20+
57K3388 - $25+
864105 - $75+
4549 - $20+
442914 - $100+
Electric Cigar Lighter - $45+
9384 - $40+
Page 10
E150 - $125+
Kramer - $100+
M166-RS - $40+
M62 - $25+
M176 - $125+
Page 11
9325 - $40+
AJ2570 - $45+
9366 - $40+
9N-639 - $70+
GG1625 - $50+
206 - $60+
502 - $50+
9348 - $100+
Page 12
M4236 - $60+
Park Lighter - $10+
GG1626 & GG1627 - $50+
4878 - $75+
3QR7561B & 3QR7562C - $40+
Page 13
3QR-G12 & 3QR-G15 - $40+
3QR-P12 - $60+
3Q-K12 - $40+
3Q-R11 - $50+
CJ4802 & CJ4803 - $50+
CJ4804 - $80+
CJ4805 - $300+
CJ4806 & CJ4807 - $40+
Page 14
All - $50+
Except 4178 - $75+
Page 15
All - 75+
Page 16
All - $50+
Except N1100-N1102 - $65+
Page 17
All - $75+
Page 18
All - $50+
Page 19
400 - $150+
403 - $125+
520 & 500 - $100+
300 - $125+
Page 20
J4253 & J4255 - $30+
J4256 - $15+
J4254 - $100+
Page 21
J93 - $30+
J92 - $75+
J3120 & J3121 - $60+
Page 22
M73 & M245 - $15+
M243-H & M239-I - $8+
M244 & M253-H - $10+
M51 - $15+
M249-S - $12+
M212-O & M60 - $20+
M43 & M53-U - $60+
M38-BO & M172 - $25+
M169 - $30+
Page 23
M35 - $35+
M25 - $50+
M37 & M32 - $20+
M30 - $40+
M69 - $45+
M72 & M59 - $30+
M250 - $100+
M177 & M91 - $20+
M33 & M64 - $25+
Page 24
3QD150 & 3QD310 - $75+
N7586 - $40+
155H250 - $80+
56V395 - $15+
Page 25
Sterling Silver Windproof - $100+
Service Lighter - $35+
Page 26
Thorens Windproof - $40+
Thorens Automatic - $50+
Foxhole Blackout - $75+
Mighty Midget - $10+
Ball of Flame - $10+
Page 27
1199 & 1197 - $40+
1181 - $25+
1195 & 1198 - $15+
3057 & 3056 - $40+
1171 & 1187 - $10+
1157 - $40+
3060 - $15+
Page 28
All - 10+
Except 1611 - $20+
1600 - $20+
1606 - $20+
Page 29
All - $10+
Page 30
All - $10+
Page 31
C600 - $20+
C340 - $15+
690 - $35+
Page 32
Top Left - $20+
Top Right - $15+
Page 33
All - $15+
Except 600 - $20+
Page 34
All - $60+
Page 35
All - $50+
Page 36
All - $50+
Page 37
All - $100+
Page 38
All - $100+
Page 39
J16431 & J16433 - $75+
J16431a - $90+
J16432 - $60+
J16432a & J16433a - $65+
J16434 - $150+
J16435 & J16436 - $60+
J16437 & J16438 - $60+
J16439 & J16439a - $65+
J16440 - $125+
J16441 & J16442 - $75+
Page 40
All - $75+
Page 41
Top Row - $75+
2nd Row - $90+
3rd Row - $75+
Bottom Row - $125+
Page 42
EA-244 - $80+
EA-246 - $90+
EA-247 - $100+
Page 43
EA-238 - $80+
EA-239 - $30+
EA-240 - $40+
EA-241 & EA-243 - $50+
EA-242 - $125+
Page 44
Both Lighters - $50+ each
Page 45
All - $75+
Except EA-234 - $100+
Page 46
All - $75+
Page 47
All - $40+
Page 48
All - $75+
Except 128 - $90+
Page 49
All - $70+
Page 50
All - $75+
Page 51
All - $75+
Page 52
3Q-E4134 & 3Q-E4139 - $40+
3Q-E4150 - $50+
3Q-E4143 - $75+
3Q-E4145 - $60+
3Q-E4160 & 3Q-E58-1 - $50+
3Q-E4113 & 3Q-E4114 - $50+
3Q-E4126 - $75
3Q-E4122 & 3Q-E36-3 - $50+
3Q-E4119 - $40+
3Q-E4145 - $70+
3Q-E4123 - $45+
3Q-E3412 - $50+
3Q-E4041 - $75+
Page 53
Top Row - $40+
Middle Row - $30+
All on Bottom Row - $50+
Except 232J84 - $40+
Page 54
All - $50+
Except N1067 & N1068 - $75+
Page 55
All - $60+
Except N1052 - $100+
Page 56
N1048 - $100+
N1049 & N1050 - $75+
N1051 - $110+
Page 57
All - $100+
Page 58
All - $100+
Page 59
T18701 & T18702 - $100+
T18703 thru T18705 - $100+
T18706 & T18707 - $80+
T18708 - $75+
T18709 - $100+
Page 60
12968 - $125+
13007 & 12790 - $100+
817 & 801 - $150+
12875 - $150+
12099 - $160+
12417 & 12280 - $150+
Ronson Smoker Set - $250+
12773 - $175+
Page 61
01151 - $60+
1151 - $35+
153 & 151 - $75+
021 - $60+
21 - $35+
1936 & 1944 - $60+
14312 & 1948 - $60+
1934 - $60+
1933 - $35+
1946 & 1940 - $60+
1938 - $60+
1102 - $35+
100 - $75+
12351 - $60+
17 - $35+
01152 - $60+
1152 - $35+
14319 - $75+
Page 62
Top Row - $50+
Middle Lighter - $10+
All Cases - $75+
Except Case CJ3230 - $50+
Page 63
All - $125+
Page 64
3Q-R6603 - $60+
3Q-R6414 - $35+
3Q-R6048 - $30+
3Q-R7070 - $60+
3Q-R15252 - $125+
3Q-R6723 - $50+
3Q-R7496 - $100+
3Q-R5232 & 3Q-R6939 - $70+
Page 65
Top Two Rows - $15+
Bottom Two Rows - $10+
Page 66
Lighter Fluid Can - $20+
All Other is Reference
Page 67
Top Two Rows - $15+
82162 - $20+
13100 & 13541 - $15+
13540 & 13806 - $15+
11951 - $400+
Page 68
Top Lighters - $15+
Table Lighters - $20+
48701 - $40+
48902 - $60+
53753 - $50+
Page 69
19572 - $20+
58783 - $15+
58784 - $25+
24611 - $15+
37610 - $20+
37759 - $25+
56600 & 51600 - $10+
51762 - $25+
30600 & 55601 - $10+
52600 & 80601 - $40+
31600 - 15+
22761 - $25+
54600 - $10+
Page 70
Top Row - $15+
18185 - $15+
18539 & 18806 - $15+
18928 - $40+
18950 & 18955 - $400+
Bottom Lighters - $10+
Page 71
All - $7+
Page 72
All - $5+
Page 73
Desk & Library Lighters - $15+
Page 74
Reference Only
Page 75
Reference Only
Page 76
Reference Only
Page 77
Reference Only
Page 78
GG1085 - $100+
GG1086 - $400+
GG1083 & GG1084 - $50+
GG1081 & GG1080 - $60+
GG1087 - $50+
3Q-Z200 - $40+
3Q-Z350 - $30+
AJ2571 & AJ2573 - $60+
AJ2572 - $40+
AJ2574 - $100+
Page 79
Reference Only
Page 80
Reference Only
Page 81
Reference Only
Page 82
Reference Only
Page 83
1. - $20+
2. - $35+
3. - $25+
4. - $25+
5. - $25+
6. - $25+
7. - $25+
8. - $25+
9. - $25+
10. - $25+
11. - $75+
Page 84
1. - $40+
2. & 3. - $25+

5+
0+
- $20+
0+
l Lighters - $200+
5
0+
- $70+
0+
25+
5+
00+
)+
0+
6
5+
0+
5+
7
t Picture - $50+
ght Pict.:
1. - $15+
2. - $20+
Left Pict.:
1. - $10+
2. - $15+
Right Pict. - $35+
8
t.:
1. - $20+
2. - $35+
Left - $25+
Right Pict.:
1. - $35+
2. - $30+
Left Pict.:
1. - $50+
2. - $20+
Right Pict.:
1. - $20+
2. - $25+
9
t Pict.:
1. & 2. - $7+
3. - $12+
4. - $7+
ght Pict.:
1. - $15+
2. - $35+
3. - $25+
Left Pict. - $25+each
Right Pict.:
Top Right Lighter - $20+
Middle Lighter - $25+
Bottom Left Lighter - $25+
0
t Pict. - $25+
ght Pict. - $40+
Left Pict. - $25+
Right Picture - $40+
1
t Pict.:
All - $20+
Except Center Right - $30+
ght Pict. - $400+
Left Pict.:
1. - $20+
2. - $30+
Right Pict.:
Both Sets 30+ each
2
t - $1000+
ers - $400+
3
ft - $400+
ght - $500+
- $500+
Left - $400+
Right - $350+
4
ce Only
5
0+
N1038 - $75+
6
& N1020 - $75+
- $90+
- $100+
- $350+
- $75+

N1024 - $200+
N1025 thru N1028 - $100+ each
N1029 - $90+
N1030 - $20+
N1032 - $75+
Page 97
Top Row - $75+
Middle Two Rows - $60+
N1000 & N1001 - $75+
N1002 - $100+
Page 98
Top Row - $50+
2nd Row - $65+
3rd Row - $70+
Bottom Row - $75+
Page 99
All - $75+
Page 100
All - $65+
Except E1608 & E1611 - $50+
E1613 - $70+
Page 101
1. - $75+
2. - $50+
3. - $60+
4. - $65+
5. - $60+
6. - $75+
7. - $60+
8. - $70+
9. - $65+
10. - $75+
11. - $100+
12. - $100+
Page 102
Filling Station - $300+
Lighters - $60+
Page 103
N1069 - $90+
N1070 & N1073 - $75+
N1071 - $60+
N1072 - $65+
N1074 - $75+
N1075 - $70+
Page 104
Ronson Sets - $125+
Lighters - $50+
Page 105
12939 - $75+
1 - $30+
4 - $50+
02 & 016 - $40+
64 & 49 - $40+
1007 - $60+
01001 - $50+
17 & 21 - $45+
151 - $40+
153 - $50+
12351 & 021 - $30+
100 - $45+
90 - $65+
Page 106
All - $100-300+
Page 107
1. - $100+
2. - $100+
3. - $100+
4. - $50+
5. - $50+
6. - $50+
7. - $40+
8. - $100+
9. - $100+
Page 108
1. - $100+
2. - $150+
3. - $200+
4. - $100+
5. - $100+
6. - $100+
7 - $75+
Page 109
Top Left Pict. - $50+
Top Middle Pict. - $125+
Top Right Pict. - $30+
Bottom Left Pict.:
1. - $40+
2. - $50+
3. - $65+
4. - $20+

Bottom Right Pict.:
1. - $75+
2. - $125+
3. - $60+
Page 110
Top Left Pict.:
1. - $20+
2. - $15+
3. - $20+
4. - $35+
5. - $5+
6. - $5+
7. - $20+
8. - $15+
9. - $5+
Top Right Pict.:
1. - $15+
2. - $10+
3. - $15+
4. - $15+
5. - $15+
6. - $10+
7. - $15+
8. - $20+
9. - $10+
Bottom Left Pict.:
1. - $40+
2. - $35+
3. - $40+
4. - $8+
5. - $15+
6. - $8+
7. - $35+
8. - $10+
9. - $65+
Bottom Right Pict.:
All - $7+
Page 111
Top Left Pict.:
1. - $7+
2. - $8+
3. - $8+
4. - $8+
5. - $15+
6. - $10+
7. - $20+
8. - $8+
9. - $8+
Top Right Pict.:
1. - $8+
2. - $8+
3. - $15+
4. - $10+
5. - $7+
6. - $8+
7. - $35+
8. - $25+
9. - $10+
Bottom Left Pict.:
1. - $8+
2. - $9+
3. - $10+
4. - $15+
5. - $8+
6. - $10+
7. - $40+
8. - $4+
9. - $15+
Bottom Right Pict.:
1. - $20+
2. - $50+
3. - $20+
4. - $10+
5. - $15+
6. - $20+
Page 112
Top Left Pict.:
1. - $25+
2. - $20+
3. - $15+
4. - $45+
5. - $15+
6. - $40+
7. - $60+
8. - $40+
Top Right Pict.:
1. - $20+
2. - $20+
3. - $35+
4. - $20+

5. - $10+
6. - $8+
7. - $8+
8. - $8+
Bottom Left Pict.:
Top - $65+
Bottom - $150+
Bottom Right Pict.:
Top - $40+
Bottom - $15+
Page 113
1. - $75+
2. - $40+
3. - $50+
4. - $50+
5. - $8+
6. - $15+
Page 114
Top Left Pict.:
1. - $20+
2. - $10+
3. - $10+
4. - $4+
5. - $10+
6. - $10+
7. - $10+
8. - $4+
9. - $10+
Top Right Pict.:
1. - $30+
2. - $35+
3. - $40+
4. - $40+
Bottom Left Pict.:
1. - $10+
2. - $15+
3. - $8+
4. - $15+
5. - $10+
6. - $7+
7. - $10+
8. - $10+
9. - $25+
Bottom Right Pict.:
1. - $15+
2. - $25+
3. - $70+
4. - $25+
5. - $20+
6. - $25+
7. - $10+
8. - $25+
9. - $10+
Page 115
Top Left Pict.:
1. - $75+
2. - $15+
3. - $10+
4. - $8+
5. - $15+
6. - $8+
7. - $75+
8. - $20+
Top Right Pict.:
1. - $10+
2. - $15+
3. - $25+
4. - $10+
5. - $20+
6. - $8+
7. - $10+
8. - $10+
9. - $5+
Bottom Left Pict.:
1. - $5+
2. - $10+
3. - $15+
4. - $40+
5. - $20+
Bottom Right Pict.:
1. - $35+
2. - $20+
3. - $50+
4. - $50+
5. - $50+
6. - $15+
7. - $20+
8. - $30+
Page 116
Top Left Pict.:

1. - $25+
2. - $10+
3. - $10+
4. - $12+
5. - $10+
6. - $8+
7. - $10+
8. - $25+
9. - $8+

Top Right Pict.:
1. - $15+
2. - $5+
3. - $10+
4. - $8+
5. - $10+
6. - $20+
7. - $10+
8. - $8+
9. - $8+

Bottom Left Pict.:
1. - $10+
2. - $55+
3. - $5+
4. - $50+
5. - $50+
6. - $5+
7. - $10+
8. - $5+
9. - $10+

Bottom Right Pict.:
1. - $12+
2. - $15+
3. - $15+
4. - $5+
5. - $5+
6. - $5+
7. - $20+
8. - $8+
9. - $7+
10. - $7+

Page 117

Top Left Pict.:
1. - $10+
2. - $50+
3. - $35+
4. - $15+
5. - $15+
6. - $8+
7. - $30+
8. - $8+
9. - $5+
10. - $5+
11. - $5+

Top Right Pict.:
1. - $20+
2. - $40+
3. - $10+
4. - $25+
5. - $5+
6. - $10+
7. - $5+
8. - $10+
9. - $10+

Bottom Left Pict.:
1. - $50+
2. - $40+
3. - $30+
4. - $45+

Bottom Right Pict.:
1. - $30+
2. - $20+
3. - $30+
4. - $20+
5. - $30+
6. - $40+

Page 118

Top Left - $150+
Top Right - $200+
Bottom Collage:
1. - $40+
2. - $30+
3. - $50+
4. - $70+
5. - $30+
6. - $20+
7. - $40+
8. - $50+
9. - $40+
10. - $20+
11. - $65+
12. - $50+
13. - $35+
14. - $35+

Page 119

Top Left Pict.:
1. - $25+
2. - $60+
3. - $50+
4. - $65+
5. - $35+
6. - $10+
7. - $50+

Top Right Pict.:
1. - $15+
2. - $30+
3. - $15+
4. - $40+
5. - $20+
6. - $15+
7. - $15+
8. - $20+

Bottom Left Pict.:
1. - $30+
2. - $8+
3. - $8+
4. - $8+
5. - $8+
6. - $8+
7. - $8+
8. - $8+
9. - $8+
10. - $8+
11. - $8+

Bottom Right Pict.:
1. - $8+
2. - $8+
3. - $15+
4. - $8+
5. - $15+
6. - $8+
7. - $8+
8. - $8+
9. - $5+
10. - $8+
11. - $8+
12. - $8+

Page 120

Top Left Pict.:
1. - $25+
2. - $25+
3. - $25+
4. - $20+
5. - $6+
6. - $10+
7. - $7+
8. - $7+
9. - $5+

Top Right Pict.:
1. - $15+
2. - $15+
3. - $15+
4. - $10+
5. - $10+
6. - $14+
7. - $8+
8. - $10+
9. - $10+

Bottom Left Pict.:
1. - $5+
2. - $5+
3. - $5+
4. - $5+
5. - $10+
6. - $5+
7. - $10+
8. - $4+
9. - $10+

Bottom Right Pict.:
1. - $9+
2. - $8+
3. - $18+
4. - $12+
5. - $10+
6. - $10+
7. - $12+
8. - $10+
9. - $5+

Page 121

Top Left Pict.:
1. - $15+
2. - $10+
3. - $15+
4. - $4+
5. - $10+
6. - $25+
7. - $10+
8. - $15+

Top Right Pict.:
All - $8+
Except #3. - $4+

Bottom Left Pict.:
1. - $25+
2. - $8+
3. - $8+
4. - $15+
5. - $8+
6. - $8+
7. - $8+
8. - $8+
9. - $8+
10. - $8+
11. - $8+
12. - $8+

Bottom Right Pict.:
1. - $10+
2. - $10+
3. - $15+
4. - $10+
5. - $15+
6. - $8+
7. - $4+
8. - $15+
9. - $10+
10. - $8+
11. - $3+
12. - $3+
13. - $10+
14. - $35+
15. - $20+

Page 122

Top - $700+
Bottom Left - $45+
Bottom Right Pict.:
Top - $100+
Bottom - $50+

Page 123

Top Left Pict.:
1. - $12+
2. - $8+
3. - $8+
4. - $8+
5. - $8+
6. - $8+
7. - $8+
8. - $8+
9. - $15+
10. - $8+
11. - $8+
12. - $10+

Top Right Pict.:
1. - $8+
2. - $15+
3. - $10+
4. - $18+
5. - $8+
6. - $8+
7. - $5+
8. - $5+
9. - $3+
10. - $8+
11. - $5+
12. - $4+

Bottom Left Pict.:
1. - $15+
2. - $8+
3. - $8+
4. - $8+
5. - $8+
6. - $8+
7. - $15+
8. - $8+

Bottom Right Pict.:
1. - $15+
2. - $20+
3. - $25+
4. - $20+
5. - $15+

Page 124

Top Left Pict. - $40+
Top Middle Pict. - $20+
Top Right Pict.:
1. - $25+
2. - $40+
3. - $15+
4. - $10+
5. - $20+
6. - $5+

Bottom Left Pict. - $100+
Bottom Right Pict.:
1. - $15+
2. - $30+
3. - $20+
4. - $10+
5. - $10+
6. - $10+
7. - $25+

Page 125

Top Left Pict.:
1. thru 3. - $15+
4. - $5+
5. - $5+
6. - $5+
7. - $10+
8. - $100+
9. - $10+

Top Right Pict.:
1. - $50+
2. - $30+
3. - $5+
4. - $45+
5. - $10+
6. - $10+
7. - $4+
8. - $4+
9. - $15+

Bottom Left Pict.:
1. - $10+
2. - $10+
3. - $30+
4. - $60+
5. - $30+
6. - $30+
7. - $20+
8. - $10+
9. - $60+
10. - $60+

Bottom Right Pict.:
1. - $10+
2. - $8+
3. - $8+
4. - $20+
5. - $15+
6. - $15+
7. - $7+
8. - $15+
9. - $20+
10. - $10+

Page 126

1. - $15+
2. - $15+
3. - $20+
4. - $20+
5. - $10+
6. - $20+
7. - $20+
8. - $20+
9. - $8+
10. - $15+
11. - $15+
12. - $15+

Page 127

1. - $20+
2. - $15+
3. - $12+
4. - $225+
5. - $20+
6. - $15+
7. - $20+

Page 128

1. - $30+
2. - $25+
3. - $30+
4. - $30+
5. - $20+
6. - $30+
7. - $20+
8. - $25+
9. - $25+
10. - $20+

Page 129

ft Pict.:
1. - $25+
2. - $20+
3. - $20+
4. - $25+
5. - $25+
6. - $25+
7. - $40+
8. - $50+
9. - $30+
ght Pict.:
1. - $6+
2. - $7+
All Others - $5+
Left Pict.:
1. - $20+
2. - $15+
3. - $25+
4. - $15+
5. - $10+
6. - $15+
7. - $10+
8. - $15+
9. - $15+
Right Pict.:
1. - $25+
2. - $20+
3. - $20+
4. - $25+
5. - $5+
6. - $20+
7. - $6+
8. - $6+
9. - $6+

30
ft Pict. - $18+ each
ght Pict. - $13+ each
Left Pict.:
1. - $25+
2. - $25+
3. - $25+
4. - $16+
5. - $16+
6. - $25+
7. - $16+
8. - $16+
9. - $25+
Right Pict.:
1. - $25+
2. - $20+
3. - $20+
4. - $30+
5. - $12+
6. - $35+
7. - $16+
8. - $15+

31
t Pict.:
1. - $18+
2. - $25+
3. - $40+
4. - $25+
5. - $30+
6. - $25+
7. - $20+
8. - $20+
9. - $30+
ght Pict.:
1. - $5+
2. - $5+
3. - $5+
4. - $10+
5. - $25+
6. - $25+
7. - $5+
Left Pict.:
1. - $20+
2. - $15+
3. - $20+
4. - $5+
5. - $5+
Right Pict.:
1. - $15+
2. - $8+
3. - $8+
4. - $8+
5. - $7+
6. - $9+

2
t Pict.:
Top - $25+
Bottom - $35+
Top Middle Pict.:
Top - $40+
Bottom - $50+
Top Right Pict.:
Top - $12+
Bottom - $25+
Bottom Left Pict.:
1. - $30+
2. - $25+
3. - $5+
Bottom Right Pict.:
1. - $35+
2. - $25+
3. - $25+
4. - $20+
5. - $30+
6. - $20+
7. - $20+
8. - $30+
9. - $30+

Page 133
Top Left Pict.:
Top - $10+
Bottom - $20+
Top Right Pict.:
1. - $50+
2. - $20+
3. - $10+
4. - $40+
5. - $25+
Bottom Left Pict.:
1. - $50+
2. - $20+
3. - $35+
4. - $60+
5. - $40+
6. - $65+
7. - $30+
Bottom Right Pict.:
Left - $20+
Right - $25+

Page 134
Top Left - $125+
Top Right - $55+
Bottom Left - $60+ each
Bottom Right Pict.:
1. - $25+
2. - $30+
3. - $20+
4. - $30+
5. - $35+
6. - $10+

Page 135
Top Left - $250+
Top Right - $200+
Bottom - $250+ Very Rare

Page 136
Top Left Pict. - $3+ each
Top Right Pict. - $3+ each
Bottom Left Pict.:
1. - $25+
2. - $15+
3. - $15+
4. - $25+
Bottom Right Pict. - $50+

Page 137
Top Left Pict. - $35+
Top Right Pict. - $35+
Bottom Left Pict. - $100+
Bottom Right Pict. - $50+

Page 138
Top Pict.:
1. - $15+
2. - $25+
3. - $35+
4. - $12+
Bottom Left Pict.:
1. - $20+
2. - $15+
3. - $40+
4. - $30+
Bottom Right Pict.:
1. - $8+
2. - $10+
3. - $8+
4. - $35+

Page 139
Top Left Pict.:
1. - $25+
2. - $40+
3. - $20+
Top Right Pict. - $40+
Bottom Left Pict. - $50+
Bottom Right Pict.:
1. - $50+
2. - $75+
3. - $25+
4. - $15+

Page 140
Top Left Pict. - $40+
Top Right Pict. - $20+ each
Bottom Left Pict. - $20+
Bottom Right Pict.:
Top Left - $100+
Bottom Left - $75+
Bottom Right - $35+

Page 141
Top Left Pict.:
Top Row - $30+ each
Middle Left - $10+
Middle Right - $15+
Bottom Left - $20+
Bottom Right - $15+
Top Right Pict.:
Top Left - $25+
Top Right - $25+
Bottom Left - $15+
Bottom Right - $35+
Bottom Left Pict.:
Top Set - $35+
Bottom Set - $30+
Bottom Right Pict.:
Top Set - $45+
Bottom Left - $20+
Bottom Right - $30+

Page 142
Top Left Pict.:
Top Left - $35+
Top Right - $10+
Bottom Left - $12+
Bottom Right - $15+
Top Right Pict.:
Top Left - $25+
Top Right - $10+
Bottom Set - $20+
Bottom Left Pict.:
Top - $30+
Bottom - $15+
Bottom Right Pict. - $15+

Page 143
Top Left Pict. - $30+ each
Top Right Pict. - $20+
Bottom Left Pict.:
Top - $30+
Bottom - $15+
Bottom Right Pict.:
Top Left - $12+
Top Right - $40+
Bottom Left - $25+
Bottom Right - $15+

Page 144
Top Left Pict.:
Top Left - $35+
Top Right - $22+
Bottom - $35+
Top Right Pict.:
Top Left - $15+
Top Right - $20+
Bottom - $15+
Bottom Left Pict.:
Top Left - $15+
Top Right - $40+
Bottom Left - $10+
Bottom Right - $15+
Bottom Right Pict.:
Top Left - $8+
Top Right - $15+
Bottom Left - $4+
Bottom Right - $20+

Page 145
Top Left Pict. - $25+
Top Right Pict. - $35+
Bottom Left Pict. - $100+
Bottom Right Pict. - $50+

Page 146
Top Left Pict. - $60+
Top Right Pict.:
1. - $40+
2. - $35+
Bottom Left Pict. - $30+
Bottom Right Pict. - $15+

Page 147
Top Left Pict.:
1. - $15+
2. - $25+
3. - $7+
4. - $7+
Top Right Pict.:
1. - $30+
2. - $20+
3. - $75+
4. - $50+
Bottom Left Pict.:
1. - $20+
2. - $10+
3. - $20+
4. - $25+
Bottom Right Pict.:
1. - $50+
2. - $10+
3. - $15+
4. - $25+

Page 148
Top Left Pict.:
Top - $150+
Bottom - $100+
Top Right Pict. - $75+
Bottom Left Pict.:
1. - $30+
2. - $45+
3. - $25+
4. - $50+
Bottom Right Pict.:
Top - $35+
Bottom - $50+

Page 149
Top Left Pict. - $200+
Top Right Pict. - $225+
Bottom Pict. - $225+

Page 150
Top Left Pict. - $15+ each
Top Right Pict. - $40+
Bottom Left Pict. - $40+
Bottom Right Pict.:
1. - $15+
2. - $10+
3. - $10+
4. - $35+

Page 151
Top Left Pict. - $75+
Top Right Pict. - $25+ each
Middle Pict.:
Top - $75+
Bottom - $40+
Bottom Left Pict.:
1. - $15+
2. - $30+
3. - $50+
4. - $40+
Bottom Right Pict.:
1. - $45+
2. - $45+
3. - $25+

Page 152
Top Left Pict.:
Top Set - $25+
Bottom - $15+
Top Right Pict.:
1. - $20+
2. - $25+
3. - $15+
4. - $15+
Bottom Left Pict.:
1. - $40+
2. - $20+
3. - $30+
Bottom Right Pict.:
1. - $20+
2. - $25+
3. - $35+
4. - $60+

Page 153
Top Left Pict.:
1. - $30+
2. - $35+
3. - $20+
4. - $20+
Top Right Pict.:

1. - $20+
2. - $25+
3. - $20+
4. - $15+
Bottom Left Pict.:
1. - $15+
2. - $20+
3. - $30+
4. - $35+
Bottom Right Pict.:
1. - $30+
2. - $15+
3. - $25+
4. - $20+

Page 154
Top Left Pict. - $60+
Top Right Pict. - $75+
Bottom Left Pict. - $60+
Bottom Right Pict. - $40+

Page 155
Top Left Pict. - $50+
Top Right Pict. - $35+
Bottom Left Pict.:
1. - $40+
2. - $15+
3. - $20+
4. - $40+
Bottom Right Pict.:
1. - $20+
2. - $35+
3. - $25+
4. - $25+

Page 156
Top Left Pict.:
Top - $25+
Bottom Left - $5+
Bottom Right - $8+
Top Right Pict.:
Top Left - $40+
Top Right - $8+
Bottom Left - $8+
Bottom Right - $15+
Bottom Left Pict.:
Top Left - $40+
Top Right - $40+
Bottom - $35+
Bottom Right pict.:
Top - $40+
Bottom - $30+

Page 157
Top Left Pict. - $40+
Top Right Pict. - $40+
Bottom Left Pict. - $50+
Bottom Right Pict. - $150+

Page 158
Top Left Pict. - $35+
Top Right Pict. - $70+
Bottom Left Pict.:
Top - $30+
Bottom - $35+
Bottom Right Pict. - $20+

Page 159
Top Left Pict. - $30+
Top Right Pict. - $25+
Bottom Left Pict.:
Top - $35+
Bottom - $30+
Bottom Right Pict. - $25+

Page 160
Top Left Pict.:
Top - $145+
Bottom - $50+
Top Right Pict. - $150+
Bottom Left Pict. - $125+
Bottom Right Pict. - $35+ each

Page 161
Top Left Pict.:
Top Left - $65+
Top Right - $65+
Bottom Left - $20+
Bottom Right - $25+
Top Right Pict.:
Top Left - $15+
Top Right - $20+
Bottom Left - $12+
Bottom Right - $20+
Bottom Left Pict.:
Top Left - $10+
Top Right - $8+
Bottom - $10+ each
Bottom Right Pict.:
Top Left - $75+
Top Right - $25+
Bottom Left - $15+
Bottom Right - $12+

Page 162
Top Left Pict.:
Top Left - $10+
Top Right - $12+
Middle - $12+
Bottom Left - $10+
Bottom Right - $10+
Top Right Pict.:
Top Left - $20+
Top Right - $50+
Bottom Left - $40+
Bottom Right - $30+
Bottom Left Pict.:
Top Left - $17+
Top Right - $10+
Bottom Left - $15+
Bottom Right - $20+
Bottom Right Pict.:
Top Left - $10+
Top Right - $25+
Bottom Left - $15+
Bottom Right - $25+

Page 163
Top Left Pict. - $40+
Top Right Pict. - $35+
Bottom Left Pict. - $100+
Bottom Right Pict. - $25+

Page 164
Top Left Pict. - $35+
Top Right Pict. - $275+
Bottom Left Pict. - $50+
Bottom Right Pict. - $100+

Page 165
Top Left Pict. - $60+
Top Right Pict. - $75+
Bottom Left Pict. - $60+
Bottom Right Pict. - $75+ set

Page 166
Top Pict. - $250+
Bottom Left Pict. - $400+
Bottom Right Pict. - $250+

Page 167
Top Left Pict.:
Top Left - $25+
Top Right - $10+
Bottom Left - $10+
Bottom Right - $15+
Top Right Pict.:
Left - $40+
Top Right - $25+
Bottom Right - $50+
Bottom Left Pict. - $35+
Bottom Right Pict.:
Top Left - $15+
Top Right - $10+
Bottom Left - $5+
Bottom Right - $15+

Page 168
Top Left Pict. - $75+
Top Right Pict. - $75+
Bottom Left Pict. - $100+
Bottom Right Pict. - $90+

Page 169
Top Left Pict. - $50+
Top Right Pict.:
Top - $25+
Bottom - $10+
Bottom - $100+

Page 170
Top Left Pict.:
1. - $50+
2. - $65+
3. - $50+
4. - $20+
Top Right Pict.:
Left - $30+
Top Right - $25+
Bottom Right - $20+
Bottom Left Pict.:
1. - $25+
2. - $20+
3. - $15+
4. - $15+
Bottom Right Pict.:
1. - $30+
2. - $35+
3. - $35+
4. - $60+

Page 171
Top Left Pict. - $10+
Top Right Pict. - $20+
Bottom Left Pict. - $45+
Bottom Right Pict. - $15+

Page 172
Top Left Pict.:
Left - $25+
Right - $35+
Top Right Pict. - $50+
Bottom Left Pict. - $20+
Bottom Right Pict. - $10+

Page 173
Top Left Pict.:
Top - $150+
Bottom - $40+
Top Right Pict. - $35+ each
Bottom Left Pict. - $60+
Bottom Right Pict. - $40+

Page 174
Top Left Pict. - $200+
Top Right Pict. - $175+
Bottom Left Pict.:
Top - $150+
Bottom - $175+
Bottom Right Pict. - $500+

Page 175
Top Left Pict. - $30+
Top Right Pict. - $100+
Bottom Left Pict.:
1. - $9+
2. - $25+
3. - $10+
Bottom Right Pict. - $75+

Page 176
Top Left Pict.:
Top Left - $50+
Right - $60+
Bottom Left - $50+
Top Right Pict.:
1. - $50+
2. - $35+
3. - $60+
4. - $35+
Bottom Left Pict.:
Top Left - $40+
Top Right - $40+
Bottom Left - $28+
Bottom Right - $45+
Bottom Right Pict.:
Left Side - $35+
Top Right - $45+
Bottom Right - $45+

Page 177
Top Left Pict.:
1. - $25+
2. - $100+
3. - $35+
4. - $30+
Top Right Pict.:
Top - $100+
Bottom - $45+
Bottom Left Pict.:
Top - $65+
Bottom - $40+
Bottom Right Pict. - $50+

Page 178
Top Pict. - $80+
Bottom Left Pict. - $125+
Bottom Right Pict. - $150+
Lighters - $10+ each

Page 179
Top Pict. - $150+
Lighters - $10+ each
Bottom Pict. - $175+
Lighters - $12+ each

Page 180
Top Left Pict. - $100+
Lighters - $15+ each
Top Right Pict. - $80+
Bottom Left Pict. - $125+
Lighters - $10+ each
Bottom Right Pict. - $100+
Lighters - $20+ each